THE ALL NEW! BATMAN

THE BRAVE AND THE BOLD

SHOLLY FISCH Writer

RICK BURCHETT Penciller

DAN DAVIS Inker

WILDSTORM FX HEROIC AGE GABE ELTAEB Colorists

TRAVIS LANHAM CARLOS M. MANGUAL Letterers

RICK BURCHETT and DAN DAVIS Covers

BATMAN created by BOB KANE

SUPERMAN created by JERRY SIEGEL & JOE SHUSTER

WONDER WOMAN created by WILLIAM MOULTON MARSTON

Scott Peterson Jim Chadwick Editors-Original Series
Chynna Clugston Flores Assistant Editor-Original Series
Ian Sattler Director Editorial, Special Projects and Archival Editions
Robbin Brosterman Design Director-Books

Eddie Berganza Executive Editor
Bob Harras VP-Editor in Chief

Diane Nelson President
Dan DiDio and **Jim Lee** Co-Publishers
Geoff Johns Chief Creative Officer
John Rood Executive VP-Sales, Marketing and Business Development
Amy Genkins Senior VP-Business and Legal Affairs
Nairi Gardiner Senior VP-Finance
Jeff Boison VP-Publishing Operations
Mark Chiarello VP-Art Direction and Design
John Cunningham VP-Marketing
Terri Cunningham VP-Talent Relations and Services
Alison Gill Senior VP-Manufacturing and Operations
David Hyde VP-Publicity
Hank Kanalz Senior VP-Digital
Jay Kogan VP-Business and Legal Affairs, Publishing
Jack Mahan VP-Business Affairs, Talent
Nick Napolitano VP-Manufacturing Administration
Ron Perazza VP-Online
Sue Pohja VP-Book Sales
Courtney Simmons Senior VP-Publicity
Bob Wayne Senior VP-Sales

THE ALL-NEW BATMAN: THE BRAVE AND THE BOLD VOLUME ONE

DC Comics, 1700 Broadway, New York, NY 10019
A Warner Bros. Entertainment Company
Printed by RR Donnelley, Willard, OH, USA. 8/26/11. First Printing.
ISBN: 978-1-4012-3272-6

SUSTAINABLE FORESTRY INITIATIVE
Certified Fiber Sourcing

Fiber used in this product line meets the sourcing requirements of the SFI program.
www.sfiprogram.org SGS-SFI/COC-US10/81072

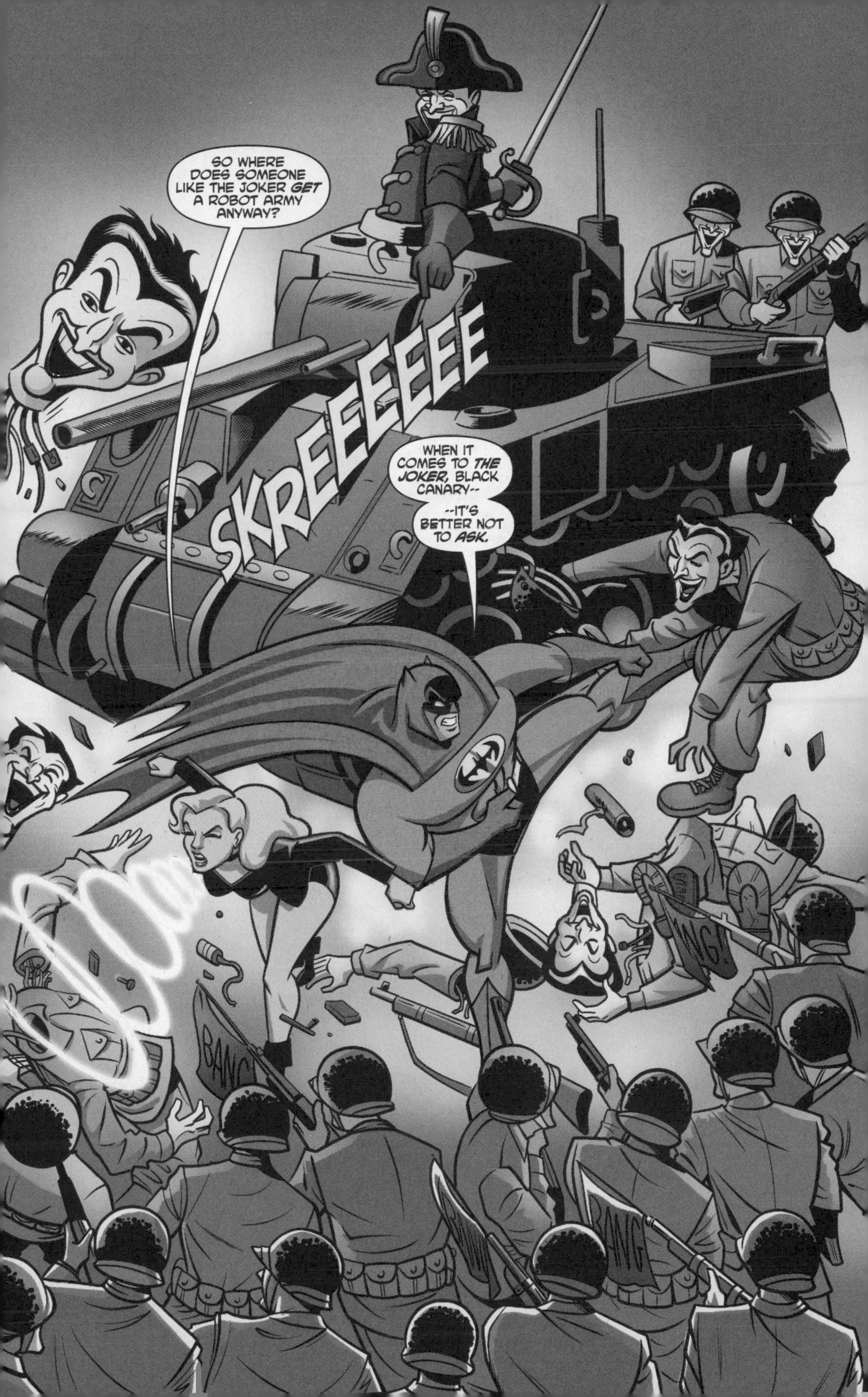
SO WHERE DOES SOMEONE LIKE THE JOKER *GET* A ROBOT ARMY ANYWAY?
SKREEEEEEE
WHEN IT COMES TO *THE JOKER*, BLACK CANARY--
--IT'S BETTER NOT TO *ASK.*
BANG

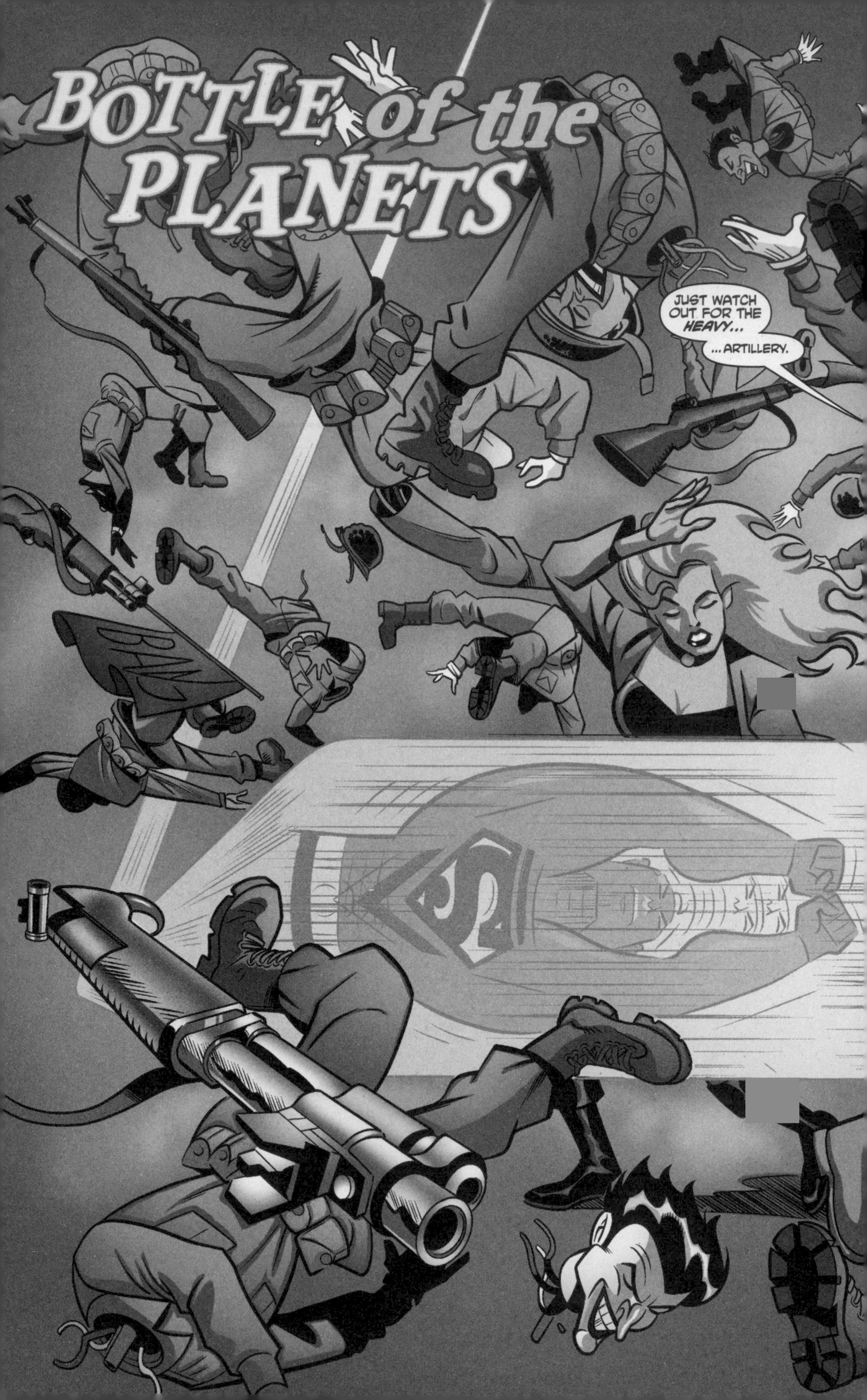
BOTTLE of the PLANETS
JUST WATCH OUT FOR THE HEAVY...
...ARTILLERY.

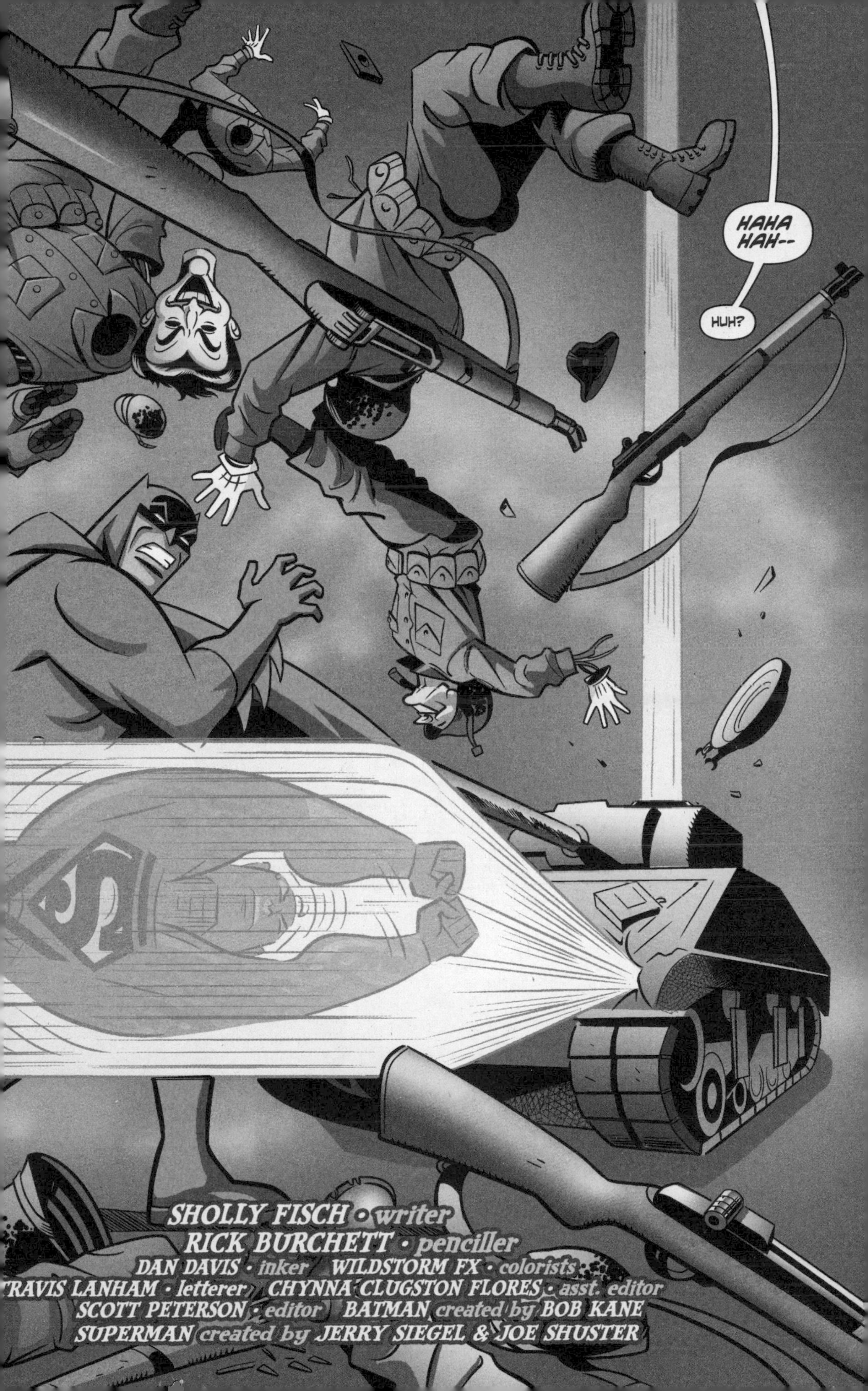
HAHA HAH--
HUH?
SHOLLY FISCH • writer
RICK BURCHETT • penciller
DAN DAVIS • inker WILDSTORM FX • colorists
TRAVIS LANHAM • letterer CHYNNA CLUGSTON FLORES • asst. editor
SCOTT PETERSON • editor BATMAN created by BOB KANE
SUPERMAN created by JERRY SIEGEL & JOE SHUSTER

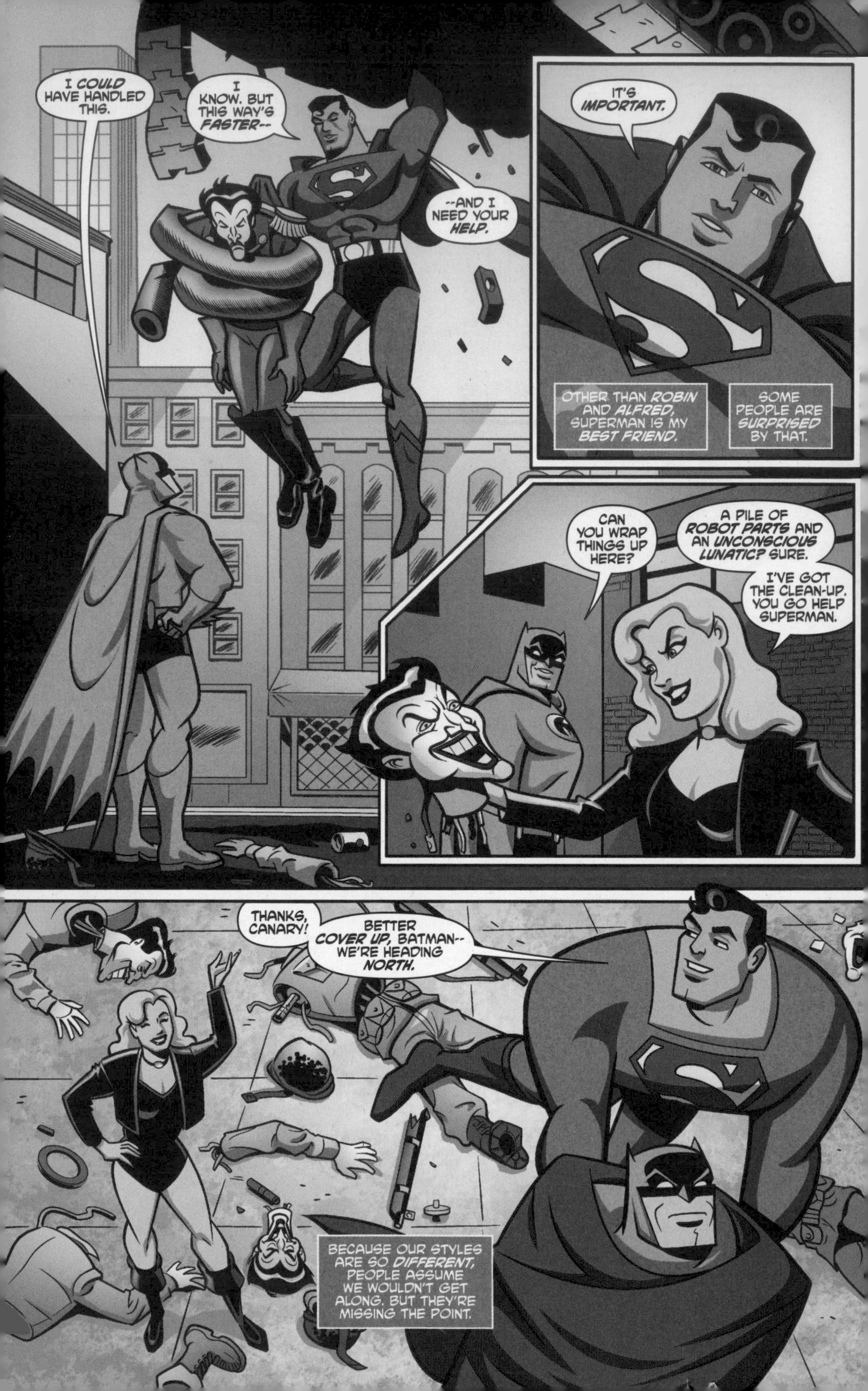

I COULD HAVE HANDLED THIS.
I KNOW. BUT THIS WAY'S FASTER--
--AND I NEED YOUR HELP.
IT'S IMPORTANT.
OTHER THAN ROBIN AND ALFRED, SUPERMAN IS MY BEST FRIEND.
SOME PEOPLE ARE SURPRISED BY THAT.
CAN YOU WRAP THINGS UP HERE?
A PILE OF ROBOT PARTS AND AN UNCONSCIOUS LUNATIC? SURE.
I'VE GOT THE CLEAN-UP. YOU GO HELP SUPERMAN.
THANKS, CANARY!
BETTER COVER UP, BATMAN-- WE'RE HEADING NORTH.
BECAUSE OUR STYLES ARE SO DIFFERENT, PEOPLE ASSUME WE WOULDN'T GET ALONG. BUT THEY'RE MISSING THE POINT.

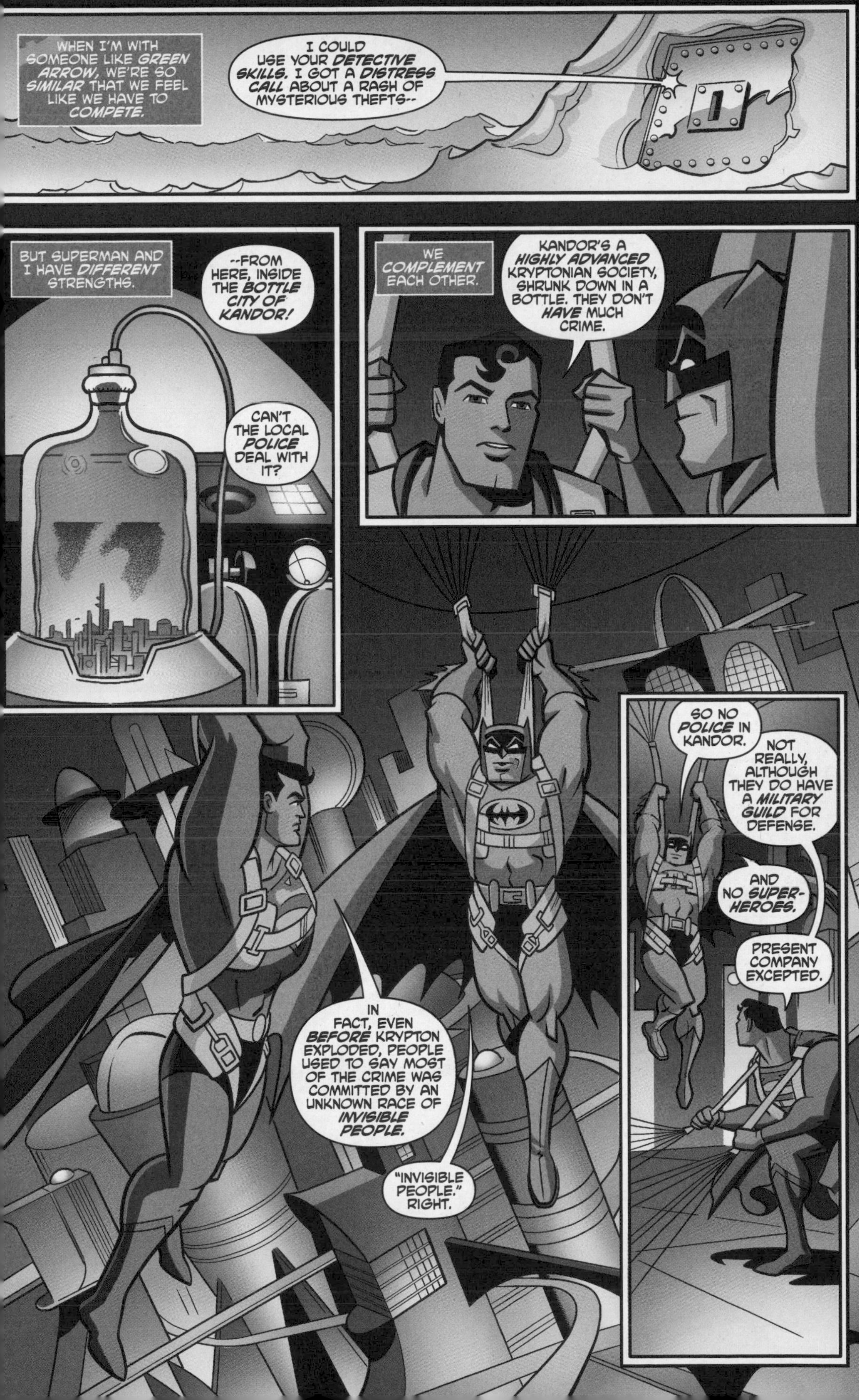
WHEN I'M WITH SOMEONE LIKE GREEN ARROW, WE'RE SO SIMILAR THAT WE FEEL LIKE WE HAVE TO COMPETE.
I COULD USE YOUR DETECTIVE SKILLS. I GOT A DISTRESS CALL ABOUT A RASH OF MYSTERIOUS THEFTS--
BUT SUPERMAN AND I HAVE DIFFERENT STRENGTHS.
--FROM HERE, INSIDE THE BOTTLE CITY OF KANDOR!
CAN'T THE LOCAL POLICE DEAL WITH IT?
WE COMPLEMENT EACH OTHER.
KANDOR'S A HIGHLY ADVANCED KRYPTONIAN SOCIETY, SHRUNK DOWN IN A BOTTLE. THEY DON'T HAVE MUCH CRIME.
IN FACT, EVEN BEFORE KRYPTON EXPLODED, PEOPLE USED TO SAY MOST OF THE CRIME WAS COMMITTED BY AN UNKNOWN RACE OF INVISIBLE PEOPLE.
"INVISIBLE PEOPLE." RIGHT.
SO NO POLICE IN KANDOR.
NOT REALLY, ALTHOUGH THEY DO HAVE A MILITARY GUILD FOR DEFENSE.
AND NO SUPER-HEROES.
PRESENT COMPANY EXCEPTED.

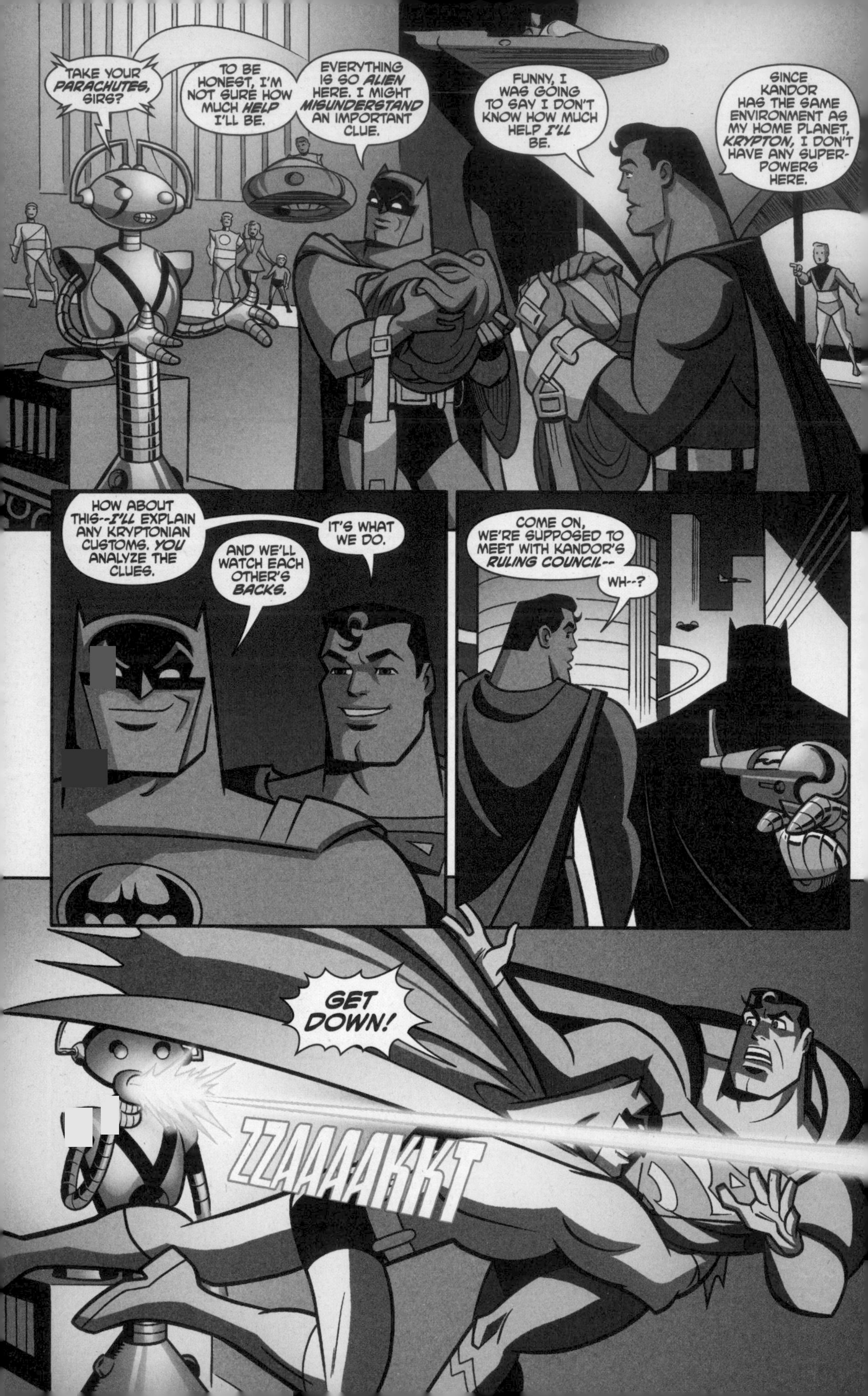
TAKE YOUR PARACHUTES, SIRS?
TO BE HONEST, I'M NOT SURE HOW MUCH HELP I'LL BE.
EVERYTHING IS SO ALIEN HERE. I MIGHT MISUNDERSTAND AN IMPORTANT CLUE.
FUNNY, I WAS GOING TO SAY I DON'T KNOW HOW MUCH HELP I'LL BE.
SINCE KANDOR HAS THE SAME ENVIRONMENT AS MY HOME PLANET, KRYPTON, I DON'T HAVE ANY SUPER-POWERS HERE.
HOW ABOUT THIS--I'LL EXPLAIN ANY KRYPTONIAN CUSTOMS. YOU ANALYZE THE CLUES.
IT'S WHAT WE DO.
AND WE'LL WATCH EACH OTHER'S BACKS.
COME ON, WE'RE SUPPOSED TO MEET WITH KANDOR'S RULING COUNCIL--
WH--?
GET DOWN!
ZZAAAAKKT

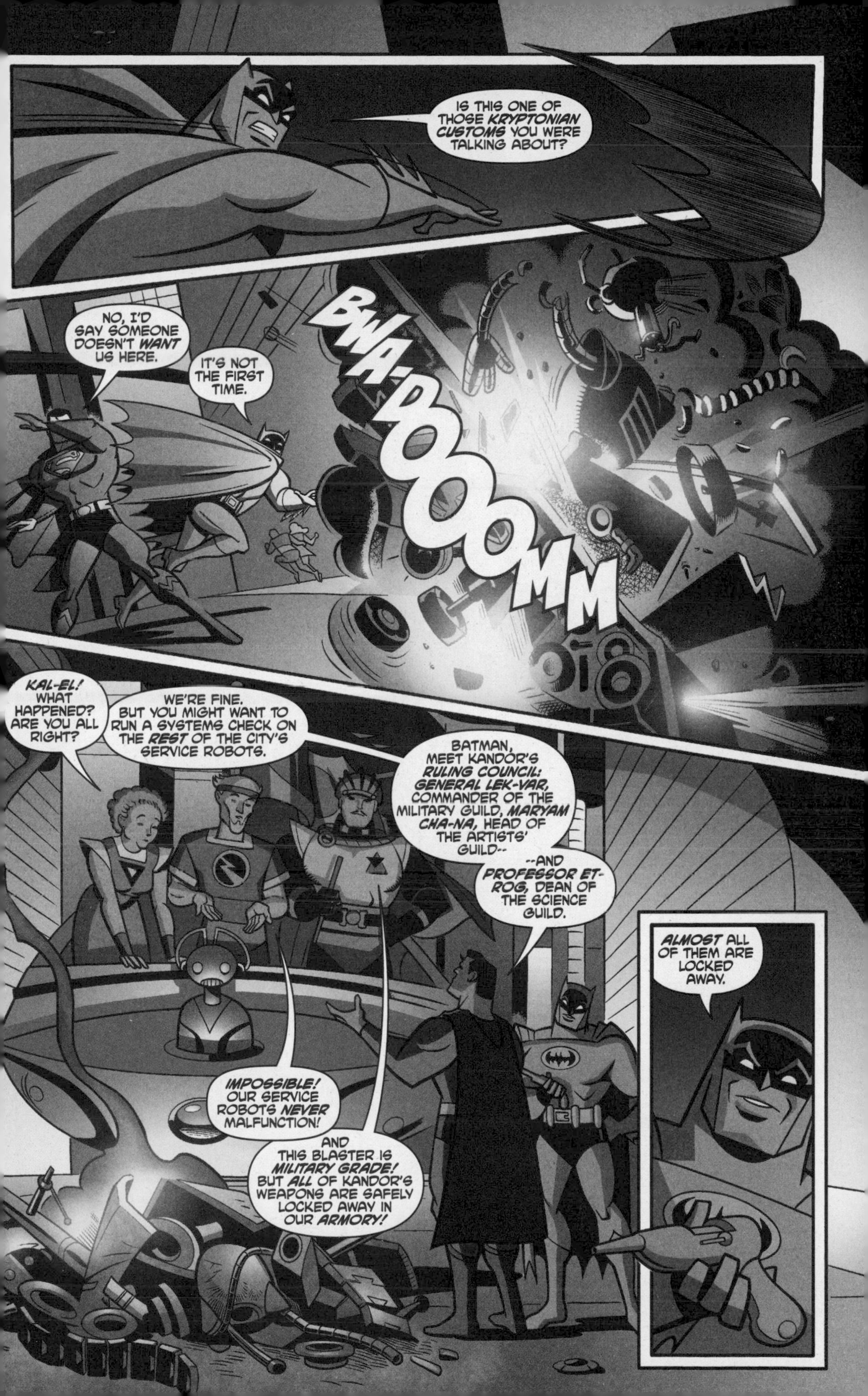
IS THIS ONE OF THOSE KRYPTONIAN CUSTOMS YOU WERE TALKING ABOUT?
BWA-DOOOMM
NO, I'D SAY SOMEONE DOESN'T WANT US HERE.
IT'S NOT THE FIRST TIME.
KAL-EL! WHAT HAPPENED? ARE YOU ALL RIGHT?
WE'RE FINE. BUT YOU MIGHT WANT TO RUN A SYSTEMS CHECK ON THE REST OF THE CITY'S SERVICE ROBOTS.
BATMAN, MEET KANDOR'S RULING COUNCIL: GENERAL LEK-VAR, COMMANDER OF THE MILITARY GUILD, MARYAM CHA-NA, HEAD OF THE ARTISTS' GUILD--
--AND PROFESSOR ET-ROG, DEAN OF THE SCIENCE GUILD.
IMPOSSIBLE! OUR SERVICE ROBOTS NEVER MALFUNCTION!
AND THIS BLASTER IS MILITARY GRADE! BUT ALL OF KANDOR'S WEAPONS ARE SAFELY LOCKED AWAY IN OUR ARMORY!
ALMOST ALL OF THEM ARE LOCKED AWAY.

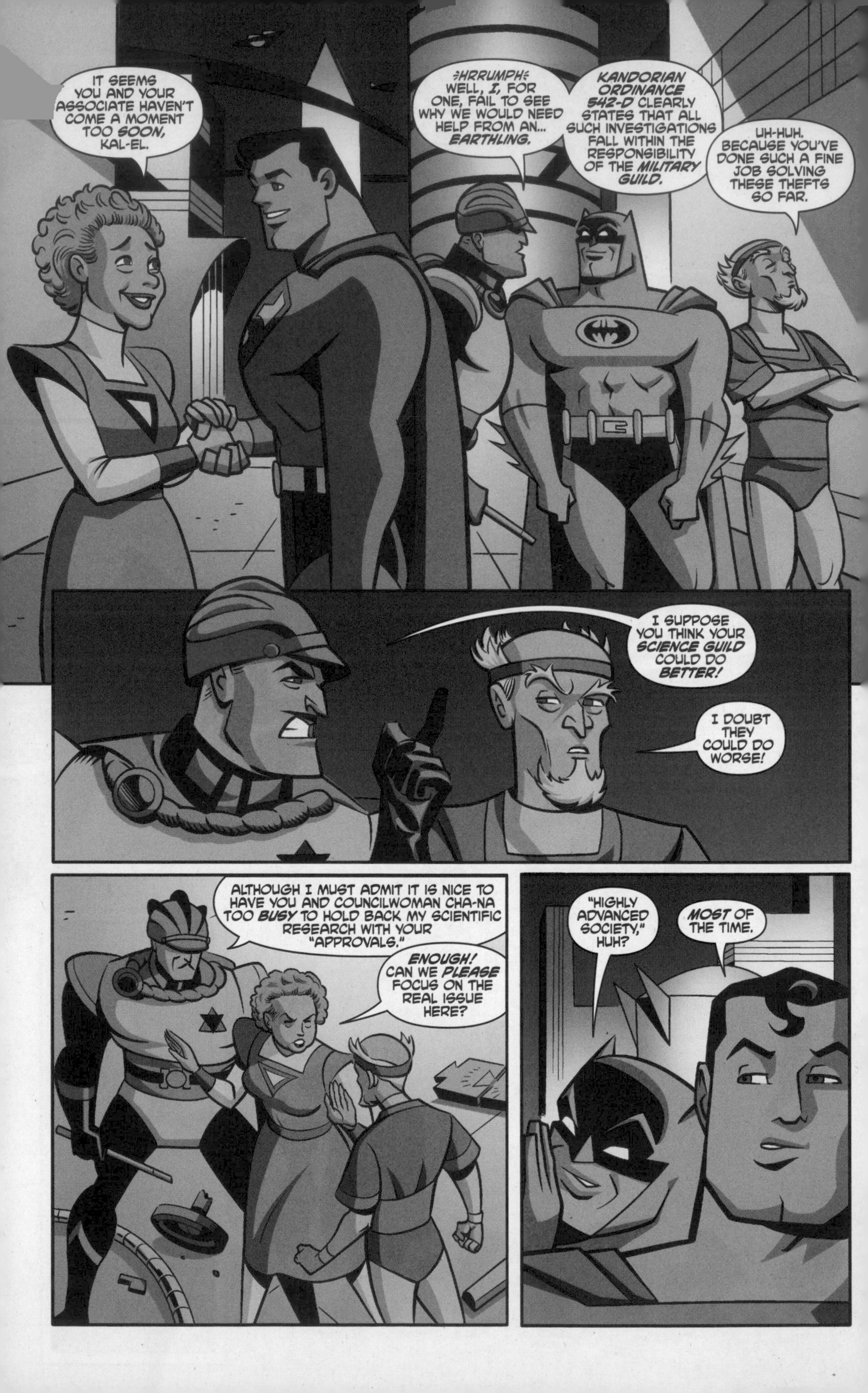
IT SEEMS YOU AND YOUR ASSOCIATE HAVEN'T COME A MOMENT TOO SOON, KAL-EL.
HRRUMPH WELL, I, FOR ONE, FAIL TO SEE WHY WE WOULD NEED HELP FROM AN... EARTHLING.
KANDORIAN ORDINANCE 542-D CLEARLY STATES THAT ALL SUCH INVESTIGATIONS FALL WITHIN THE RESPONSIBILITY OF THE MILITARY GUILD.
UH-HUH. BECAUSE YOU'VE DONE SUCH A FINE JOB SOLVING THESE THEFTS SO FAR.
I SUPPOSE YOU THINK YOUR SCIENCE GUILD COULD DO BETTER!
I DOUBT THEY COULD DO WORSE!
ALTHOUGH I MUST ADMIT IT IS NICE TO HAVE YOU AND COUNCILWOMAN CHA-NA TOO BUSY TO HOLD BACK MY SCIENTIFIC RESEARCH WITH YOUR "APPROVALS."
ENOUGH! CAN WE PLEASE FOCUS ON THE REAL ISSUE HERE?
"HIGHLY ADVANCED SOCIETY," HUH?
MOST OF THE TIME.

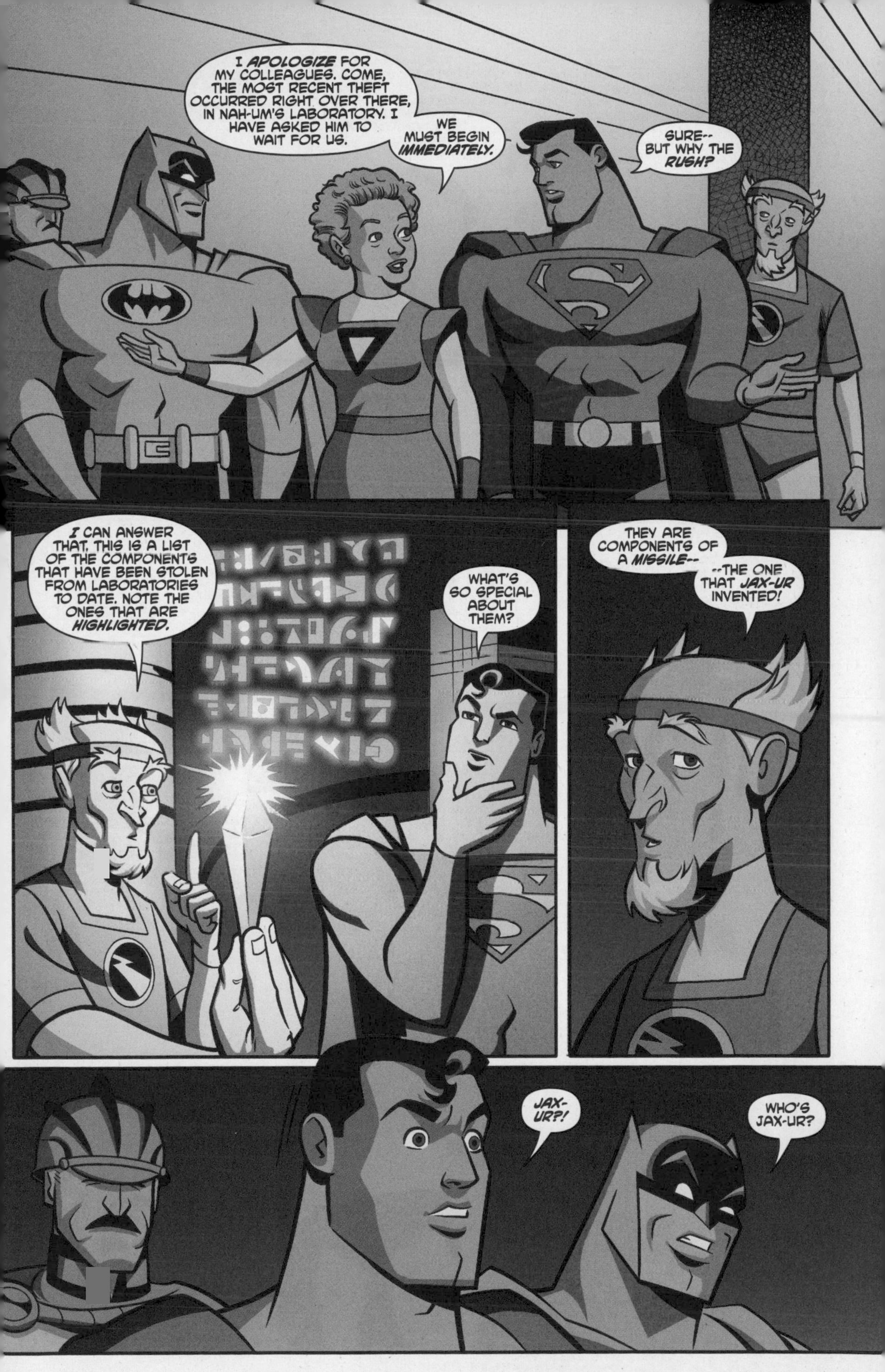

I APOLOGIZE FOR MY COLLEAGUES. COME, THE MOST RECENT THEFT OCCURRED RIGHT OVER THERE, IN NAH-UM'S LABORATORY. I HAVE ASKED HIM TO WAIT FOR US.
WE MUST BEGIN IMMEDIATELY.
SURE-- BUT WHY THE RUSH?
I CAN ANSWER THAT. THIS IS A LIST OF THE COMPONENTS THAT HAVE BEEN STOLEN FROM LABORATORIES TO DATE. NOTE THE ONES THAT ARE HIGHLIGHTED.
WHAT'S SO SPECIAL ABOUT THEM?
THEY ARE COMPONENTS OF A MISSILE--
--THE ONE THAT JAX-UR INVENTED!
JAX-UR?!
WHO'S JAX-UR?

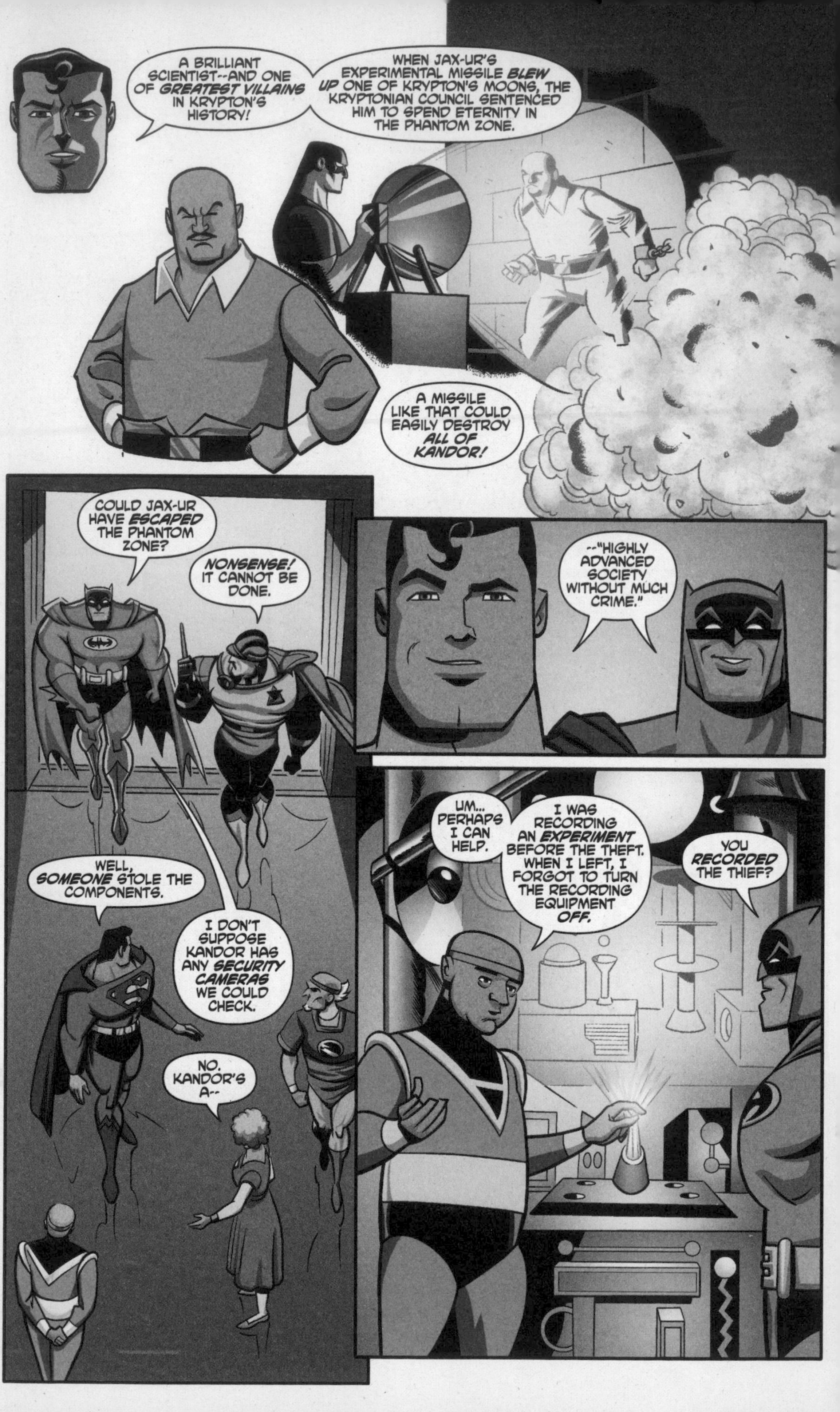
A BRILLIANT SCIENTIST--AND ONE OF GREATEST VILLAINS IN KRYPTON'S HISTORY!
WHEN JAX-UR'S EXPERIMENTAL MISSILE BLEW UP ONE OF KRYPTON'S MOONS, THE KRYPTONIAN COUNCIL SENTENCED HIM TO SPEND ETERNITY IN THE PHANTOM ZONE.
A MISSILE LIKE THAT COULD EASILY DESTROY ALL OF KANDOR!
COULD JAX-UR HAVE ESCAPED THE PHANTOM ZONE?
NONSENSE! IT CANNOT BE DONE.
WELL, SOMEONE STOLE THE COMPONENTS.
I DON'T SUPPOSE KANDOR HAS ANY SECURITY CAMERAS WE COULD CHECK.
NO. KANDOR'S A--
--"HIGHLY ADVANCED SOCIETY WITHOUT MUCH CRIME."
UM... PERHAPS I CAN HELP.
I WAS RECORDING AN EXPERIMENT BEFORE THE THEFT. WHEN I LEFT, I FORGOT TO TURN THE RECORDING EQUIPMENT OFF.
YOU RECORDED THE THIEF?

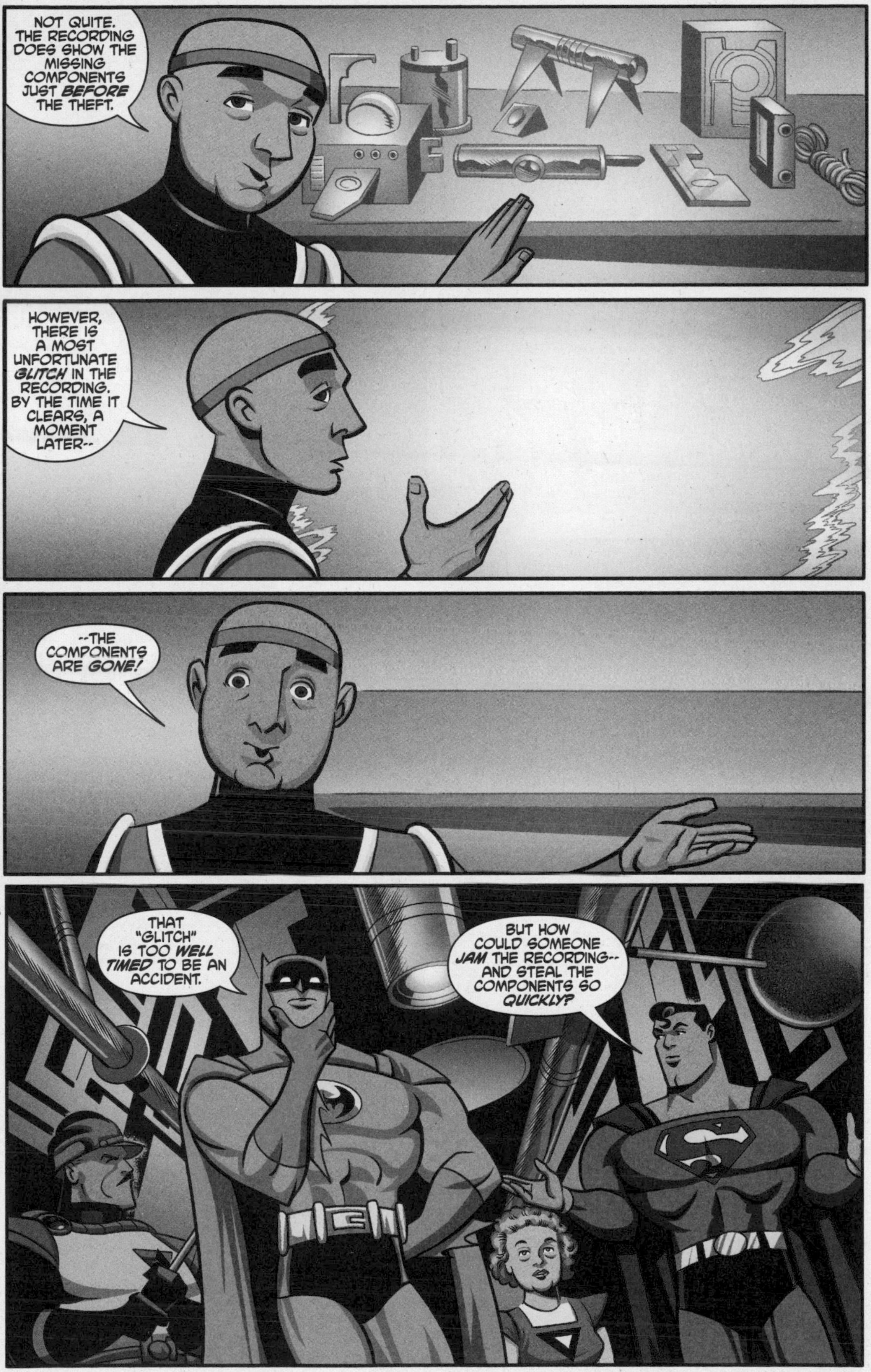

NOT QUITE. THE RECORDING DOES SHOW THE MISSING COMPONENTS JUST *BEFORE* THE THEFT.
HOWEVER, THERE IS A MOST UNFORTUNATE *GLITCH* IN THE RECORDING. BY THE TIME IT CLEARS, A MOMENT LATER--
--THE COMPONENTS ARE *GONE!*
THAT "GLITCH" IS TOO *WELL TIMED* TO BE AN ACCIDENT.
BUT HOW COULD SOMEONE *JAM* THE RECORDING-- AND STEAL THE COMPONENTS SO *QUICKLY?*

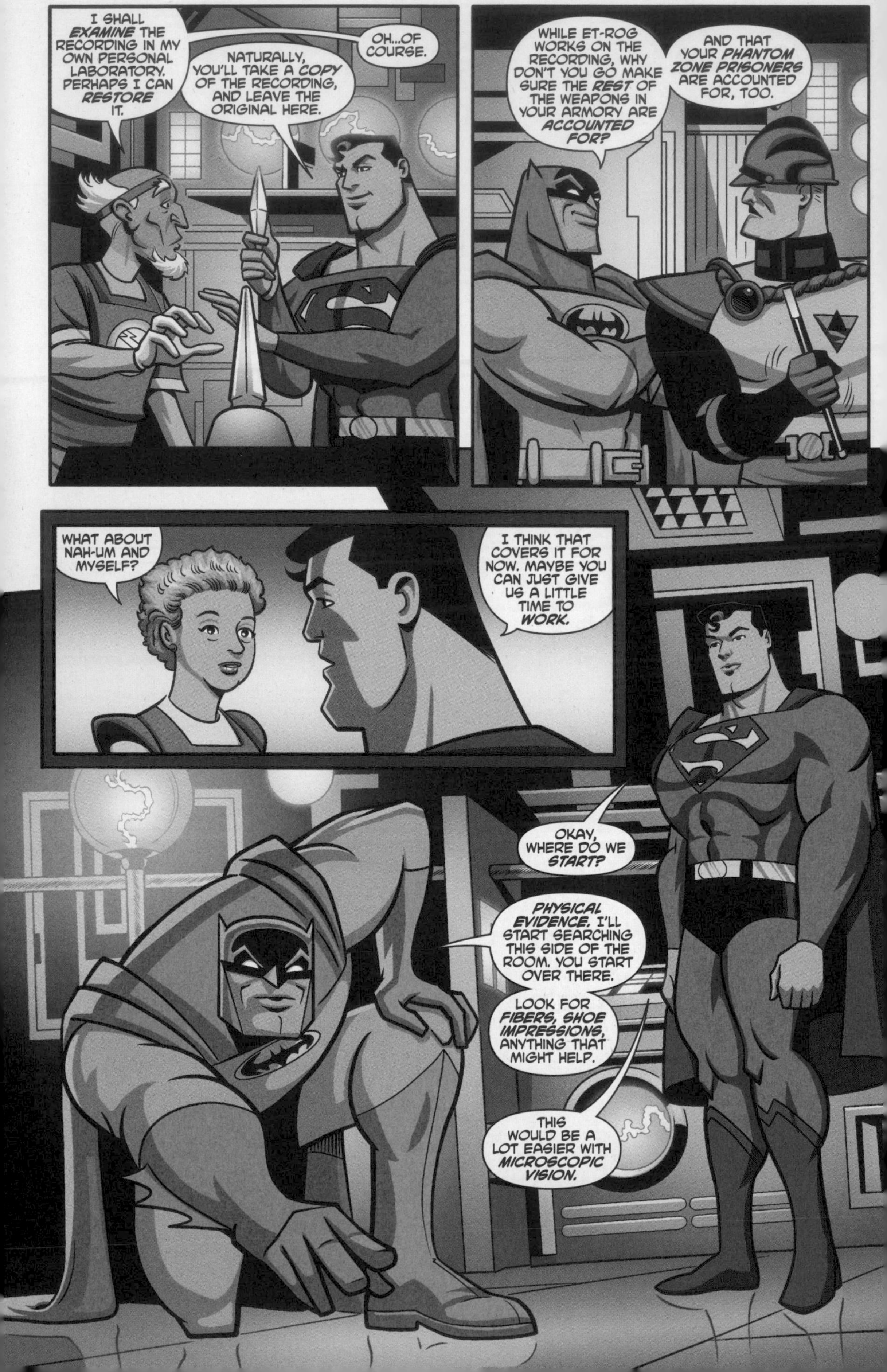

I SHALL EXAMINE THE RECORDING IN MY OWN PERSONAL LABORATORY. PERHAPS I CAN RESTORE IT.
NATURALLY, YOU'LL TAKE A COPY OF THE RECORDING, AND LEAVE THE ORIGINAL HERE.
OH...OF COURSE.
WHILE ET-ROG WORKS ON THE RECORDING, WHY DON'T YOU GO MAKE SURE THE REST OF THE WEAPONS IN YOUR ARMORY ARE ACCOUNTED FOR?
AND THAT YOUR PHANTOM ZONE PRISONERS ARE ACCOUNTED FOR, TOO.
WHAT ABOUT NAH-UM AND MYSELF?
I THINK THAT COVERS IT FOR NOW. MAYBE YOU CAN JUST GIVE US A LITTLE TIME TO WORK.
OKAY, WHERE DO WE START?
PHYSICAL EVIDENCE. I'LL START SEARCHING THIS SIDE OF THE ROOM. YOU START OVER THERE.
LOOK FOR FIBERS, SHOE IMPRESSIONS, ANYTHING THAT MIGHT HELP.
THIS WOULD BE A LOT EASIER WITH MICROSCOPIC VISION.

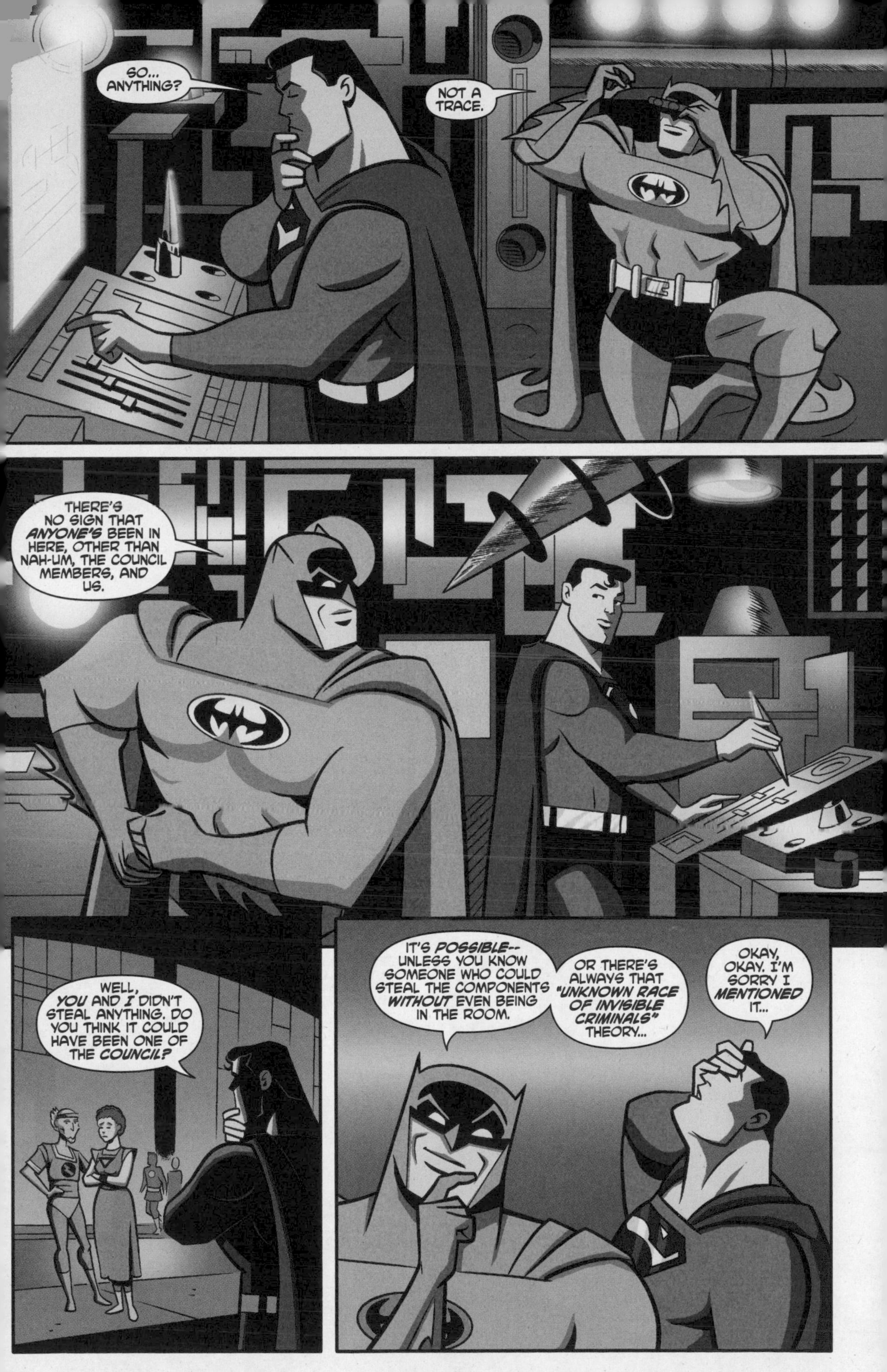
SO... ANYTHING?
NOT A TRACE.
THERE'S NO SIGN THAT *ANYONE'S* BEEN IN HERE, OTHER THAN NAH-UM, THE COUNCIL MEMBERS, AND US.
WELL, *YOU* AND *I* DIDN'T STEAL ANYTHING. DO YOU THINK IT COULD HAVE BEEN ONE OF THE *COUNCIL?*
IT'S *POSSIBLE*-- UNLESS YOU KNOW SOMEONE WHO COULD STEAL THE COMPONENTS *WITHOUT* EVEN BEING IN THE ROOM.
OR THERE'S ALWAYS THAT *"UNKNOWN RACE OF INVISIBLE CRIMINALS"* THEORY...
OKAY, OKAY. I'M SORRY I *MENTIONED* IT...

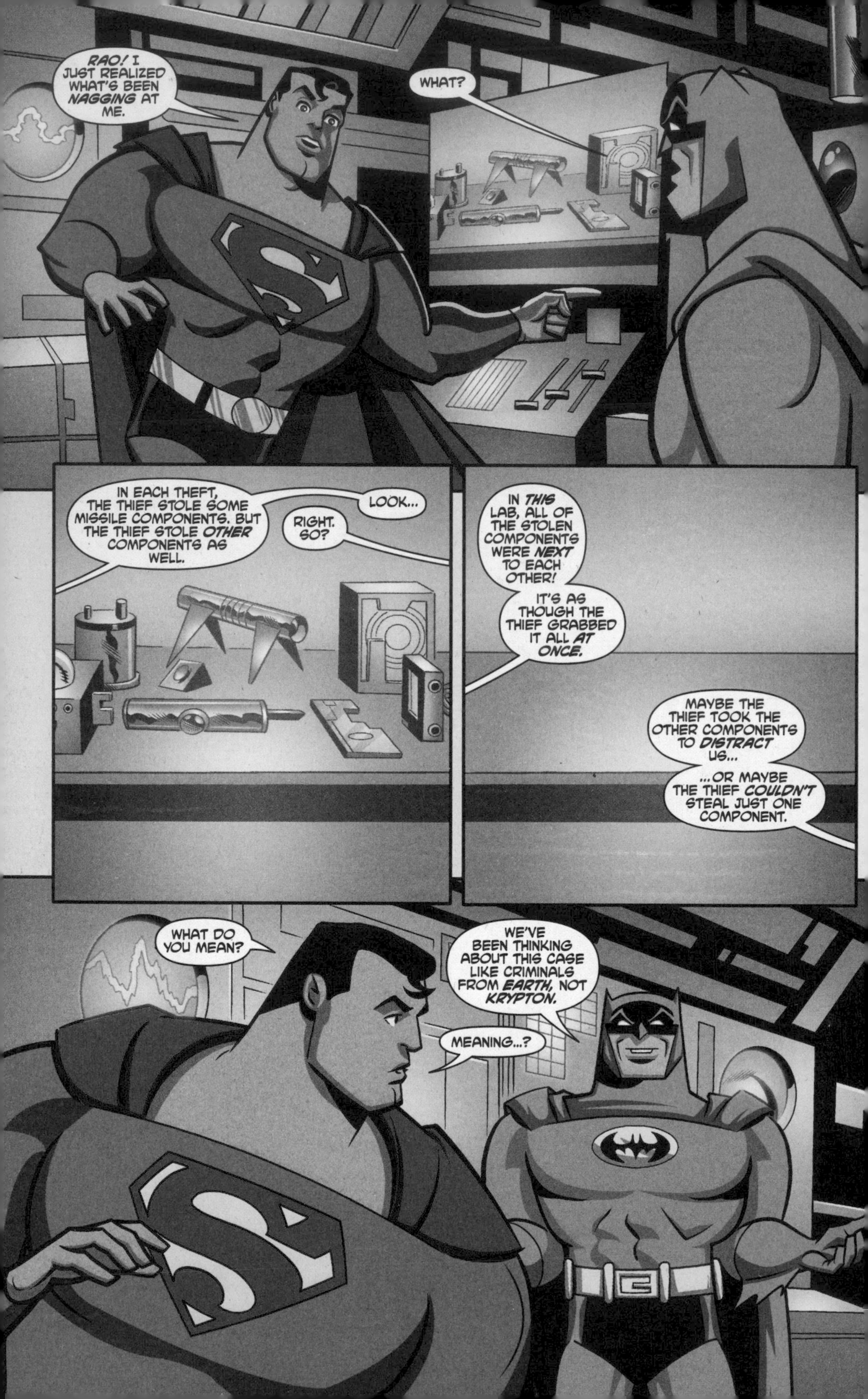
RAO! I JUST REALIZED WHAT'S BEEN NAGGING AT ME.
WHAT?
IN EACH THEFT, THE THIEF STOLE SOME MISSILE COMPONENTS. BUT THE THIEF STOLE OTHER COMPONENTS AS WELL.
LOOK...
RIGHT. SO?
IN THIS LAB, ALL OF THE STOLEN COMPONENTS WERE NEXT TO EACH OTHER!
IT'S AS THOUGH THE THIEF GRABBED IT ALL AT ONCE.
MAYBE THE THIEF TOOK THE OTHER COMPONENTS TO DISTRACT US...
...OR MAYBE THE THIEF COULDN'T STEAL JUST ONE COMPONENT.
WHAT DO YOU MEAN?
WE'VE BEEN THINKING ABOUT THIS CASE LIKE CRIMINALS FROM EARTH, NOT KRYPTON.
MEANING...?

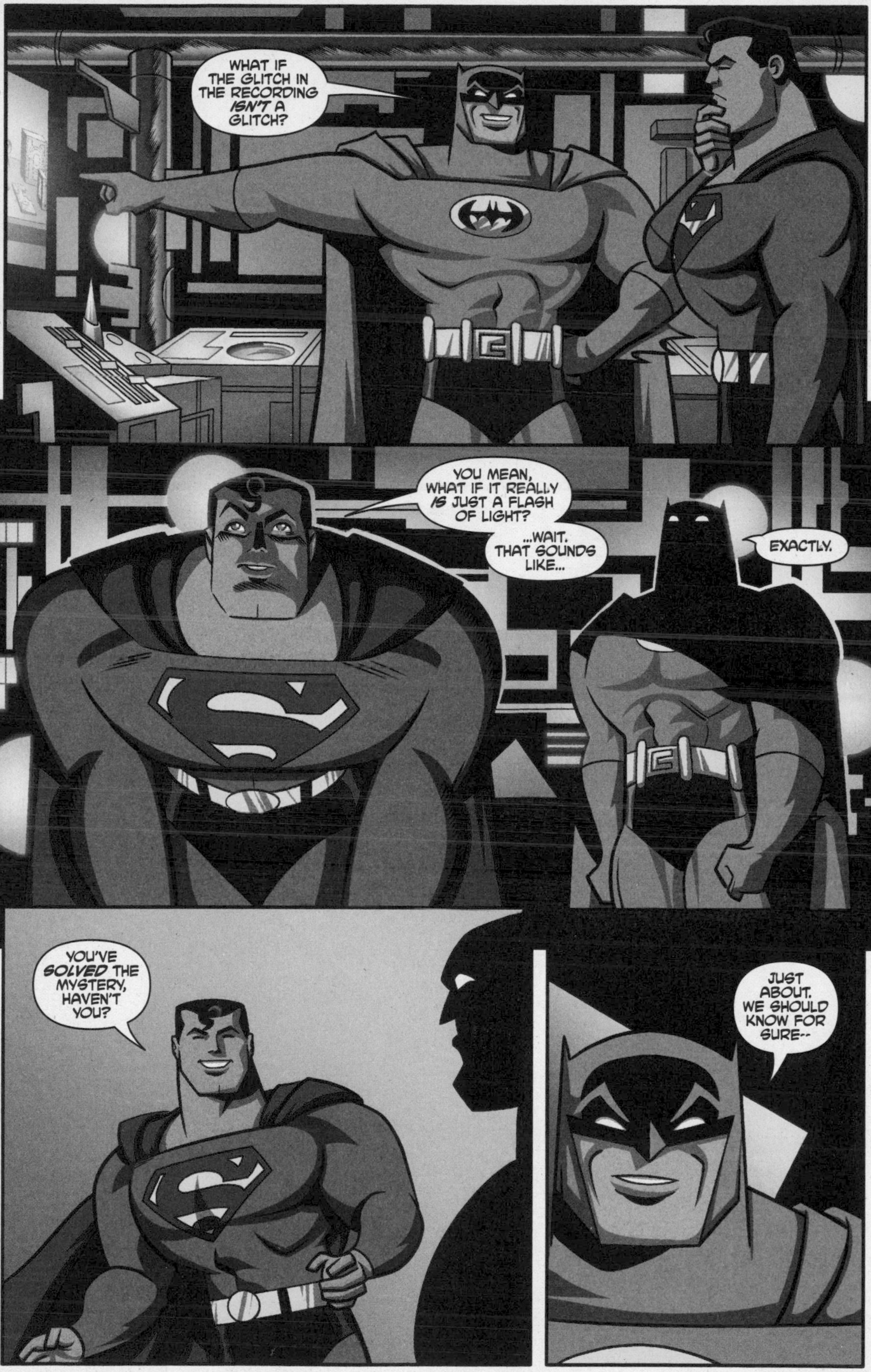
WHAT IF THE GLITCH IN THE RECORDING *ISN'T* A GLITCH?
YOU MEAN, WHAT IF IT REALLY *IS* JUST A FLASH OF LIGHT?
...WAIT. THAT SOUNDS LIKE...
EXACTLY.
YOU'VE *SOLVED* THE MYSTERY, HAVEN'T YOU?
JUST ABOUT. WE SHOULD KNOW FOR SURE--

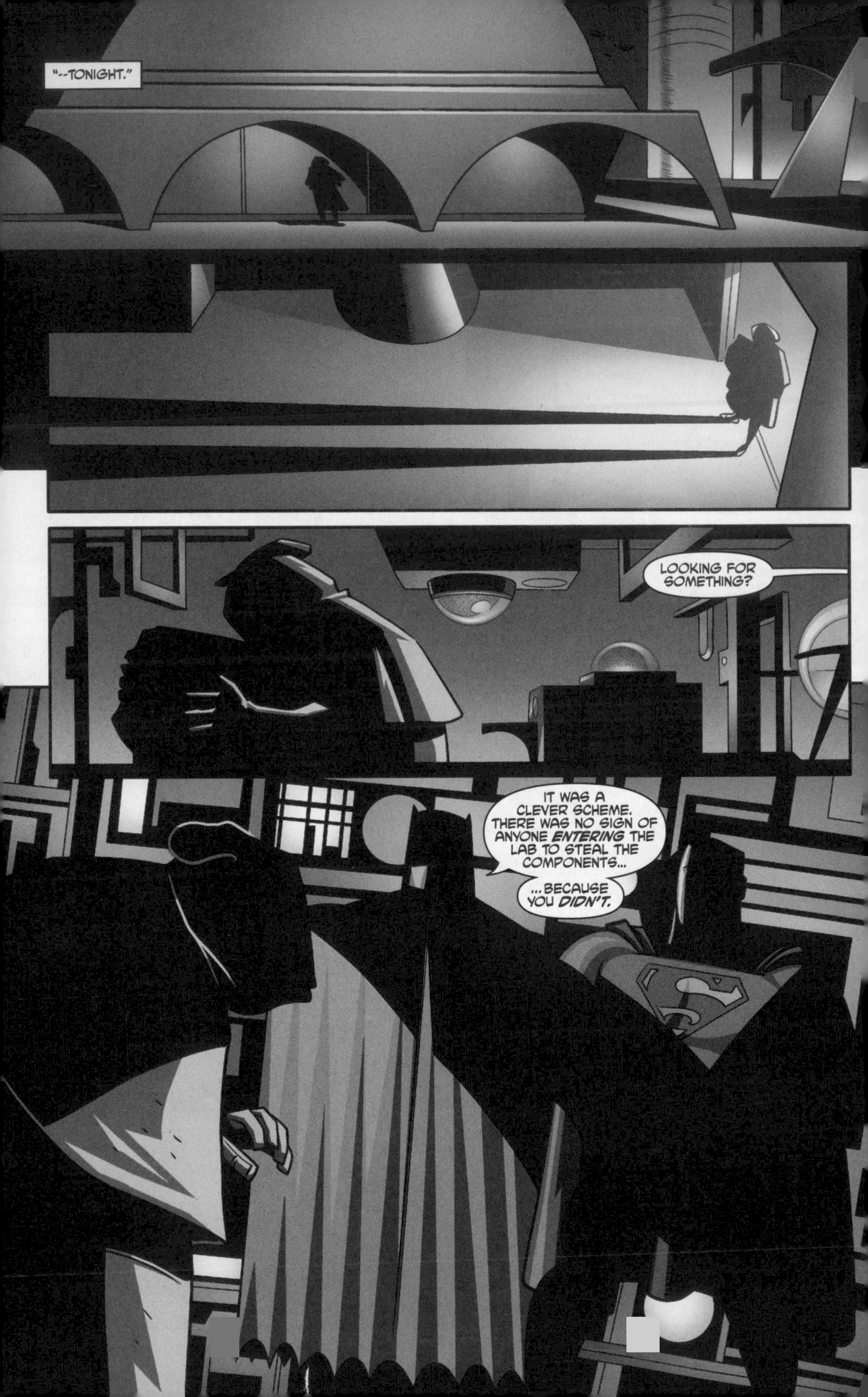
"--TONIGHT."
LOOKING FOR SOMETHING?
IT WAS A CLEVER SCHEME. THERE WAS NO SIGN OF ANYONE *ENTERING* THE LAB TO STEAL THE COMPONENTS...
...BECAUSE YOU *DIDN'T*.

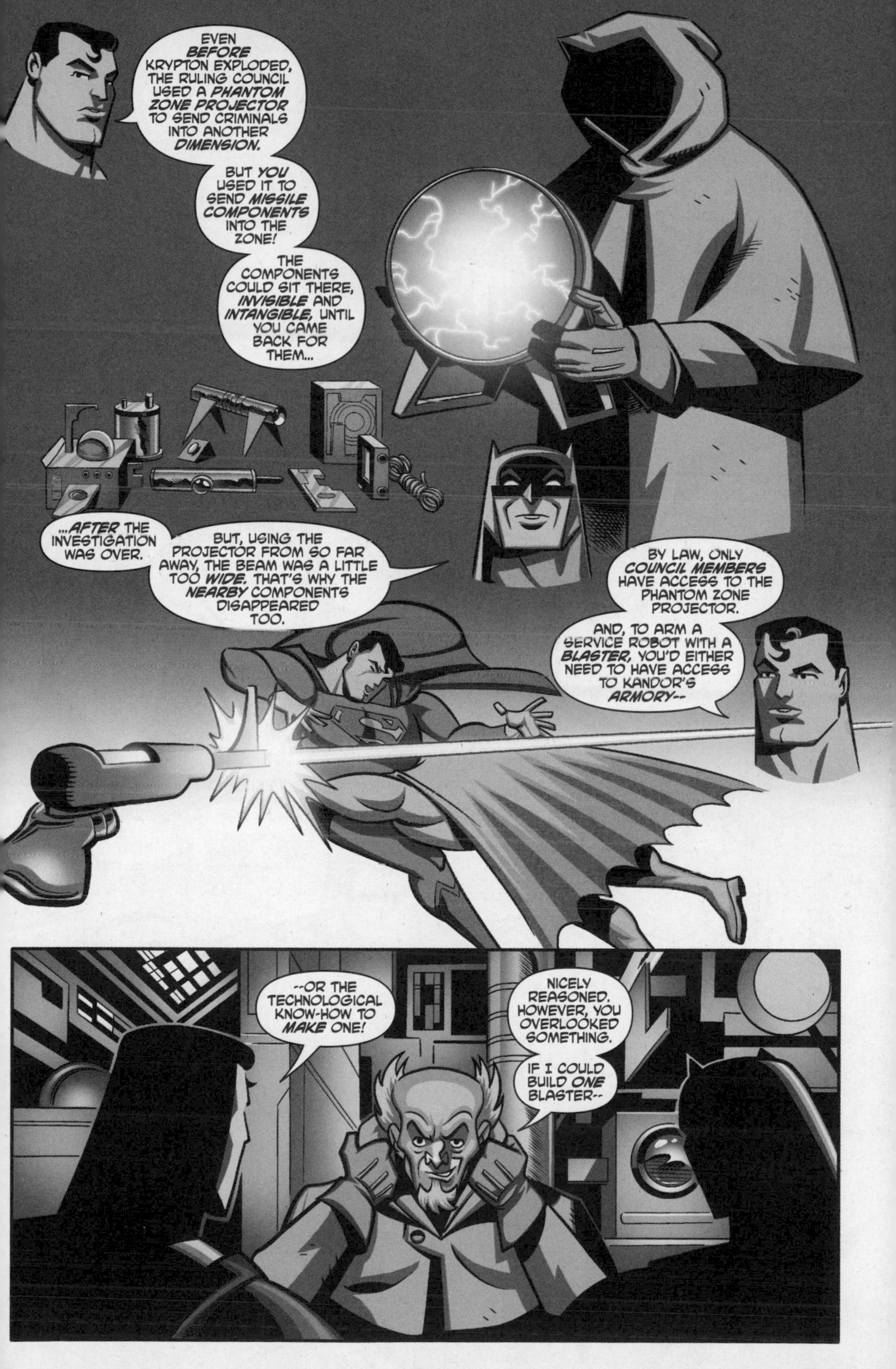
EVEN BEFORE KRYPTON EXPLODED, THE RULING COUNCIL USED A PHANTOM ZONE PROJECTOR TO SEND CRIMINALS INTO ANOTHER DIMENSION.
BUT YOU USED IT TO SEND MISSILE COMPONENTS INTO THE ZONE!
THE COMPONENTS COULD SIT THERE, INVISIBLE AND INTANGIBLE, UNTIL YOU CAME BACK FOR THEM...
...AFTER THE INVESTIGATION WAS OVER.
BUT, USING THE PROJECTOR FROM SO FAR AWAY, THE BEAM WAS A LITTLE TOO WIDE. THAT'S WHY THE NEARBY COMPONENTS DISAPPEARED TOO.
BY LAW, ONLY COUNCIL MEMBERS HAVE ACCESS TO THE PHANTOM ZONE PROJECTOR.
AND, TO ARM A SERVICE ROBOT WITH A BLASTER, YOU'D EITHER NEED TO HAVE ACCESS TO KANDOR'S ARMORY--
--OR THE TECHNOLOGICAL KNOW-HOW TO MAKE ONE!
NICELY REASONED. HOWEVER, YOU OVERLOOKED SOMETHING.
IF I COULD BUILD ONE BLASTER--

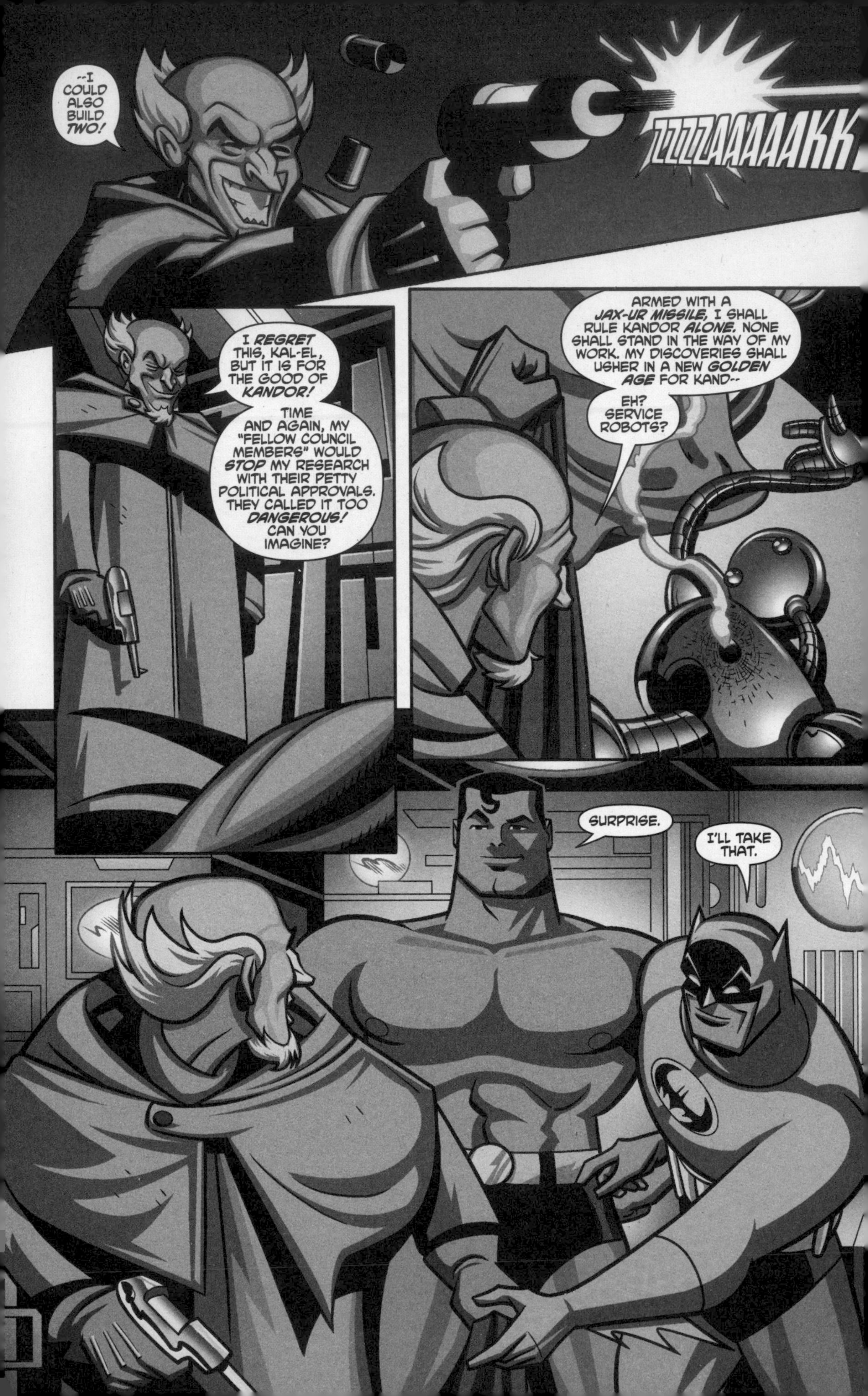
--I COULD ALSO BUILD TWO!
ZZZZAAAAAAKK
I REGRET THIS, KAL-EL, BUT IT IS FOR THE GOOD OF KANDOR!
TIME AND AGAIN, MY "FELLOW COUNCIL MEMBERS" WOULD STOP MY RESEARCH WITH THEIR PETTY POLITICAL APPROVALS. THEY CALLED IT TOO DANGEROUS! CAN YOU IMAGINE?
ARMED WITH A JAX-UR MISSILE, I SHALL RULE KANDOR ALONE. NONE SHALL STAND IN THE WAY OF MY WORK. MY DISCOVERIES SHALL USHER IN A NEW GOLDEN AGE FOR KAND--
EH? SERVICE ROBOTS?
SURPRISE.
I'LL TAKE THAT.

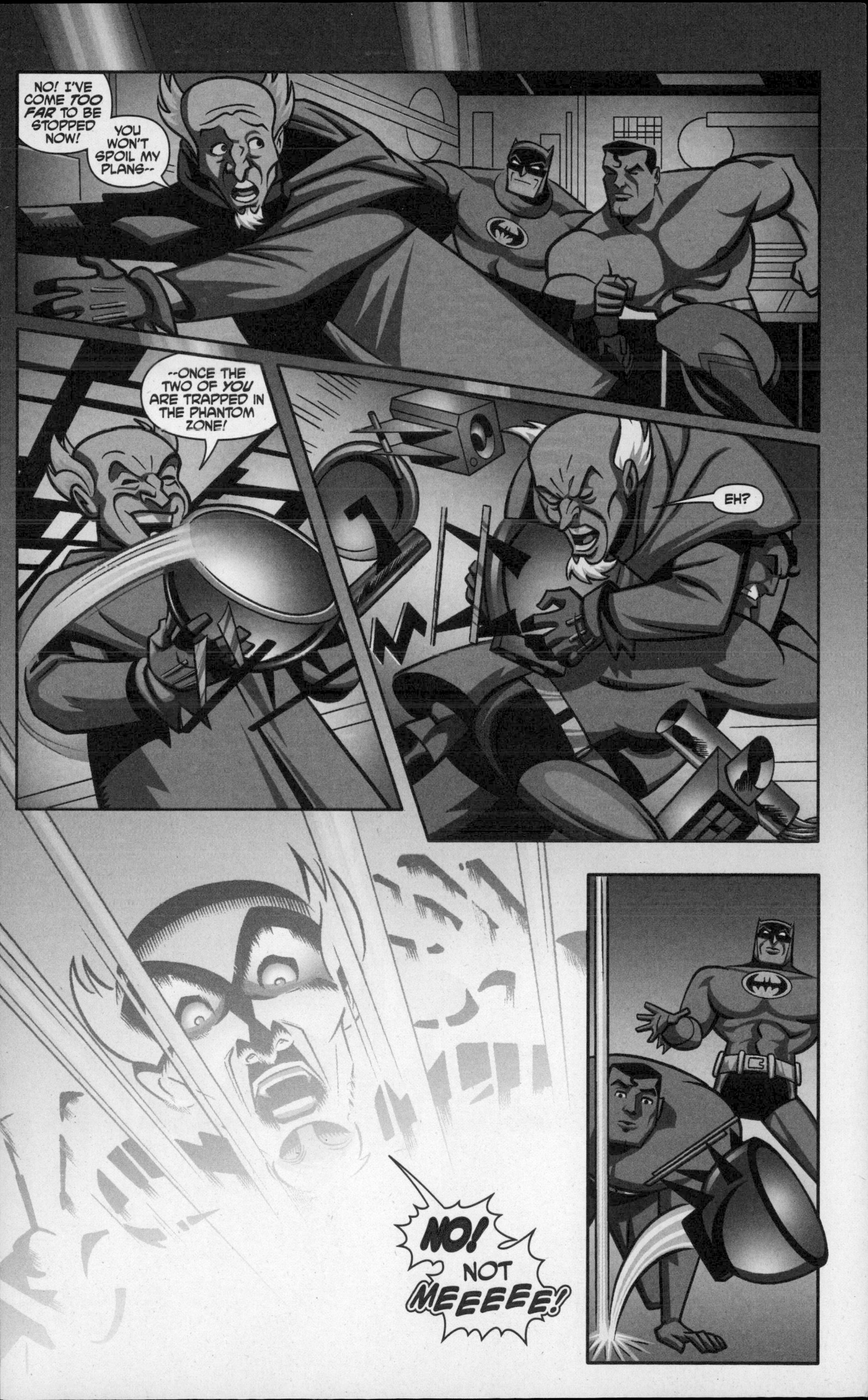
NO! I'VE COME TOO FAR TO BE STOPPED NOW!
YOU WON'T SPOIL MY PLANS--
--ONCE THE TWO OF YOU ARE TRAPPED IN THE PHANTOM ZONE!
EH?
NO! NOT MEEEEEE!

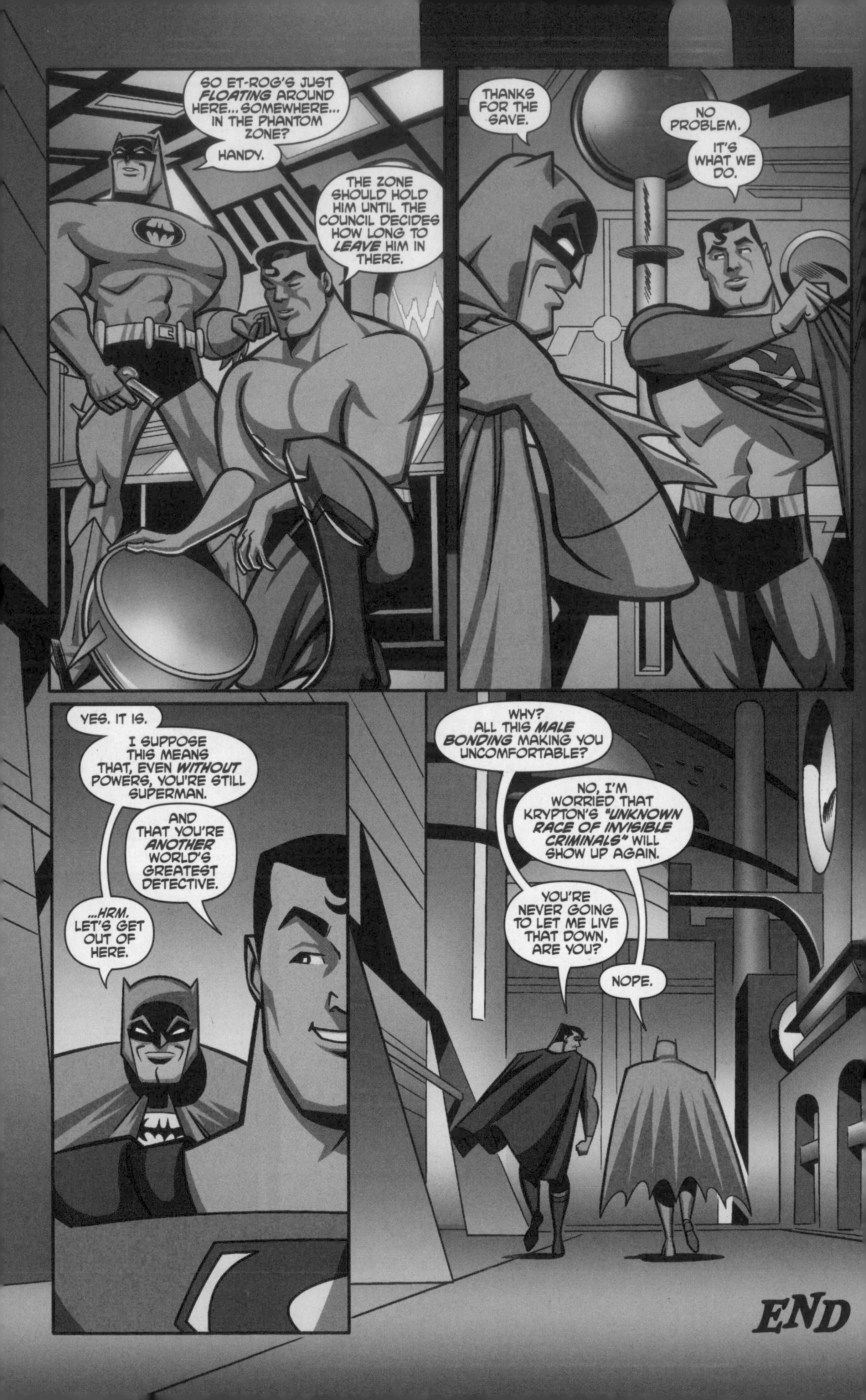
SO ET-ROG'S JUST FLOATING AROUND HERE... SOMEWHERE... IN THE PHANTOM ZONE?
HANDY.
THE ZONE SHOULD HOLD HIM UNTIL THE COUNCIL DECIDES HOW LONG TO LEAVE HIM IN THERE.
THANKS FOR THE SAVE.
NO PROBLEM.
IT'S WHAT WE DO.
YES. IT IS.
I SUPPOSE THIS MEANS THAT, EVEN WITHOUT POWERS, YOU'RE STILL SUPERMAN.
AND THAT YOU'RE ANOTHER WORLD'S GREATEST DETECTIVE.
...HRM. LET'S GET OUT OF HERE.
WHY? ALL THIS MALE BONDING MAKING YOU UNCOMFORTABLE?
NO, I'M WORRIED THAT KRYPTON'S "UNKNOWN RACE OF INVISIBLE CRIMINALS" WILL SHOW UP AGAIN.
YOU'RE NEVER GOING TO LET ME LIVE THAT DOWN, ARE YOU?
NOPE.
END

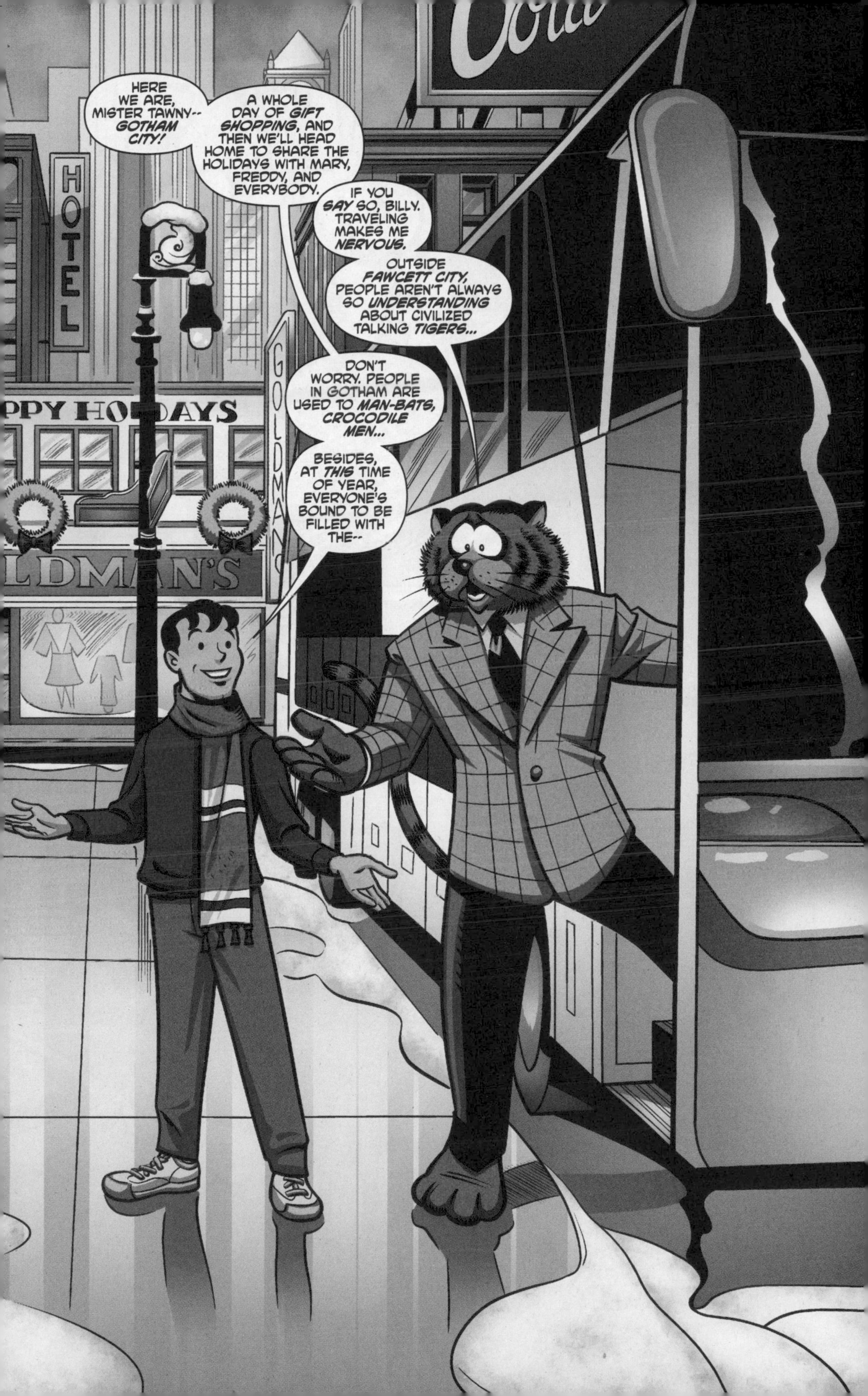

HERE WE ARE, MISTER TAWNY-- GOTHAM CITY!
A WHOLE DAY OF GIFT SHOPPING, AND THEN WE'LL HEAD HOME TO SHARE THE HOLIDAYS WITH MARY, FREDDY, AND EVERYBODY.
IF YOU SAY SO, BILLY. TRAVELING MAKES ME NERVOUS.
OUTSIDE FAWCETT CITY, PEOPLE AREN'T ALWAYS SO UNDERSTANDING ABOUT CIVILIZED TALKING TIGERS...
DON'T WORRY. PEOPLE IN GOTHAM ARE USED TO MAN-BATS, CROCODILE MEN...
BESIDES, AT THIS TIME OF YEAR, EVERYONE'S BOUND TO BE FILLED WITH THE--
HOTEL
PPY HOLIDAYS
LDMAN'S
GOLDMAN'S

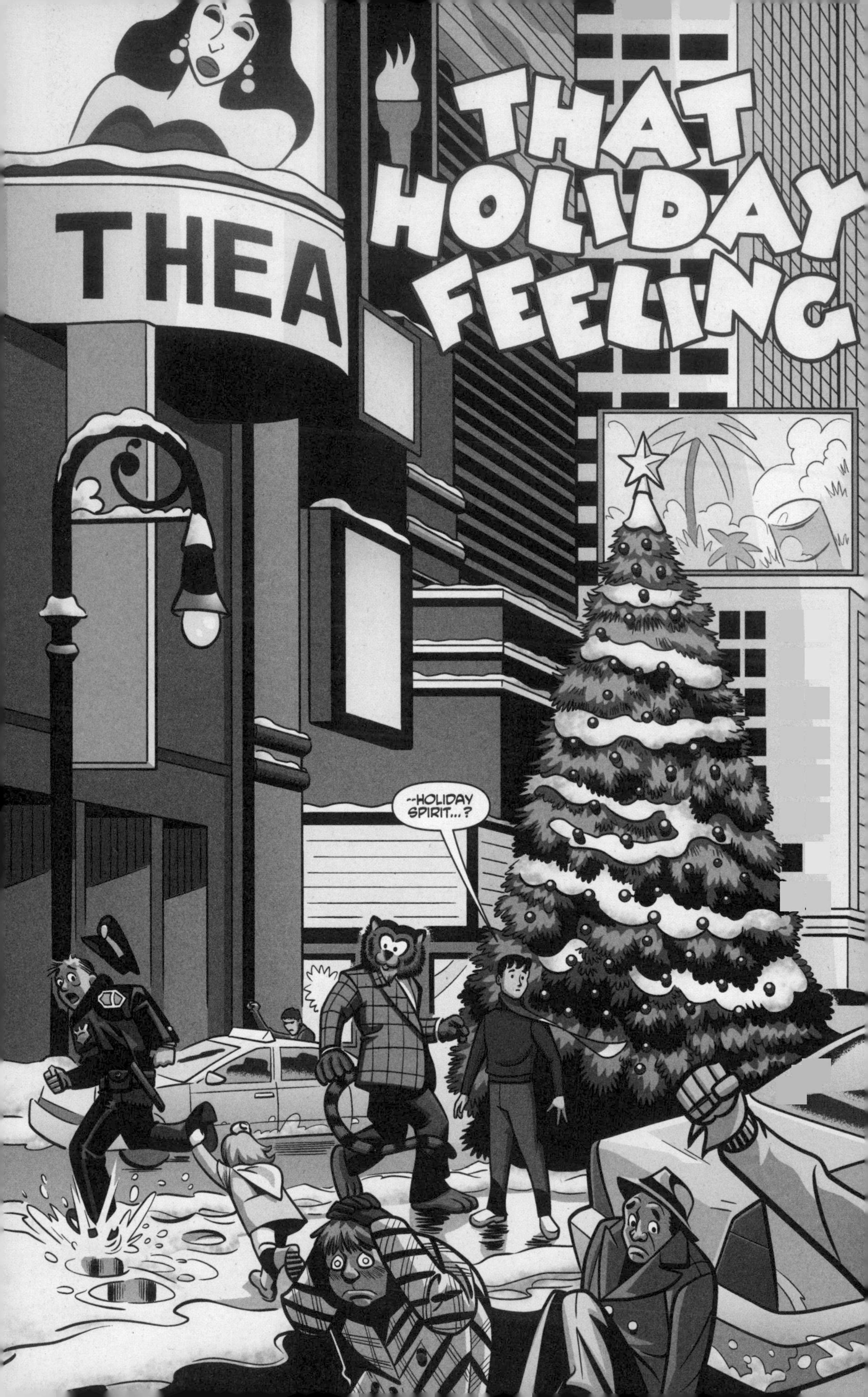
THAT HOLIDAY FEELING
THEA
--HOLIDAY SPIRIT...?

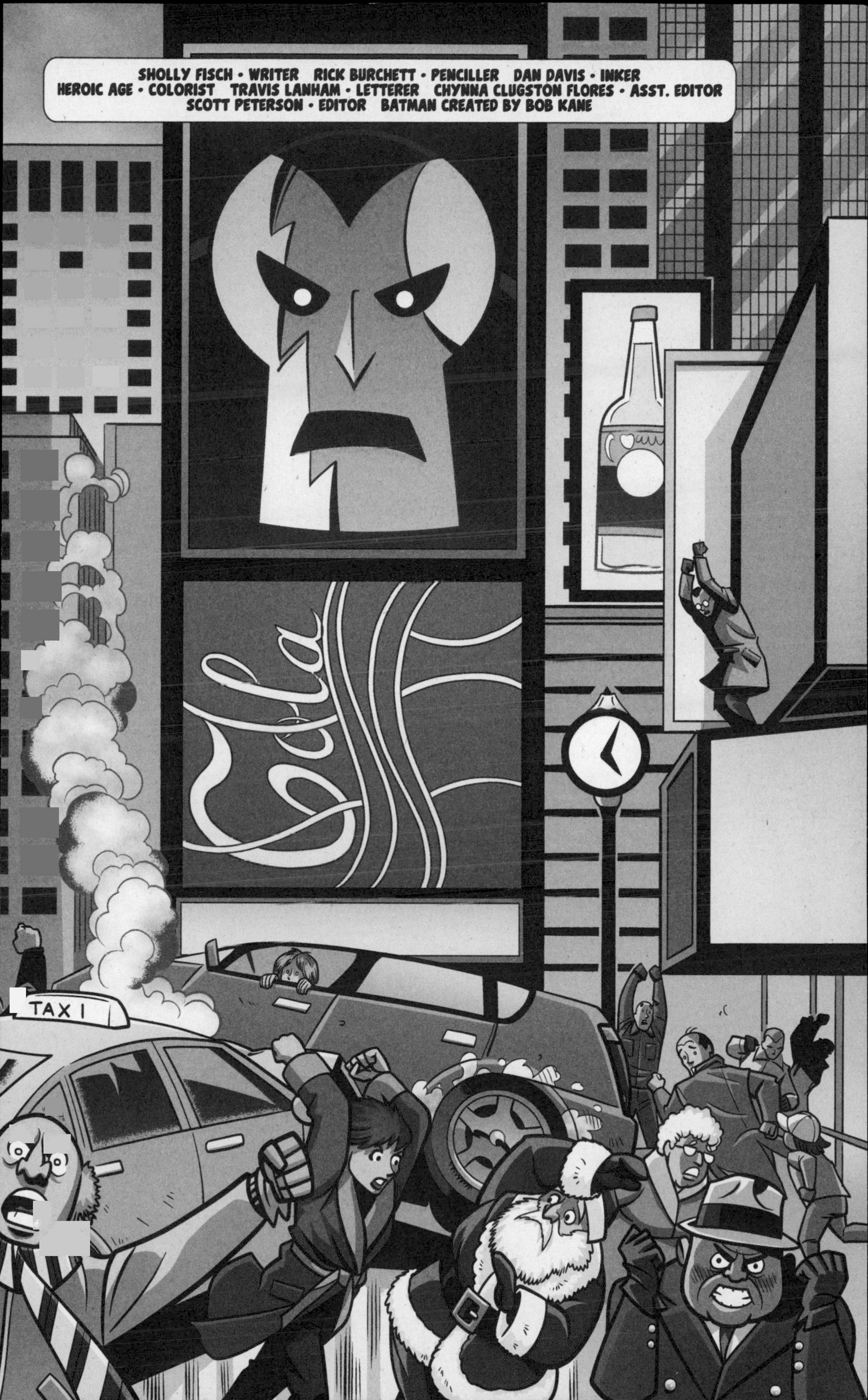
SHOLLY FISCH • WRITER RICK BURCHETT • PENCILLER DAN DAVIS • INKER
HEROIC AGE • COLORIST TRAVIS LANHAM • LETTERER CHYNNA CLUGSTON FLORES • ASST. EDITOR
SCOTT PETERSON • EDITOR BATMAN CREATED BY BOB KANE
TAXI

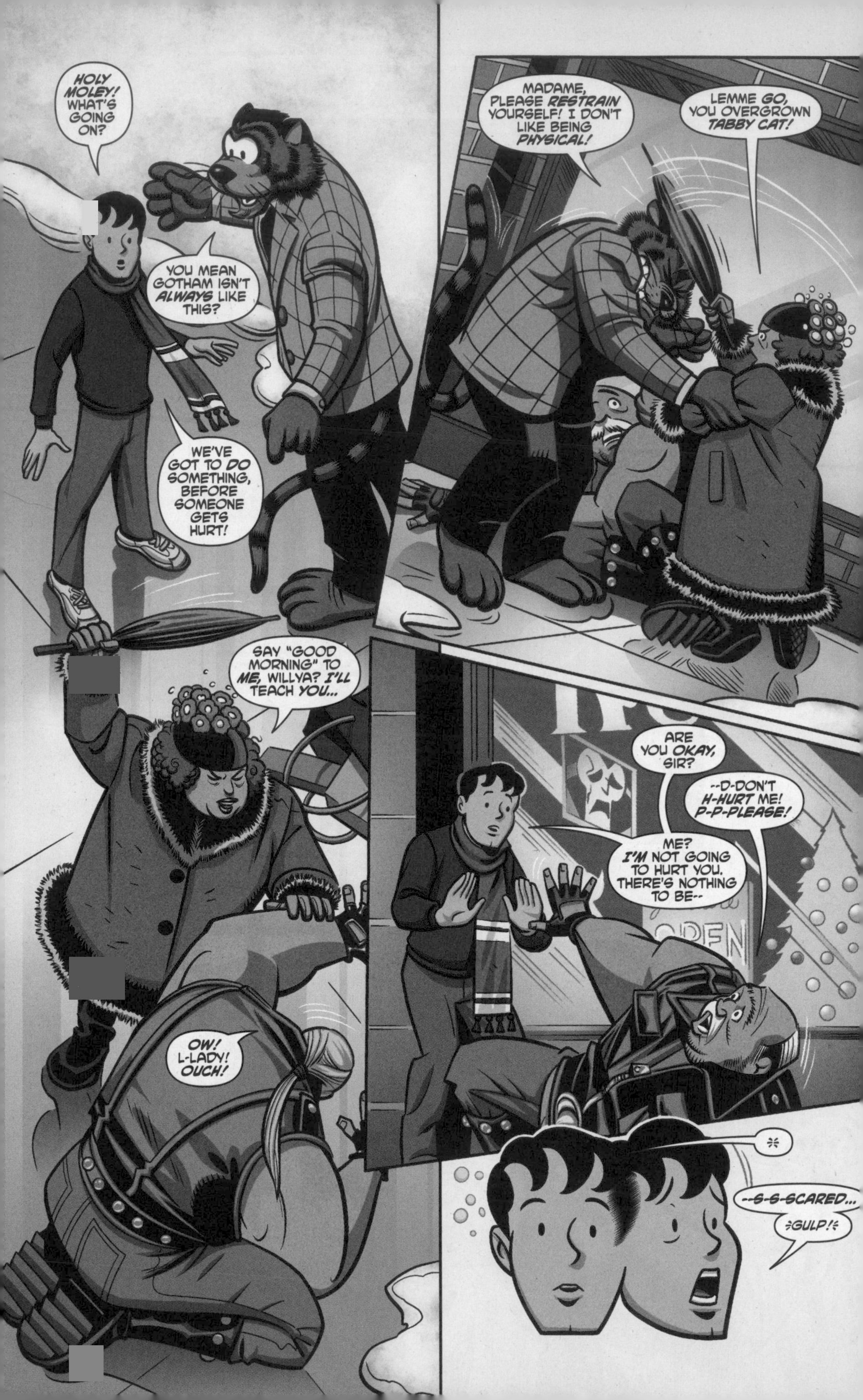
HOLY MOLEY! WHAT'S GOING ON?
YOU MEAN GOTHAM ISN'T ALWAYS LIKE THIS?
WE'VE GOT TO DO SOMETHING, BEFORE SOMEONE GETS HURT!
MADAME, PLEASE RESTRAIN YOURSELF! I DON'T LIKE BEING PHYSICAL!
LEMME GO, YOU OVERGROWN TABBY CAT!
SAY "GOOD MORNING" TO ME, WILLYA? I'LL TEACH YOU...
OW! L-LADY! OUCH!
ARE YOU OKAY, SIR?
--D-DON'T H-HURT ME! P-P-PLEASE!
ME? I'M NOT GOING TO HURT YOU. THERE'S NOTHING TO BE--
OPEN
--S-S-SCARED...
GULP!

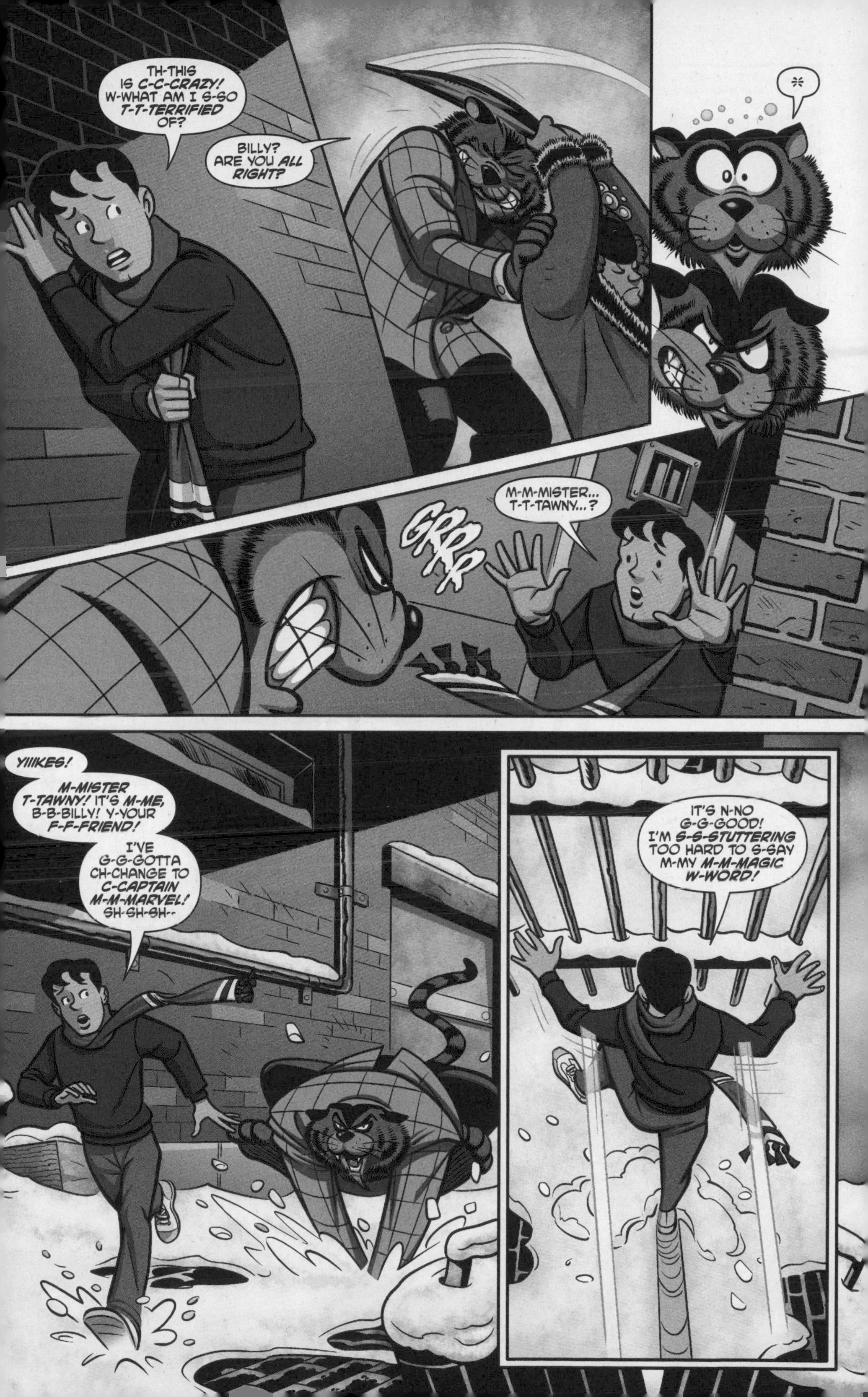

TH-THIS IS C-C-CRAZY! W-WHAT AM I S-SO T-T-TERRIFIED OF?
BILLY? ARE YOU ALL RIGHT?
M-M-MISTER... T-T-TAWNY...?
GRRR
YIIIKES!
M-MISTER T-TAWNY! IT'S M-ME, B-B-BILLY! Y-YOUR F-F-FRIEND!
I'VE G-G-GOTTA CH-CHANGE TO C-CAPTAIN M-M-MARVEL! SH-SH-SH--
IT'S N-NO G-G-GOOD! I'M S-S-STUTTERING TOO HARD TO S-SAY M-MY M-M-MAGIC W-WORD!

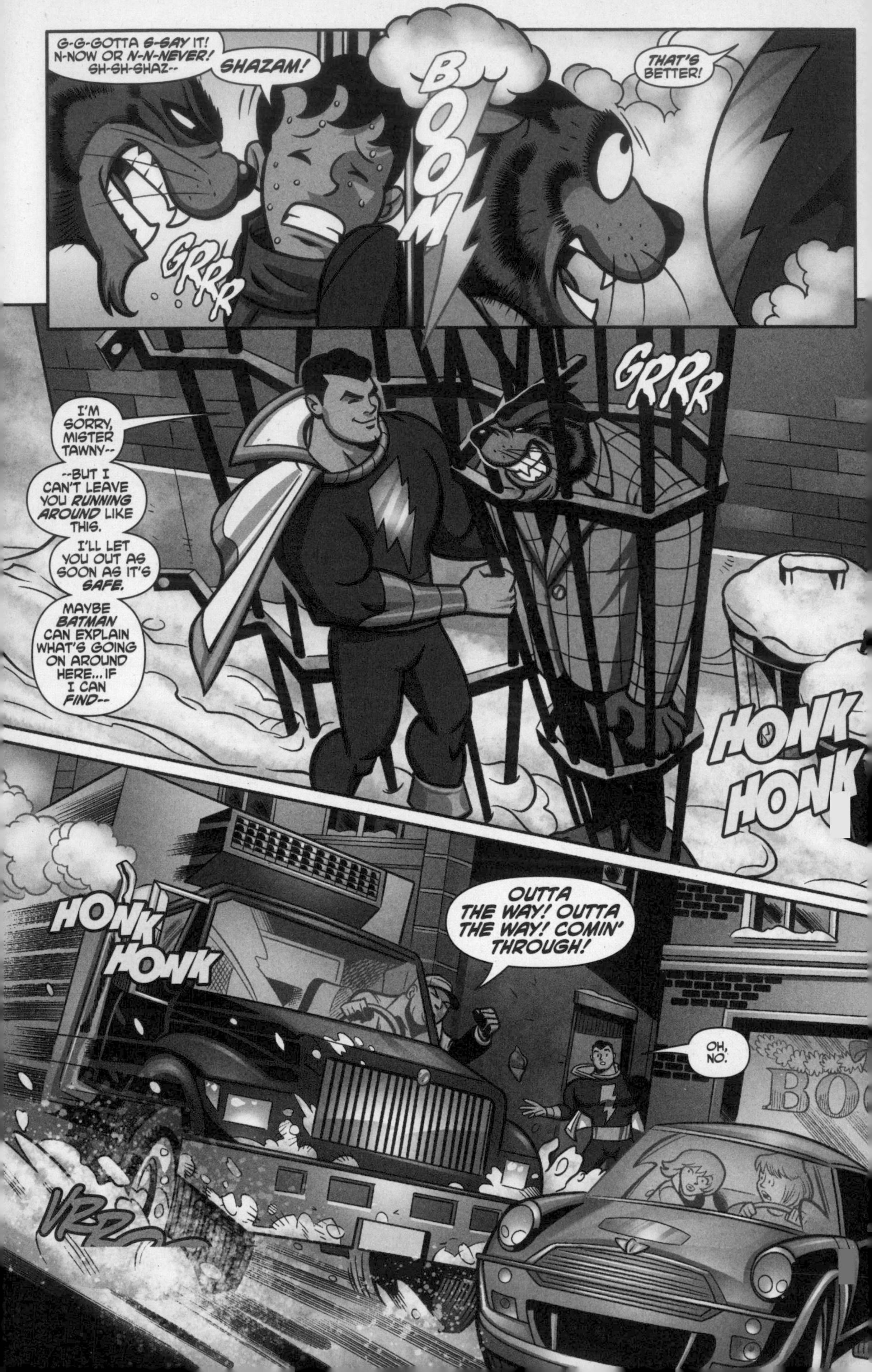
G-G-GOTTA S-SAY IT! N-NOW OR N-N-NEVER! SH-SH-SHAZ--
SHAZAM!
BOOM
THAT'S BETTER!
GRRR
GRRR
I'M SORRY, MISTER TAWNY--
--BUT I CAN'T LEAVE YOU RUNNING AROUND LIKE THIS.
I'LL LET YOU OUT AS SOON AS IT'S SAFE.
MAYBE BATMAN CAN EXPLAIN WHAT'S GOING ON AROUND HERE... IF I CAN FIND--
HONK HONK
HONK HONK
OUTTA THE WAY! OUTTA THE WAY! COMIN' THROUGH!
OH, NO.
VRRR

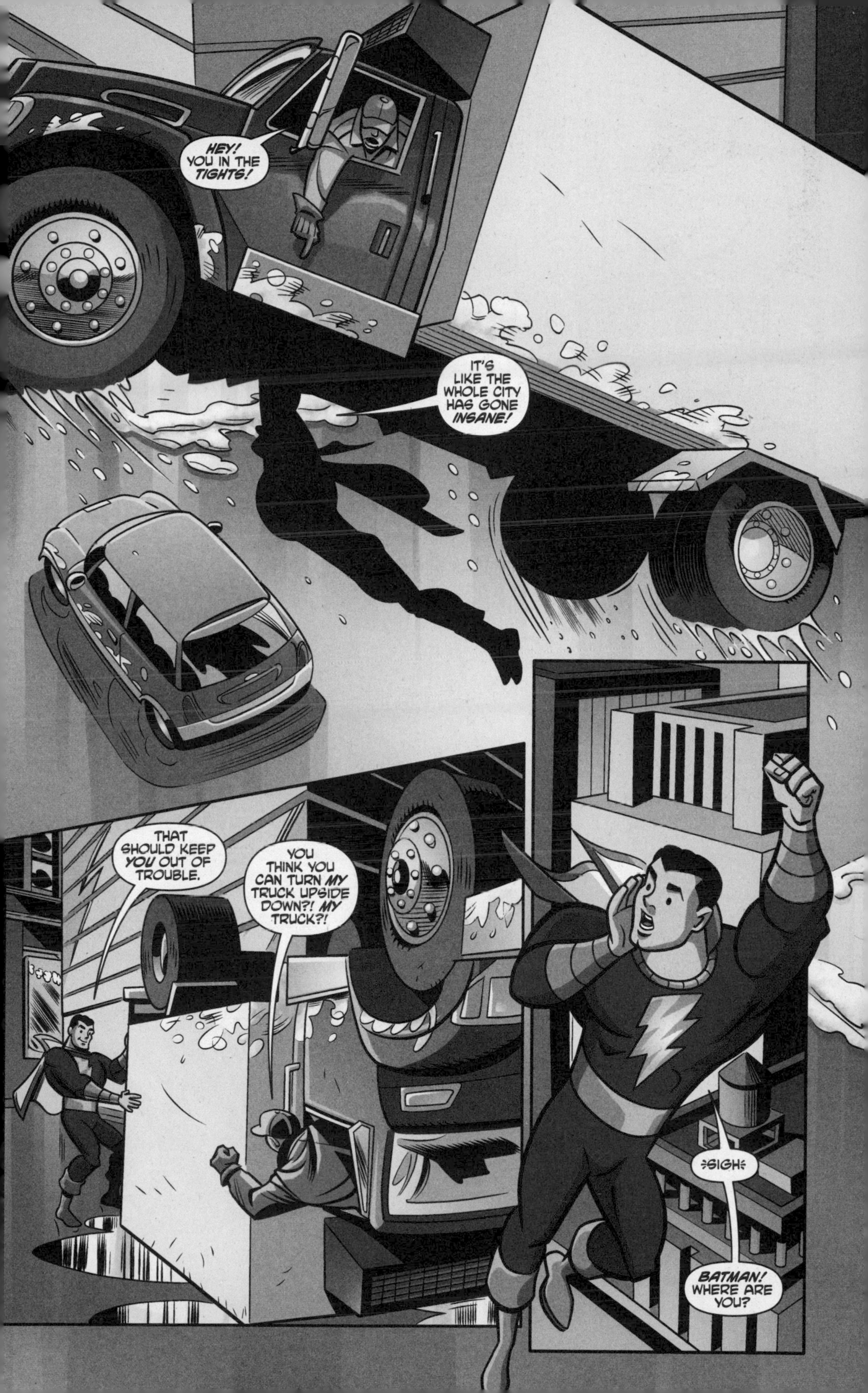
HEY! YOU IN THE TIGHTS!
IT'S LIKE THE WHOLE CITY HAS GONE INSANE!
THAT SHOULD KEEP YOU OUT OF TROUBLE.
YOU THINK YOU CAN TURN MY TRUCK UPSIDE DOWN?! MY TRUCK?!
SIGH
BATMAN! WHERE ARE YOU?

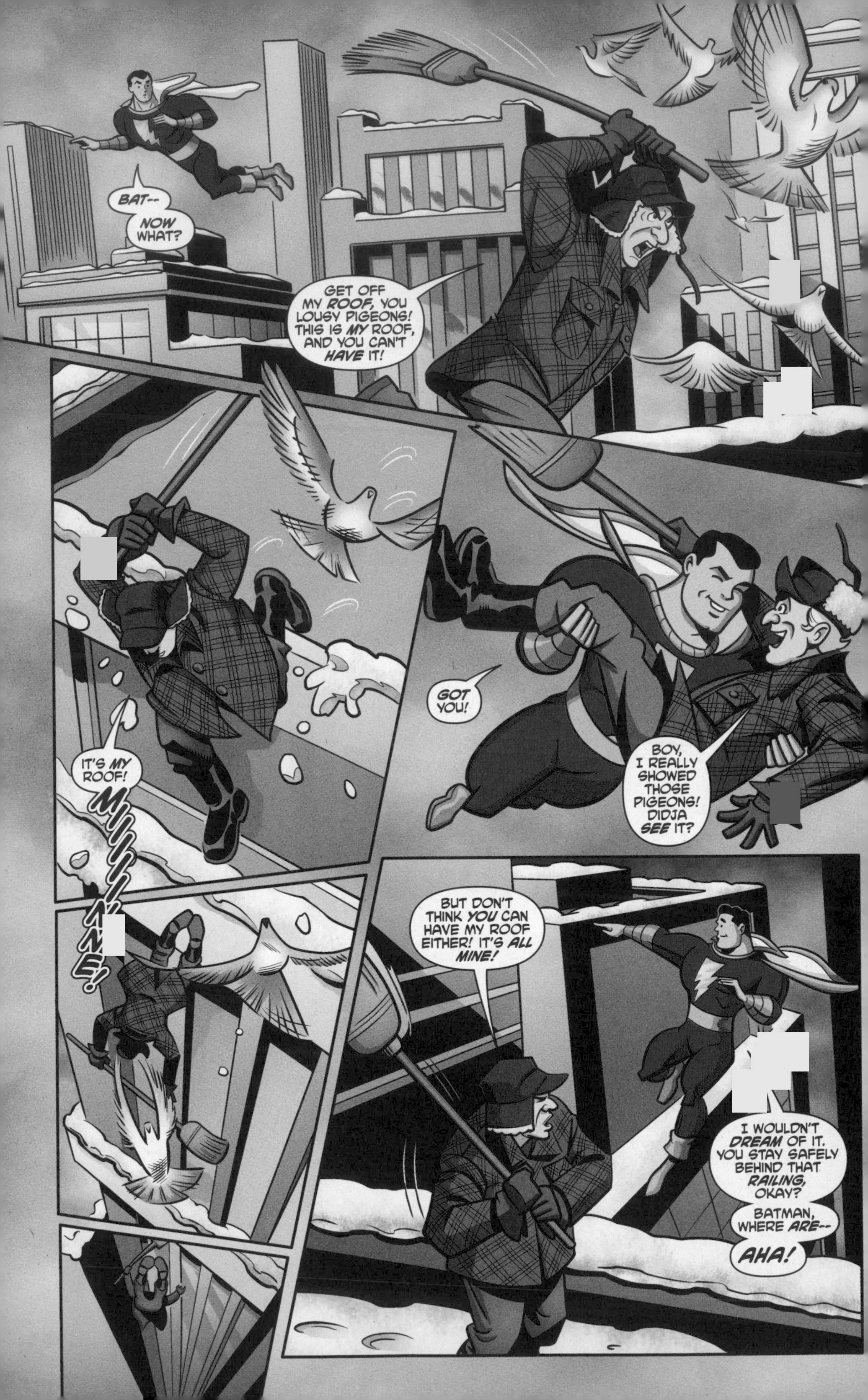
BAT-- NOW WHAT?
GET OFF MY ROOF, YOU LOUSY PIGEONS! THIS IS MY ROOF, AND YOU CAN'T HAVE IT!
IT'S MY ROOF!
MIIIIIINE!
GOT YOU!
BOY, I REALLY SHOWED THOSE PIGEONS! DIDJA SEE IT?
BUT DON'T THINK YOU CAN HAVE MY ROOF EITHER! IT'S ALL MINE!
I WOULDN'T DREAM OF IT. YOU STAY SAFELY BEHIND THAT RAILING, OKAY?
BATMAN, WHERE ARE--
AHA!

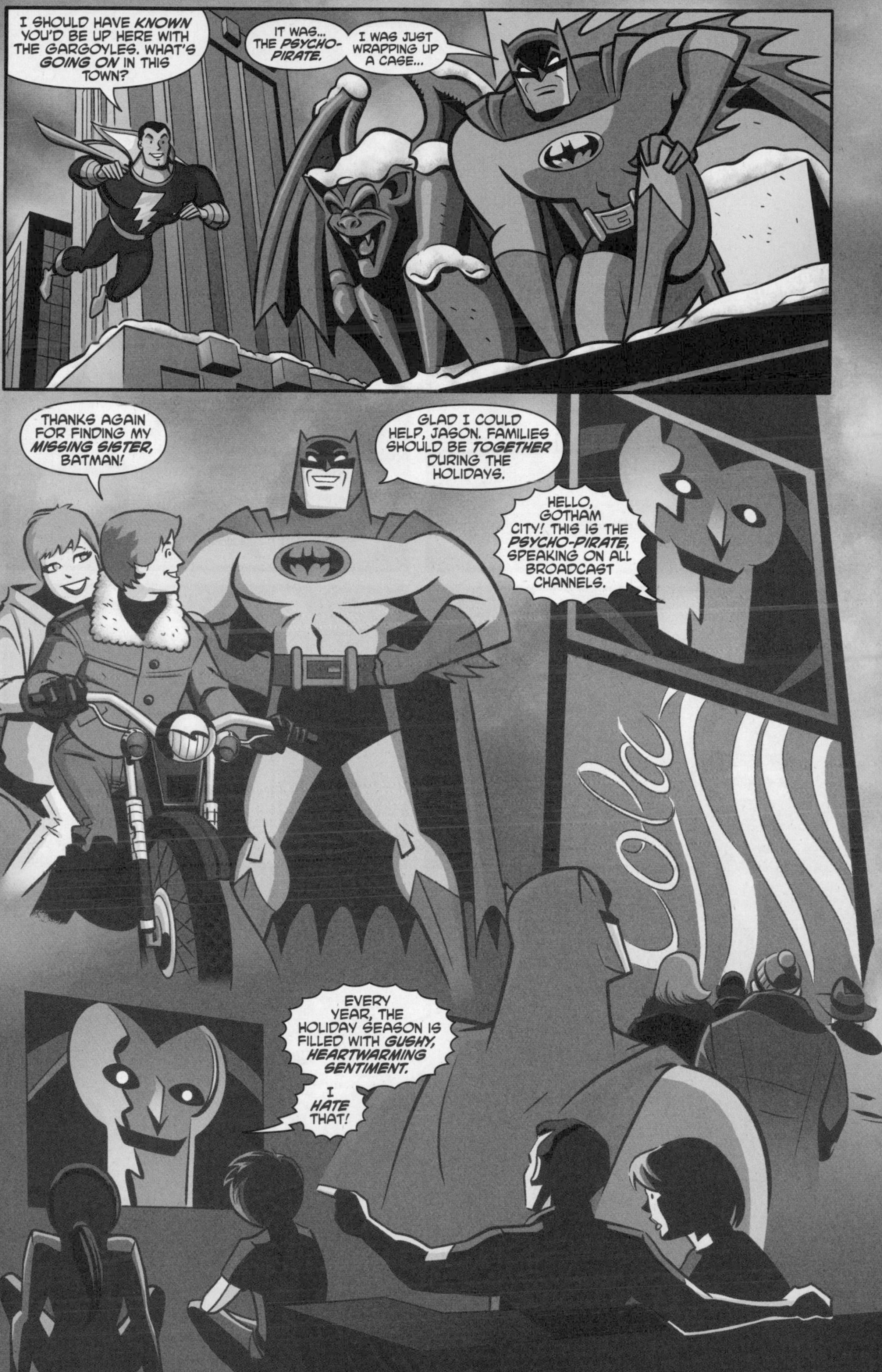
I SHOULD HAVE KNOWN YOU'D BE UP HERE WITH THE GARGOYLES. WHAT'S GOING ON IN THIS TOWN?
IT WAS... THE PSYCHO-PIRATE.
I WAS JUST WRAPPING UP A CASE...
THANKS AGAIN FOR FINDING MY MISSING SISTER, BATMAN!
GLAD I COULD HELP, JASON. FAMILIES SHOULD BE TOGETHER DURING THE HOLIDAYS.
HELLO, GOTHAM CITY! THIS IS THE PSYCHO-PIRATE, SPEAKING ON ALL BROADCAST CHANNELS.
EVERY YEAR, THE HOLIDAY SEASON IS FILLED WITH GUSHY, HEARTWARMING SENTIMENT.
I HATE THAT!

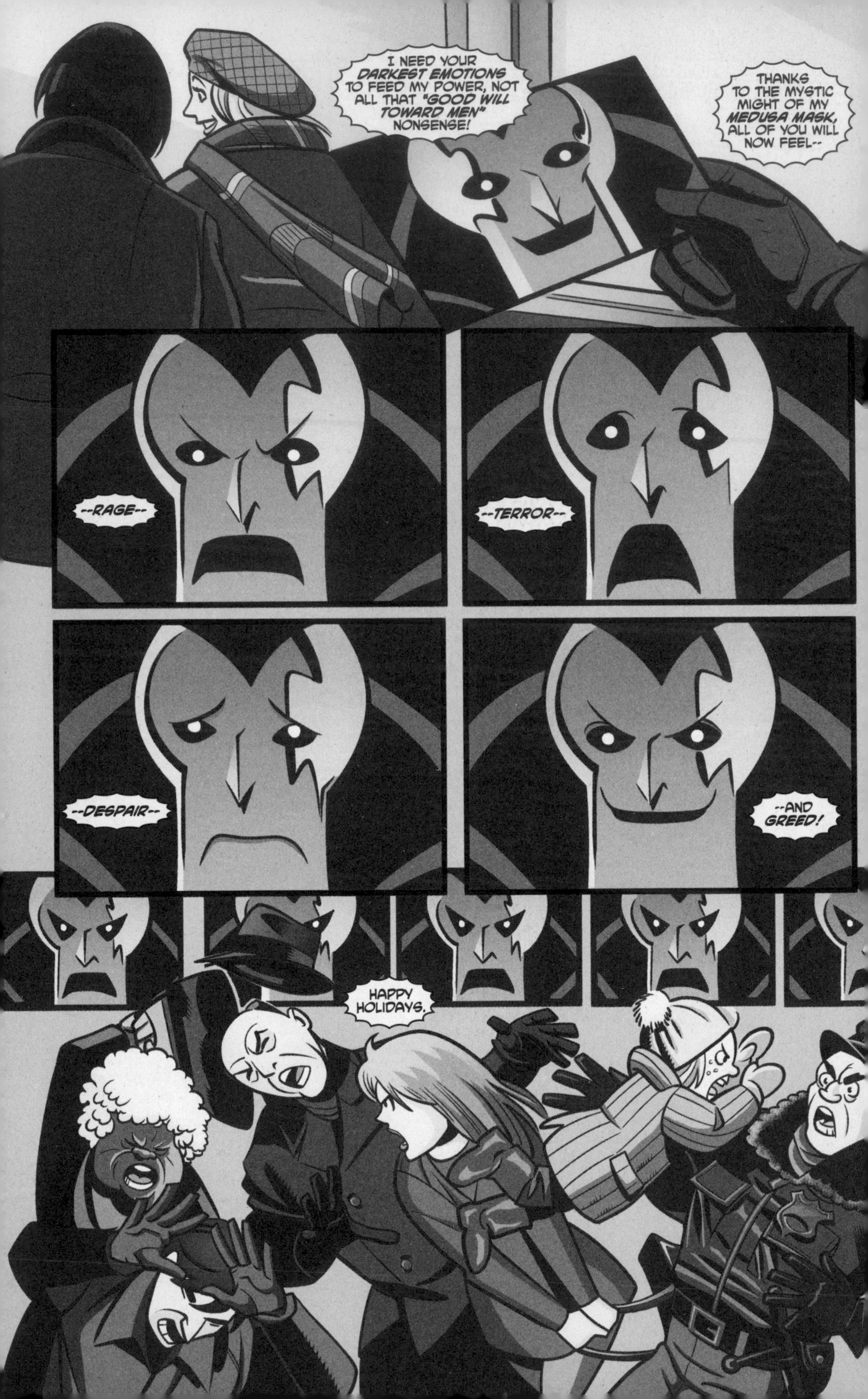
I NEED YOUR DARKEST EMOTIONS TO FEED MY POWER, NOT ALL THAT "GOOD WILL TOWARD MEN" NONSENSE!
THANKS TO THE MYSTIC MIGHT OF MY MEDUSA MASK, ALL OF YOU WILL NOW FEEL--
--RAGE--
--TERROR--
--DESPAIR--
--AND GREED!
HAPPY HOLIDAYS.

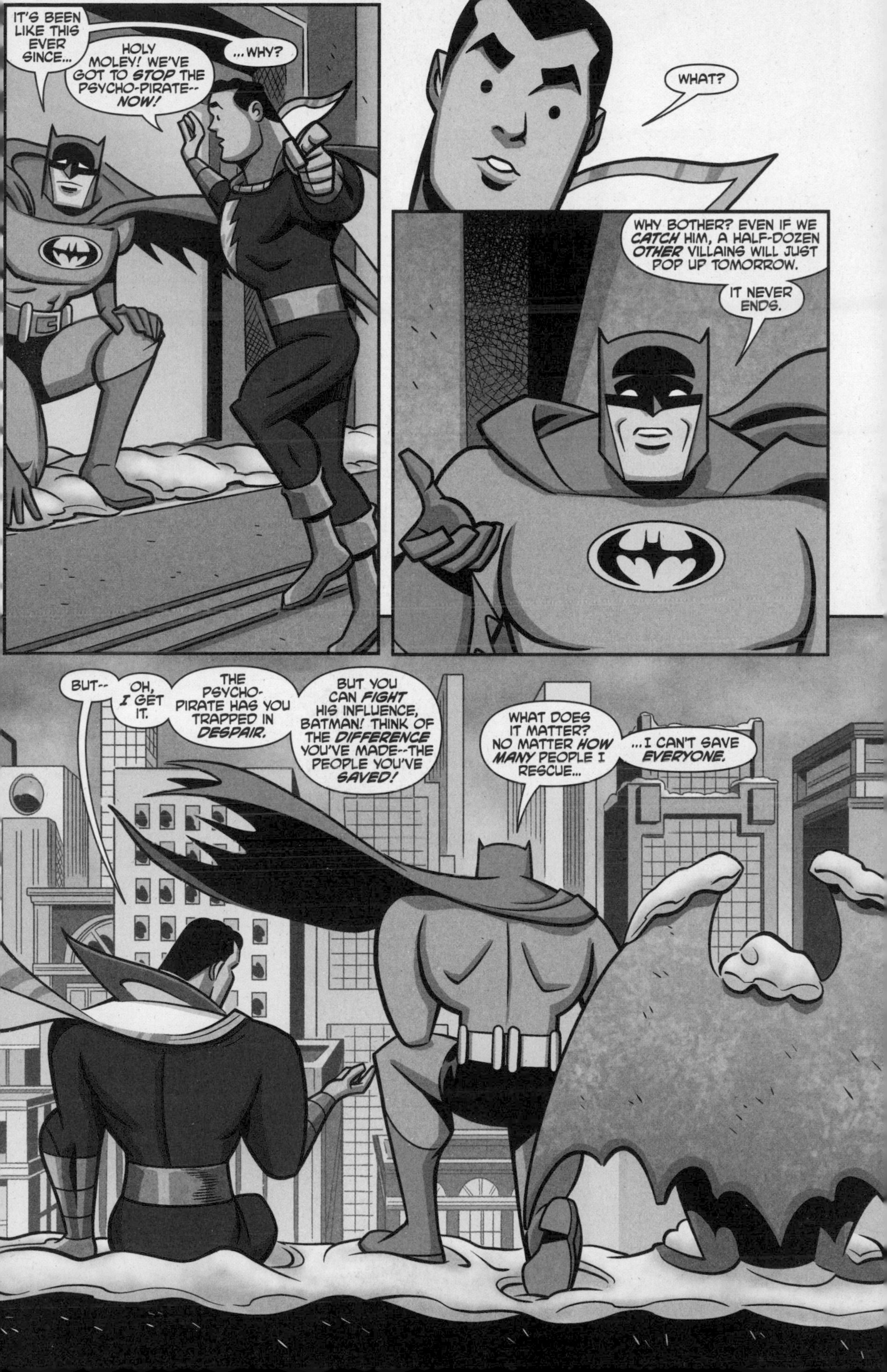
IT'S BEEN LIKE THIS EVER SINCE...
HOLY MOLEY! WE'VE GOT TO STOP THE PSYCHO-PIRATE-- NOW!
...WHY?
WHAT?
WHY BOTHER? EVEN IF WE CATCH HIM, A HALF-DOZEN OTHER VILLAINS WILL JUST POP UP TOMORROW.
IT NEVER ENDS.
BUT--
OH, I GET IT.
THE PSYCHO-PIRATE HAS YOU TRAPPED IN DESPAIR.
BUT YOU CAN FIGHT HIS INFLUENCE, BATMAN! THINK OF THE DIFFERENCE YOU'VE MADE--THE PEOPLE YOU'VE SAVED!
WHAT DOES IT MATTER? NO MATTER HOW MANY PEOPLE I RESCUE...
...I CAN'T SAVE EVERYONE.

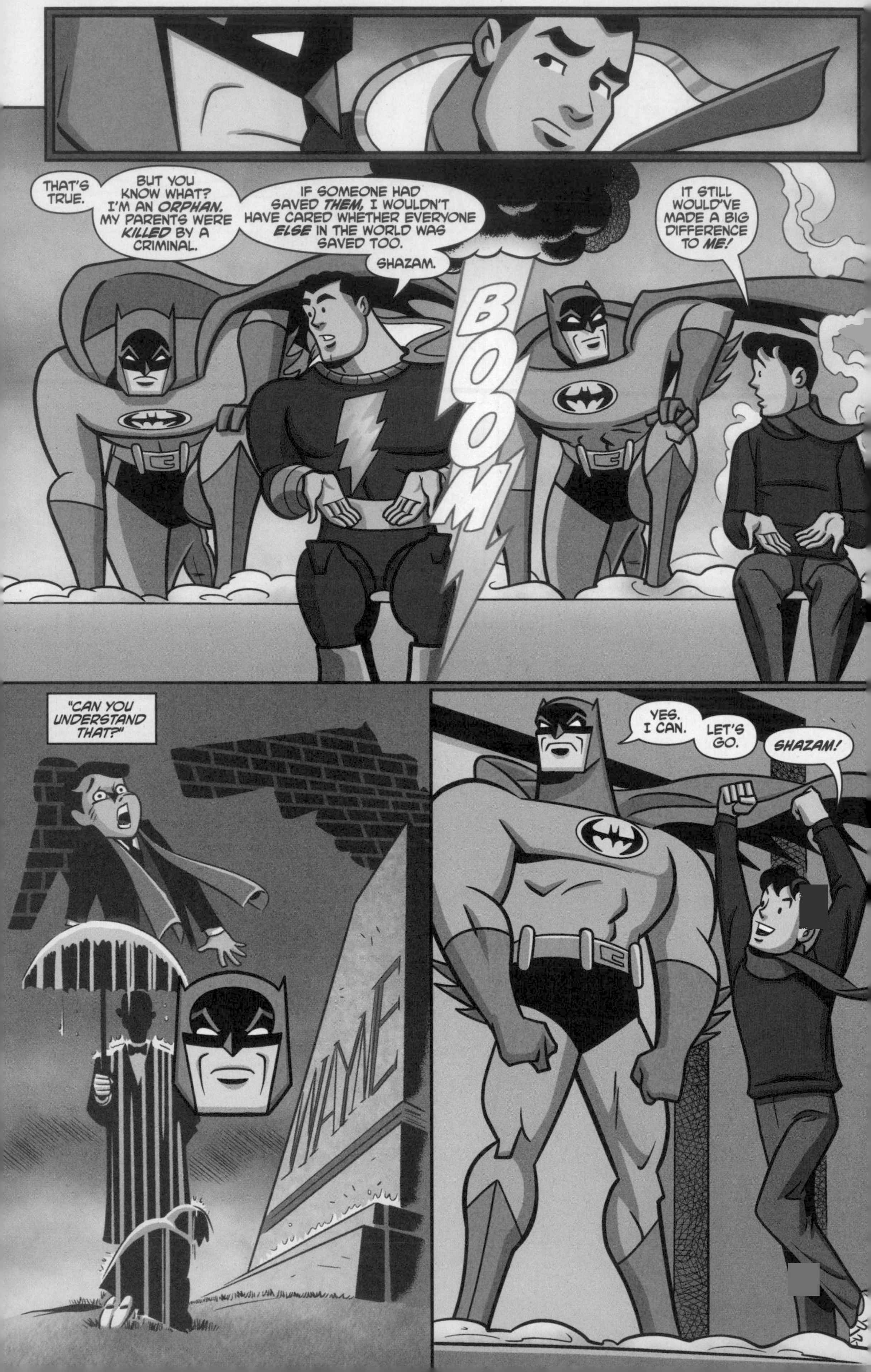
THAT'S TRUE.
BUT YOU KNOW WHAT? I'M AN *ORPHAN.* MY PARENTS WERE *KILLED* BY A CRIMINAL.
IF SOMEONE HAD SAVED *THEM,* I WOULDN'T HAVE CARED WHETHER EVERYONE *ELSE* IN THE WORLD WAS SAVED TOO.
SHAZAM.
BOOM
IT STILL WOULD'VE MADE A BIG DIFFERENCE TO *ME!*
"CAN YOU UNDERSTAND THAT?"
YES. I CAN.
LET'S GO.
SHAZAM!

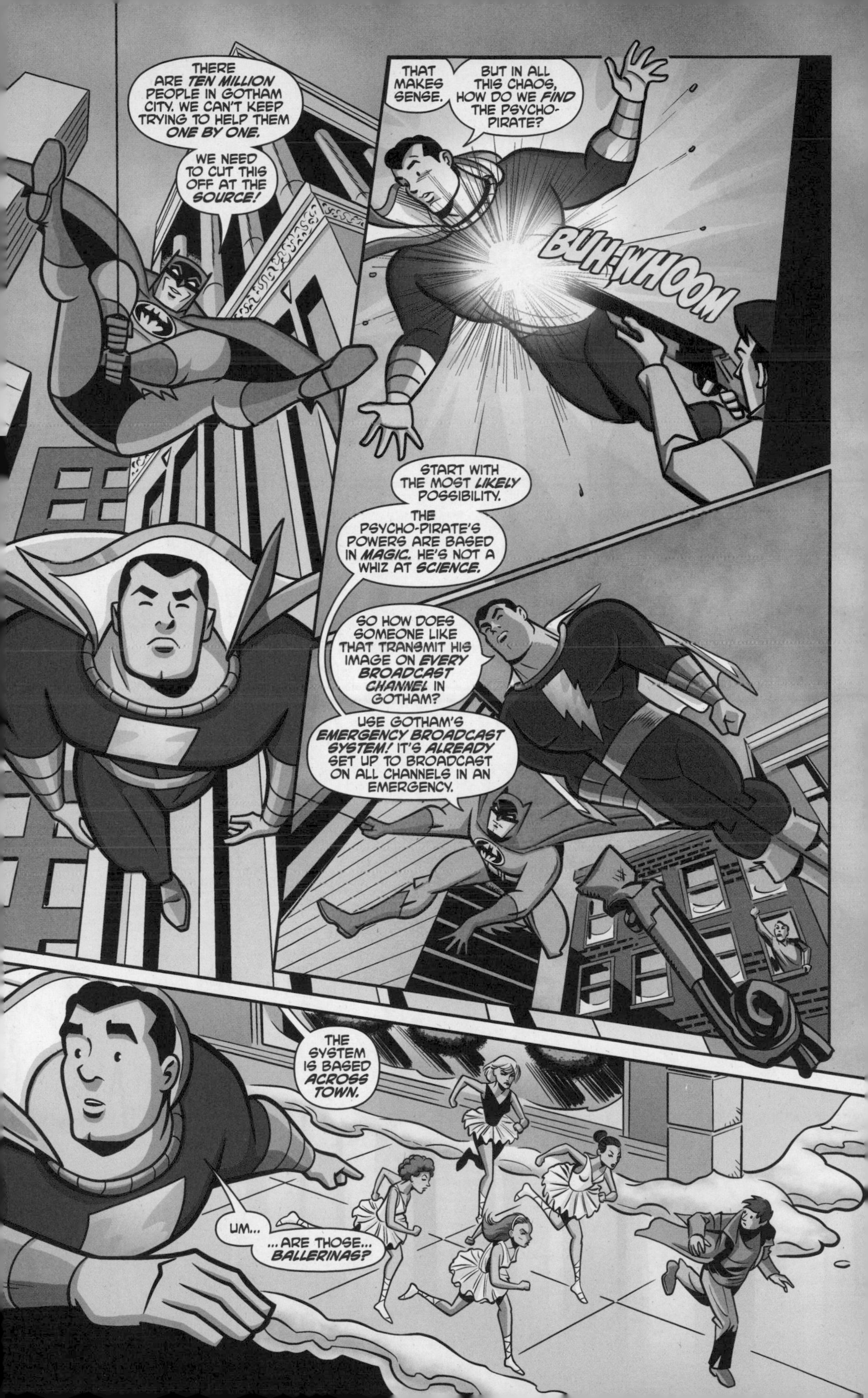
THERE ARE TEN MILLION PEOPLE IN GOTHAM CITY. WE CAN'T KEEP TRYING TO HELP THEM ONE BY ONE.
WE NEED TO CUT THIS OFF AT THE SOURCE!
THAT MAKES SENSE.
BUT IN ALL THIS CHAOS, HOW DO WE FIND THE PSYCHO-PIRATE?
BUH-WHOOM
START WITH THE MOST LIKELY POSSIBILITY.
THE PSYCHO-PIRATE'S POWERS ARE BASED IN MAGIC. HE'S NOT A WHIZ AT SCIENCE.
SO HOW DOES SOMEONE LIKE THAT TRANSMIT HIS IMAGE ON EVERY BROADCAST CHANNEL IN GOTHAM?
USE GOTHAM'S EMERGENCY BROADCAST SYSTEM! IT'S ALREADY SET UP TO BROADCAST ON ALL CHANNELS IN AN EMERGENCY.
THE SYSTEM IS BASED ACROSS TOWN.
UM...
...ARE THOSE... BALLERINAS?

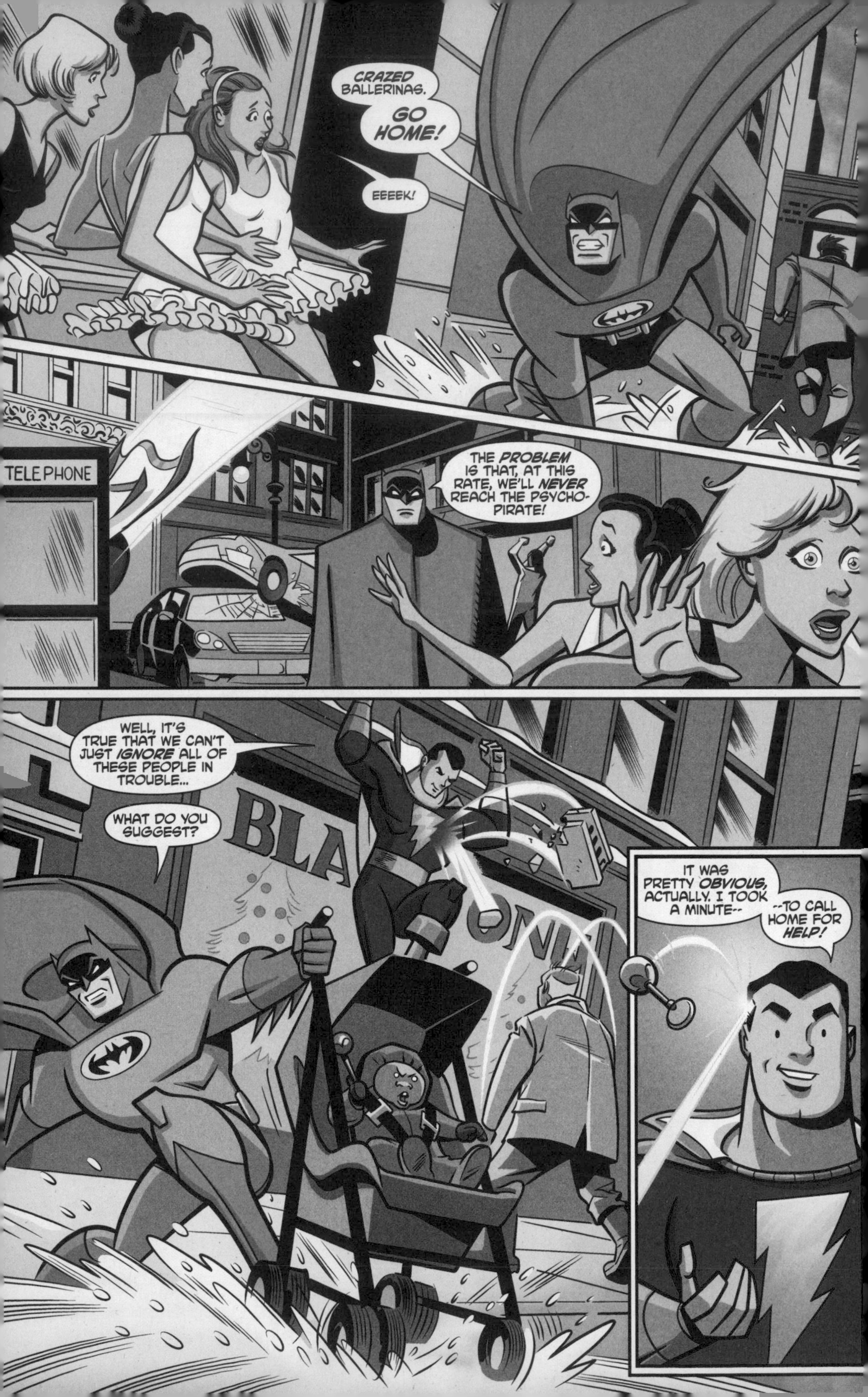
CRAZED BALLERINAS. GO HOME!
EEEEK!
TELEPHONE
THE PROBLEM IS THAT, AT THIS RATE, WE'LL NEVER REACH THE PSYCHO-PIRATE!
WELL, IT'S TRUE THAT WE CAN'T JUST IGNORE ALL OF THESE PEOPLE IN TROUBLE...
WHAT DO YOU SUGGEST?
BLA
IT WAS PRETTY OBVIOUS, ACTUALLY. I TOOK A MINUTE--
--TO CALL HOME FOR HELP!

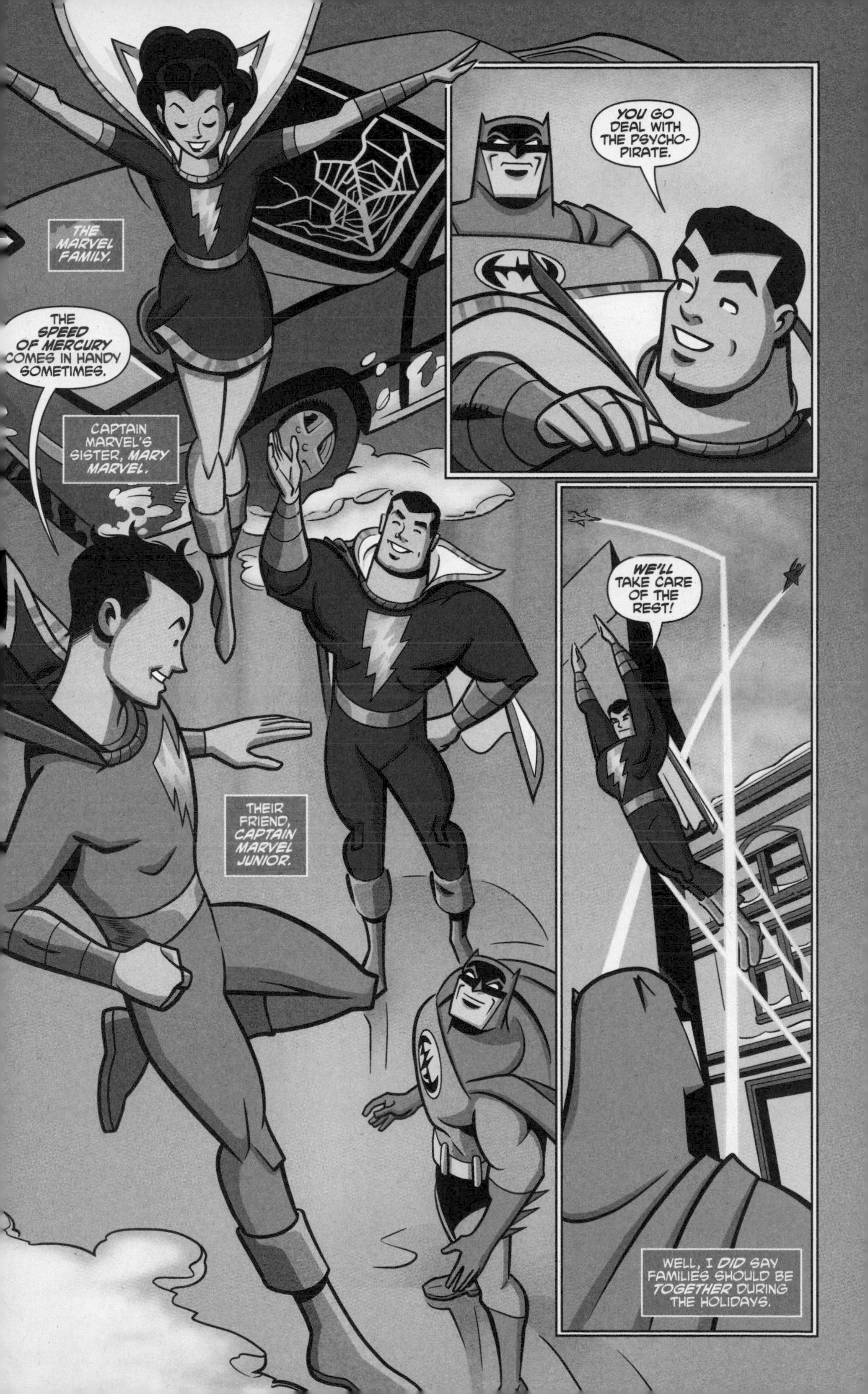
THE MARVEL FAMILY.
THE SPEED OF MERCURY COMES IN HANDY SOMETIMES.
CAPTAIN MARVEL'S SISTER, MARY MARVEL.
THEIR FRIEND, CAPTAIN MARVEL JUNIOR.
YOU GO DEAL WITH THE PSYCHO-PIRATE.
WE'LL TAKE CARE OF THE REST!
WELL, I DID SAY FAMILIES SHOULD BE TOGETHER DURING THE HOLIDAYS.

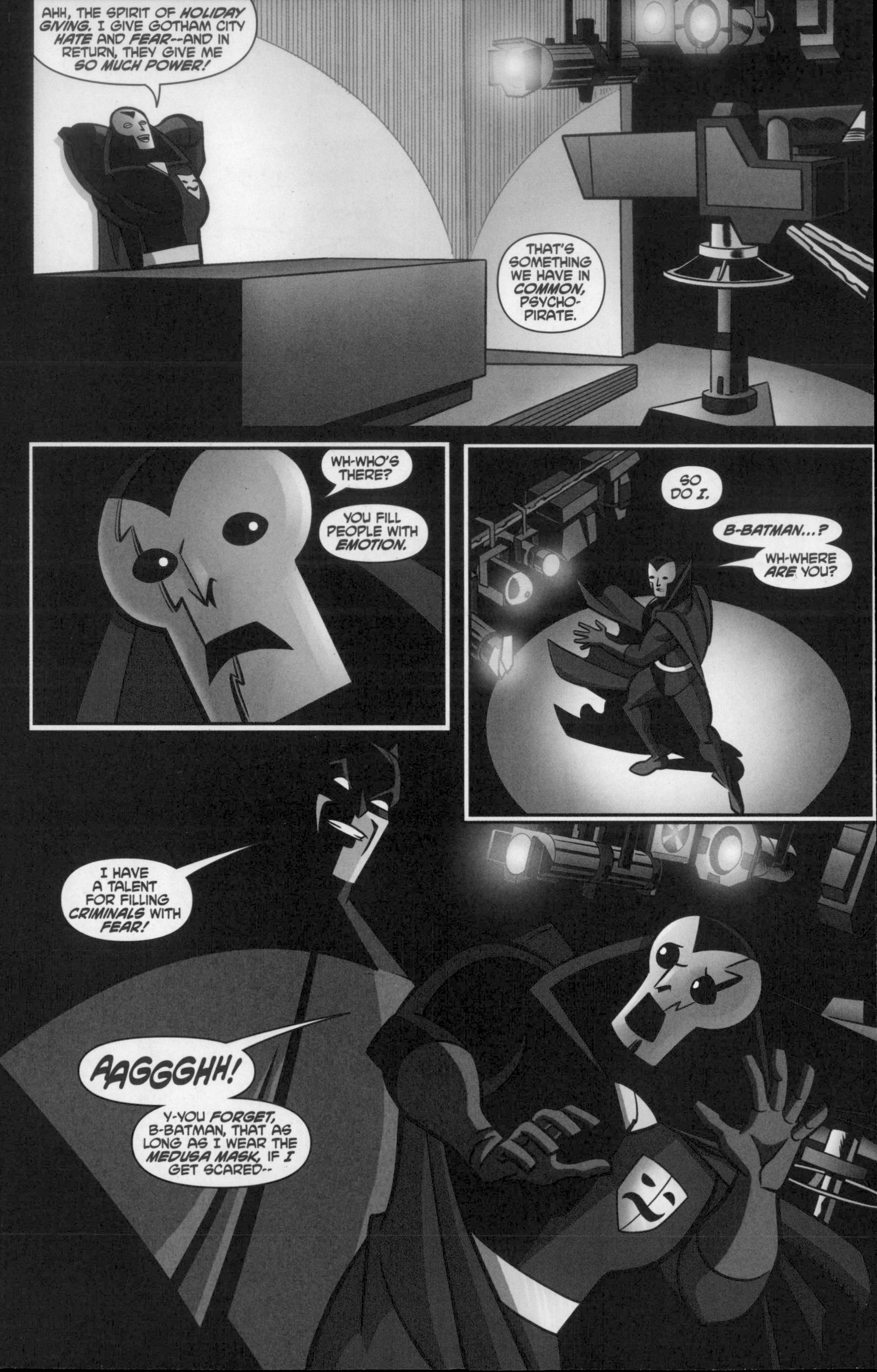
AHH, THE SPIRIT OF HOLIDAY GIVING. I GIVE GOTHAM CITY HATE AND FEAR--AND IN RETURN, THEY GIVE ME SO MUCH POWER!
THAT'S SOMETHING WE HAVE IN COMMON, PSYCHO-PIRATE.
WH-WHO'S THERE?
YOU FILL PEOPLE WITH EMOTION.
SO DO I.
B-BATMAN...?
WH-WHERE ARE YOU?
I HAVE A TALENT FOR FILLING CRIMINALS WITH FEAR!
AAGGGHH!
Y-YOU FORGET, B-BATMAN, THAT AS LONG AS I WEAR THE MEDUSA MASK, IF I GET SCARED--

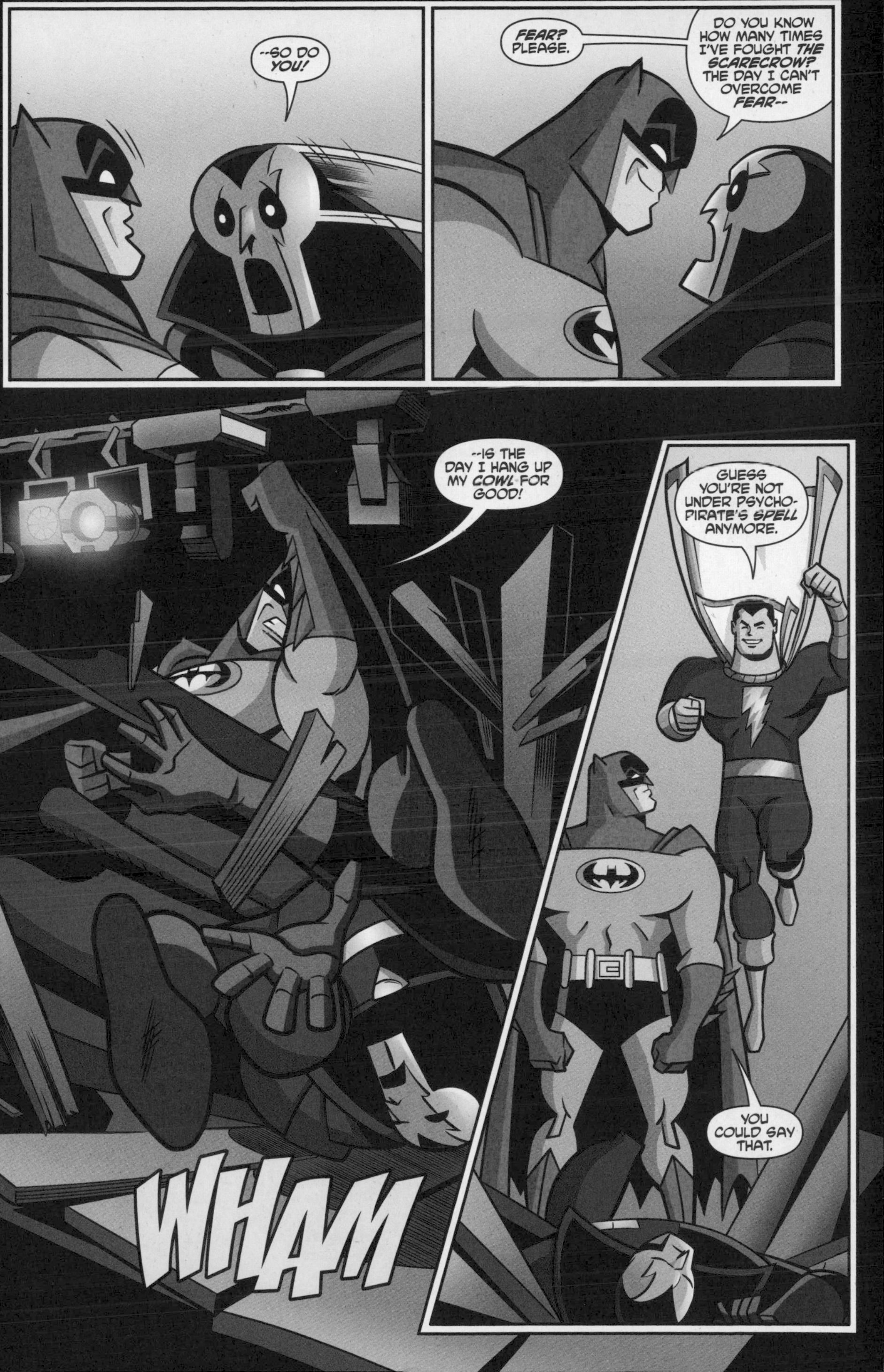
--SO DO YOU!
FEAR? PLEASE.
DO YOU KNOW HOW MANY TIMES I'VE FOUGHT THE SCARECROW? THE DAY I CAN'T OVERCOME FEAR--
--IS THE DAY I HANG UP MY COWL FOR GOOD!
WHAM
GUESS YOU'RE NOT UNDER PSYCHO-PIRATE'S SPELL ANYMORE.
YOU COULD SAY THAT.

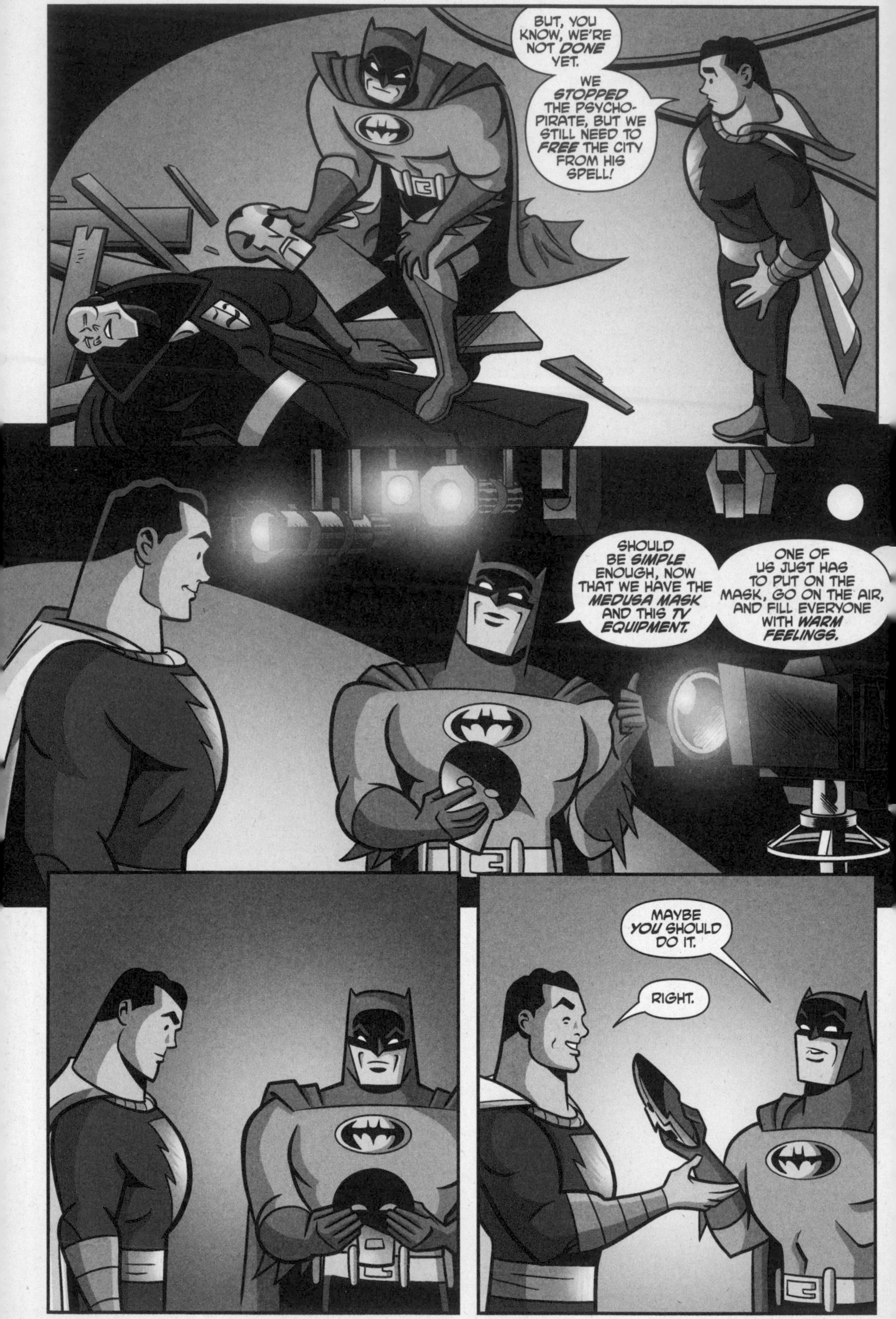
BUT, YOU KNOW, WE'RE NOT *DONE* YET.
WE *STOPPED* THE PSYCHO-PIRATE, BUT WE STILL NEED TO *FREE* THE CITY FROM HIS SPELL!
SHOULD BE *SIMPLE* ENOUGH, NOW THAT WE HAVE THE *MEDUSA MASK* AND THIS *TV EQUIPMENT.*
ONE OF US JUST HAS TO PUT ON THE MASK, GO ON THE AIR, AND FILL EVERYONE WITH *WARM FEELINGS.*
MAYBE *YOU* SHOULD DO IT.
RIGHT.

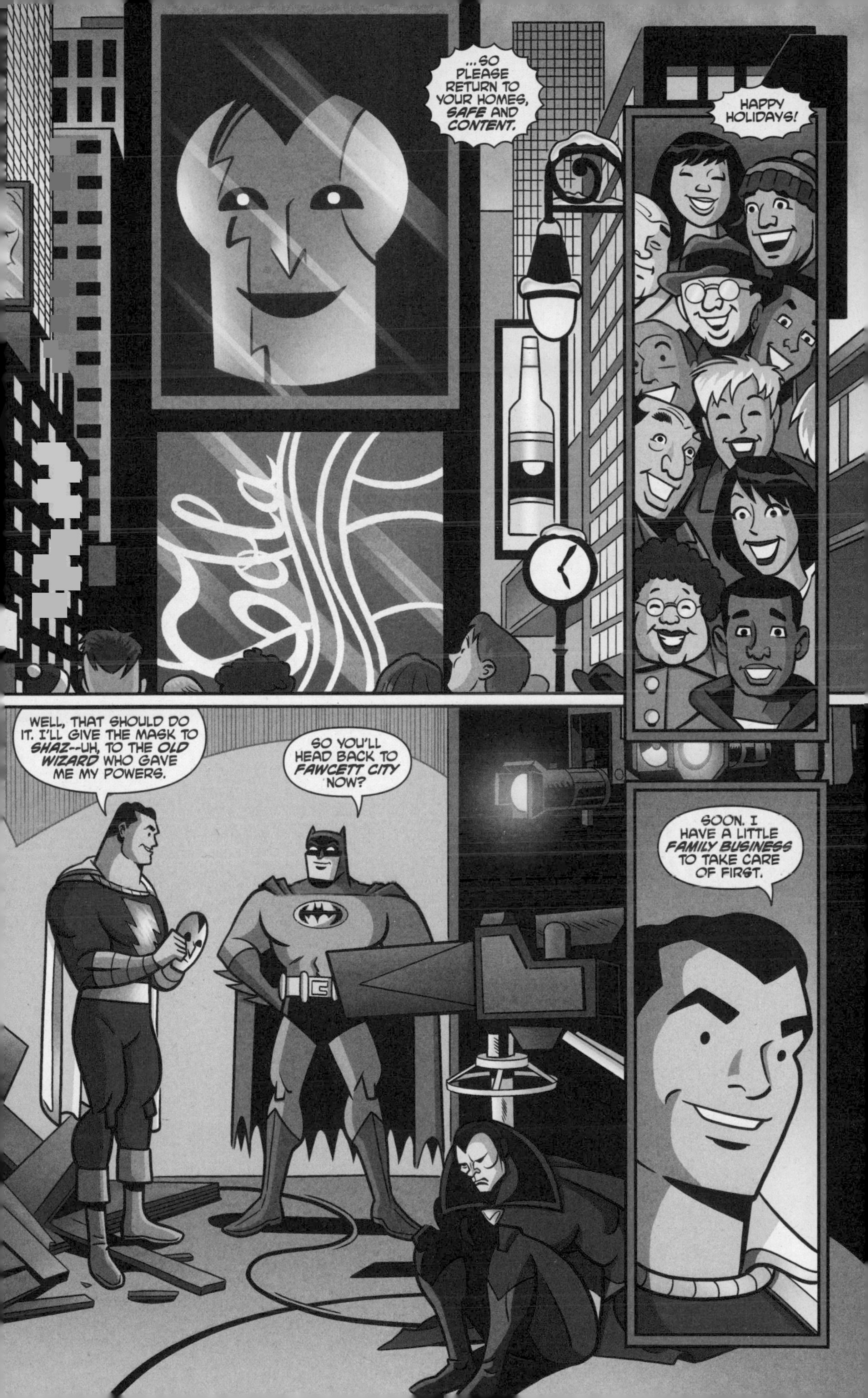
...SO PLEASE RETURN TO YOUR HOMES, SAFE AND CONTENT.
HAPPY HOLIDAYS!
WELL, THAT SHOULD DO IT. I'LL GIVE THE MASK TO SHAZ--UH, TO THE OLD WIZARD WHO GAVE ME MY POWERS.
SO YOU'LL HEAD BACK TO FAWCETT CITY NOW?
SOON. I HAVE A LITTLE FAMILY BUSINESS TO TAKE CARE OF FIRST.

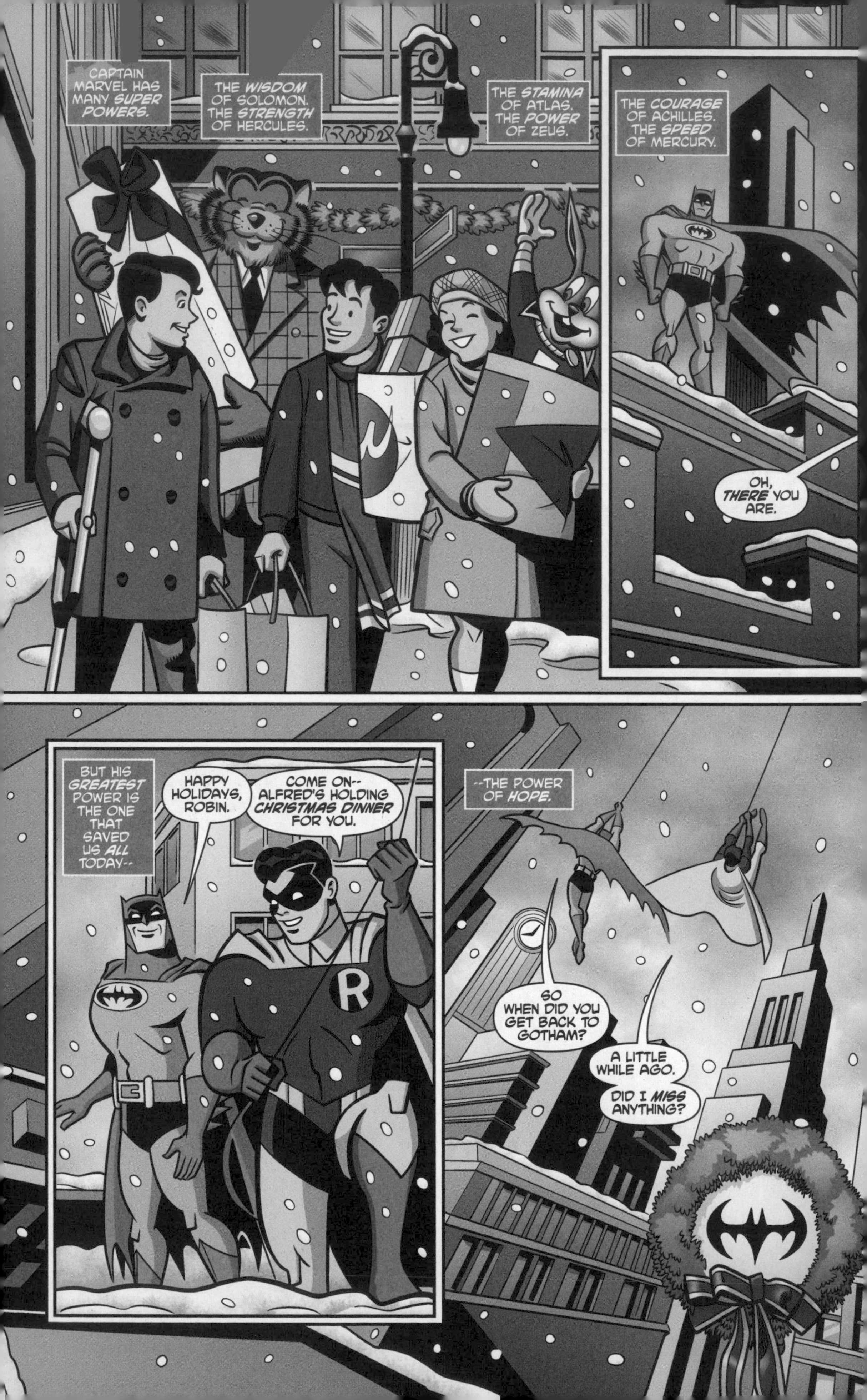
CAPTAIN MARVEL HAS MANY SUPER POWERS.
THE WISDOM OF SOLOMON. THE STRENGTH OF HERCULES.
THE STAMINA OF ATLAS. THE POWER OF ZEUS.
THE COURAGE OF ACHILLES. THE SPEED OF MERCURY.
OH, THERE YOU ARE.
BUT HIS GREATEST POWER IS THE ONE THAT SAVED US ALL TODAY--
HAPPY HOLIDAYS, ROBIN.
COME ON-- ALFRED'S HOLDING CHRISTMAS DINNER FOR YOU.
--THE POWER OF HOPE.
SO WHEN DID YOU GET BACK TO GOTHAM?
A LITTLE WHILE AGO.
DID I MISS ANYTHING?

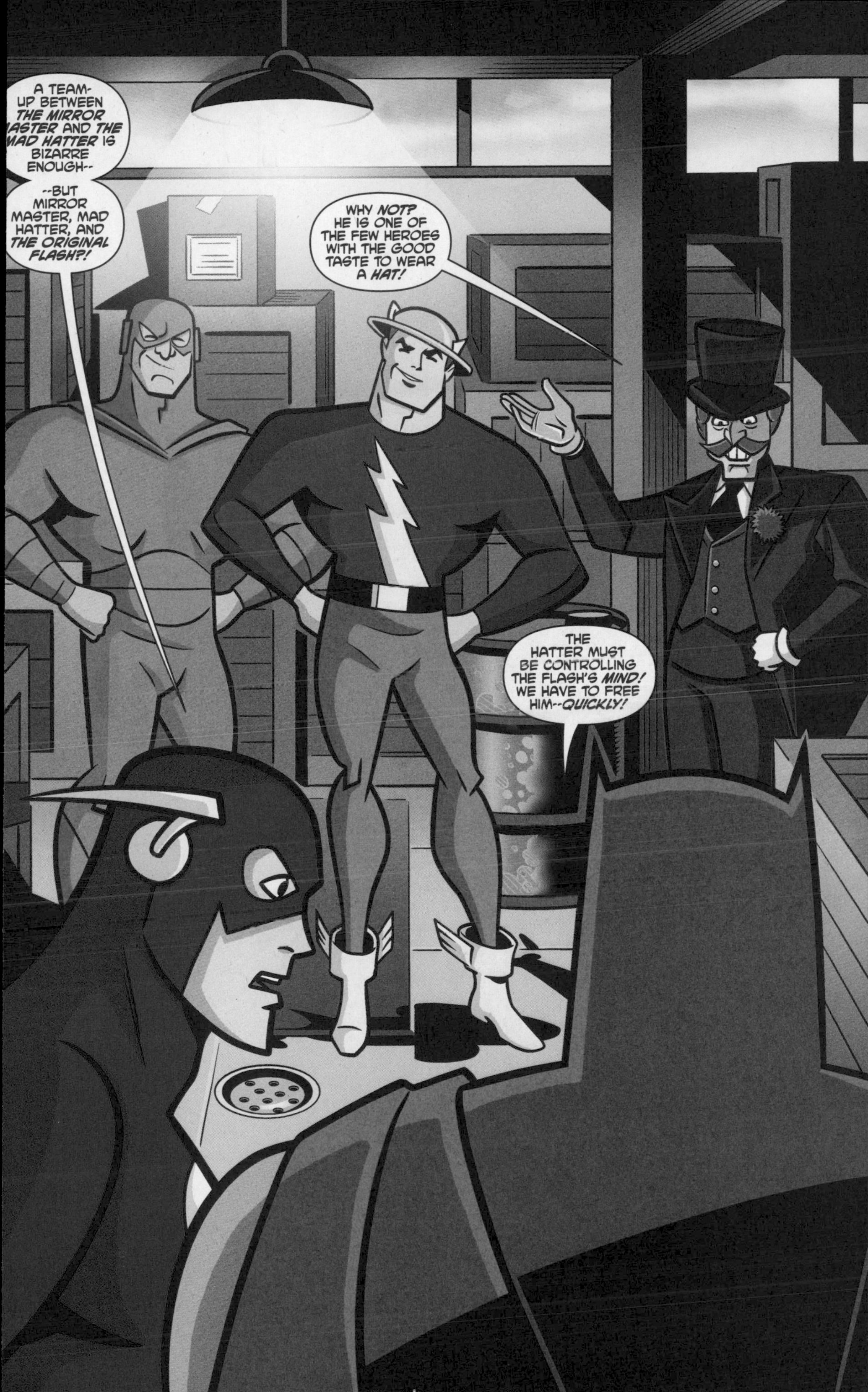
A TEAM-UP BETWEEN THE MIRROR MASTER AND THE MAD HATTER IS BIZARRE ENOUGH--
--BUT MIRROR MASTER, MAD HATTER, AND THE ORIGINAL FLASH?!
WHY NOT? HE IS ONE OF THE FEW HEROES WITH THE GOOD TASTE TO WEAR A HAT!
THE HATTER MUST BE CONTROLLING THE FLASH'S MIND! WE HAVE TO FREE HIM--QUICKLY!

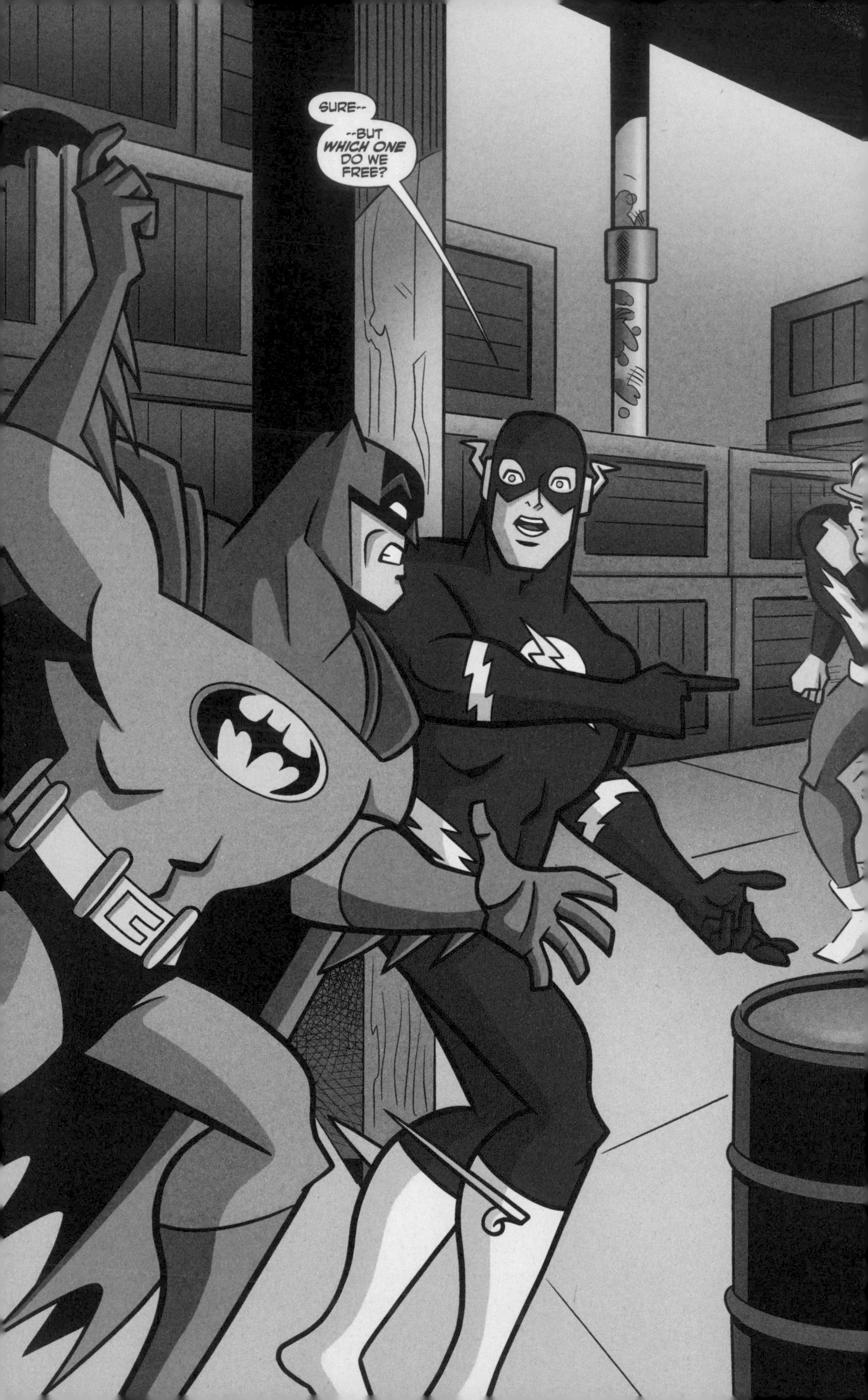
SURE--
--BUT *WHICH ONE* DO WE FREE?

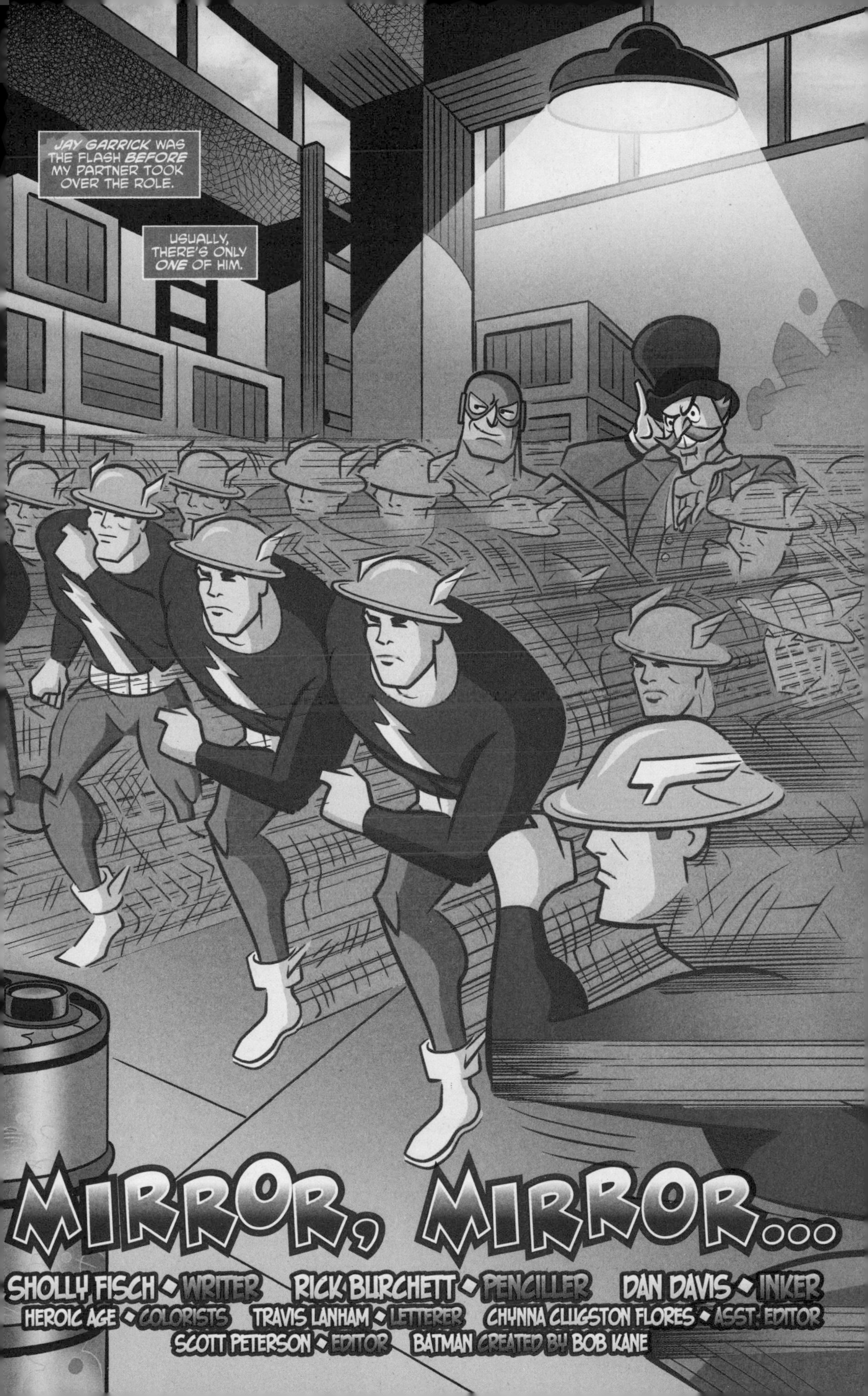
JAY GARRICK WAS THE FLASH BEFORE MY PARTNER TOOK OVER THE ROLE.
USUALLY, THERE'S ONLY ONE OF HIM.
MIRROR, MIRROR...
SHOLLY FISCH • WRITER RICK BURCHETT • PENCILLER DAN DAVIS • INKER
HEROIC AGE • COLORISTS TRAVIS LANHAM • LETTERER CHYNNA CLUGSTON FLORES • ASST. EDITOR
SCOTT PETERSON • EDITOR BATMAN CREATED BY BOB KANE

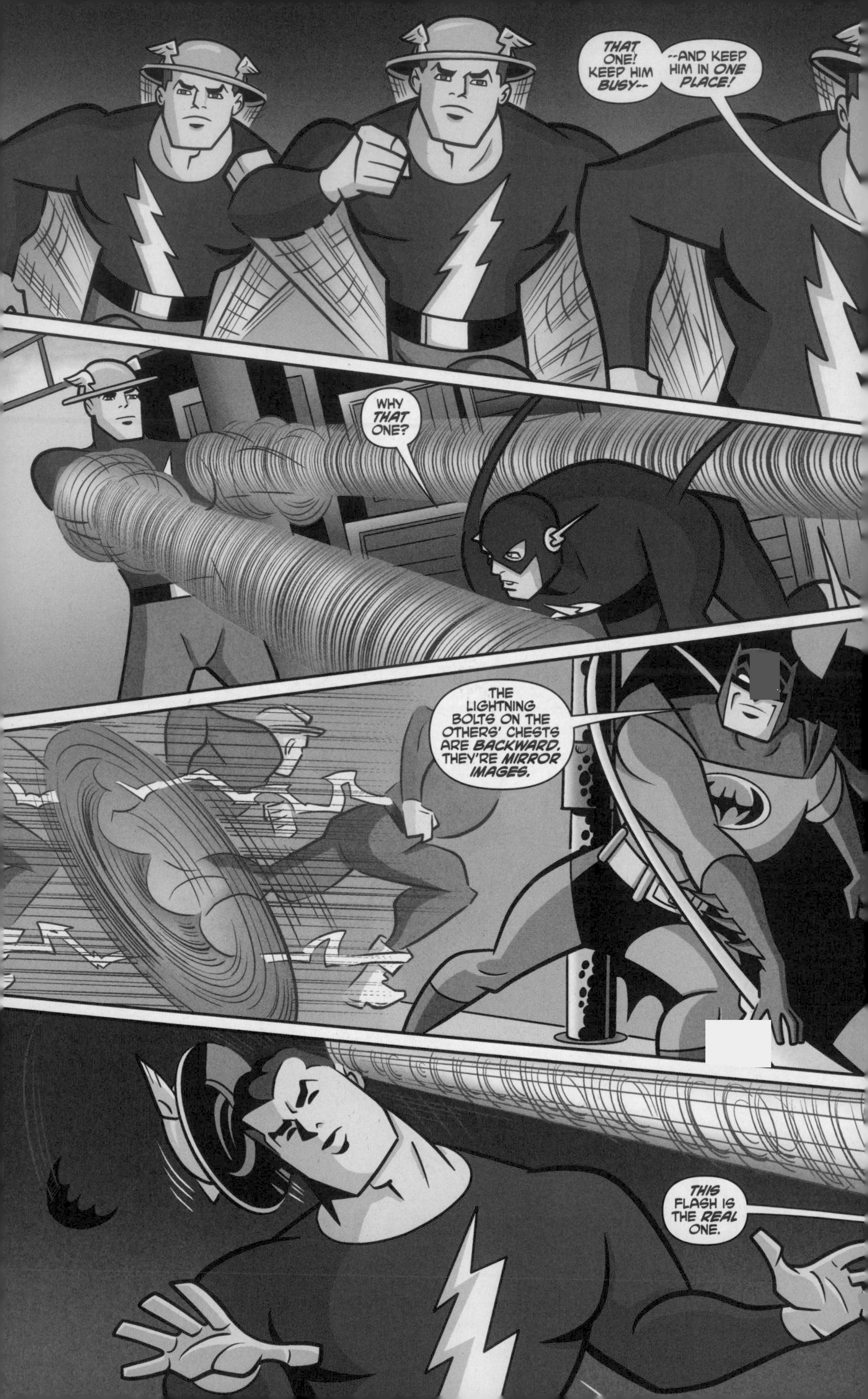
THAT ONE! KEEP HIM BUSY--
--AND KEEP HIM IN ONE PLACE!
WHY THAT ONE?
THE LIGHTNING BOLTS ON THE OTHERS' CHESTS ARE BACKWARD. THEY'RE MIRROR IMAGES.
THIS FLASH IS THE REAL ONE.

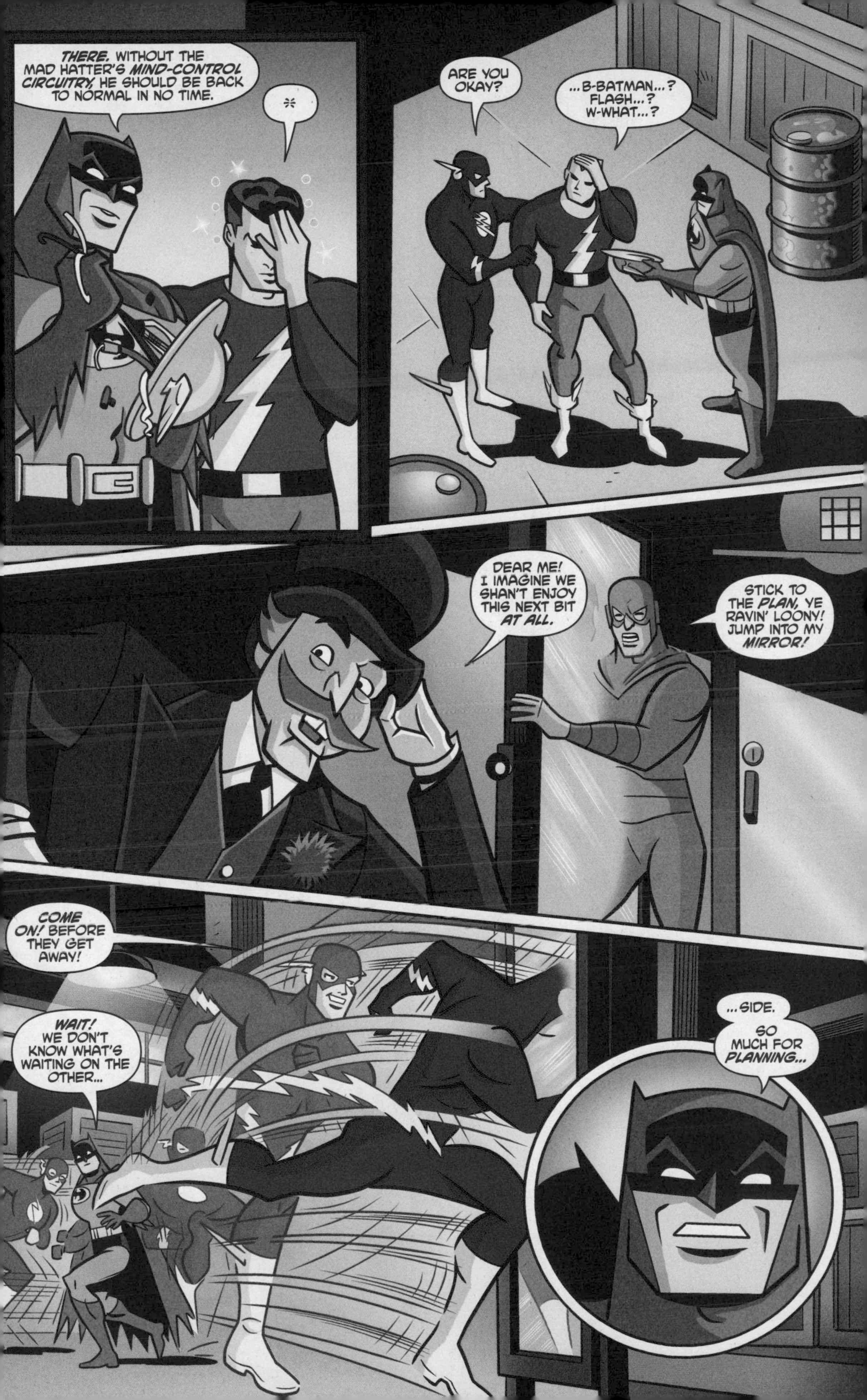
THERE. WITHOUT THE MAD HATTER'S MIND-CONTROL CIRCUITRY, HE SHOULD BE BACK TO NORMAL IN NO TIME.
ARE YOU OKAY?
...B-BATMAN...? FLASH...? W-WHAT...?
DEAR ME! I IMAGINE WE SHAN'T ENJOY THIS NEXT BIT AT ALL.
STICK TO THE PLAN, YE RAVIN' LOONY! JUMP INTO MY MIRROR!
COME ON! BEFORE THEY GET AWAY!
WAIT! WE DON'T KNOW WHAT'S WAITING ON THE OTHER...
...SIDE.
SO MUCH FOR PLANNING...

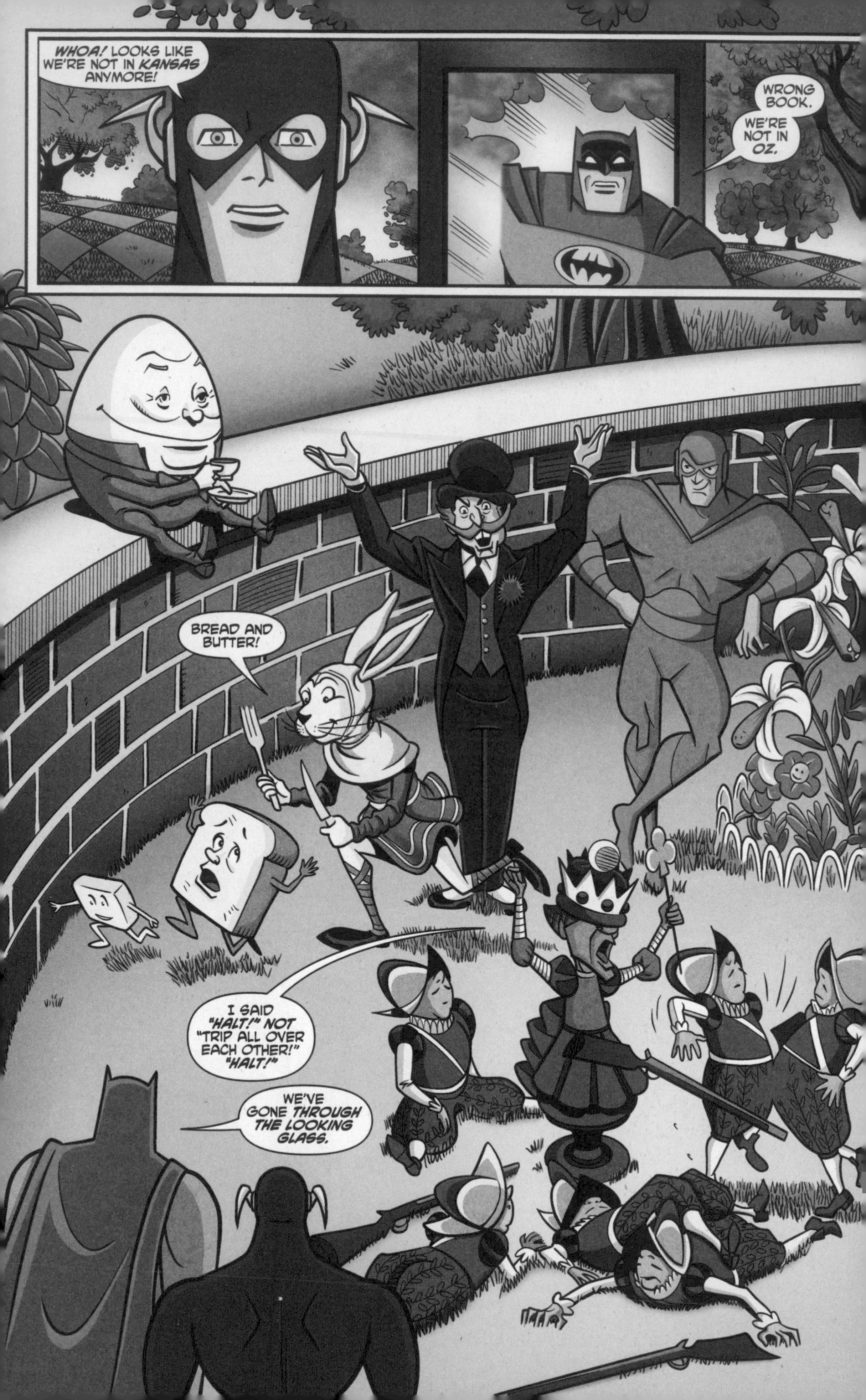
WHOA! LOOKS LIKE WE'RE NOT IN KANSAS ANYMORE!
WRONG BOOK. WE'RE NOT IN OZ.
BREAD AND BUTTER!
I SAID "HALT!" NOT "TRIP ALL OVER EACH OTHER!" "HALT!"
WE'VE GONE THROUGH THE LOOKING GLASS.

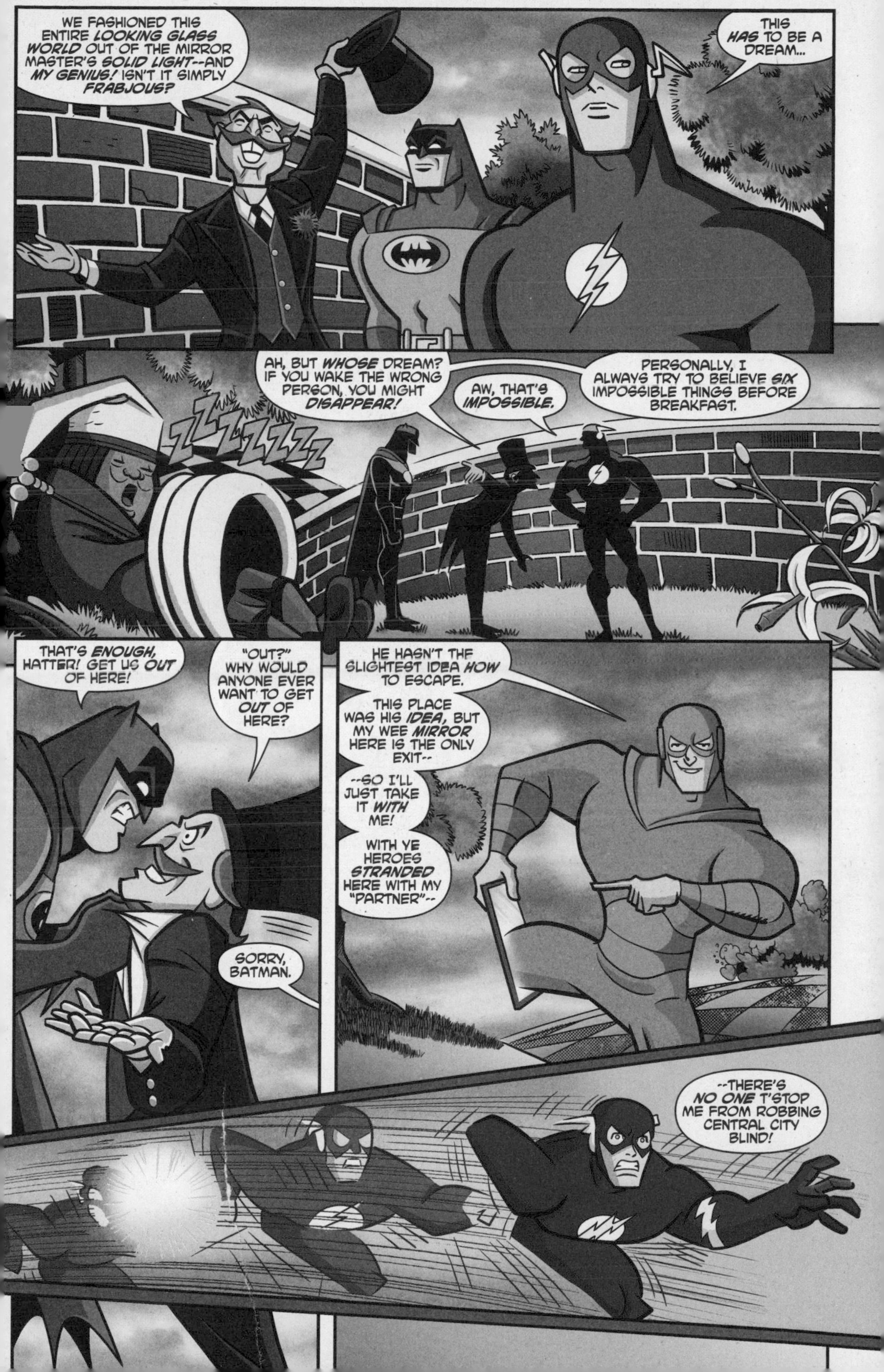

WE FASHIONED THIS ENTIRE LOOKING GLASS WORLD OUT OF THE MIRROR MASTER'S SOLID LIGHT--AND MY GENIUS! ISN'T IT SIMPLY FRABJOUS?
THIS HAS TO BE A DREAM...
AH, BUT WHOSE DREAM? IF YOU WAKE THE WRONG PERSON, YOU MIGHT DISAPPEAR!
AW, THAT'S IMPOSSIBLE.
PERSONALLY, I ALWAYS TRY TO BELIEVE SIX IMPOSSIBLE THINGS BEFORE BREAKFAST.
ZZZZZZZZ
THAT'S ENOUGH, HATTER! GET US OUT OF HERE!
"OUT?" WHY WOULD ANYONE EVER WANT TO GET OUT OF HERE?
SORRY, BATMAN.
HE HASN'T THE SLIGHTEST IDEA HOW TO ESCAPE.
THIS PLACE WAS HIS IDEA, BUT MY WEE MIRROR HERE IS THE ONLY EXIT--
--SO I'LL JUST TAKE IT WITH ME!
WITH YE HEROES STRANDED HERE WITH MY "PARTNER"--
--THERE'S NO ONE T'STOP ME FROM ROBBING CENTRAL CITY BLIND!

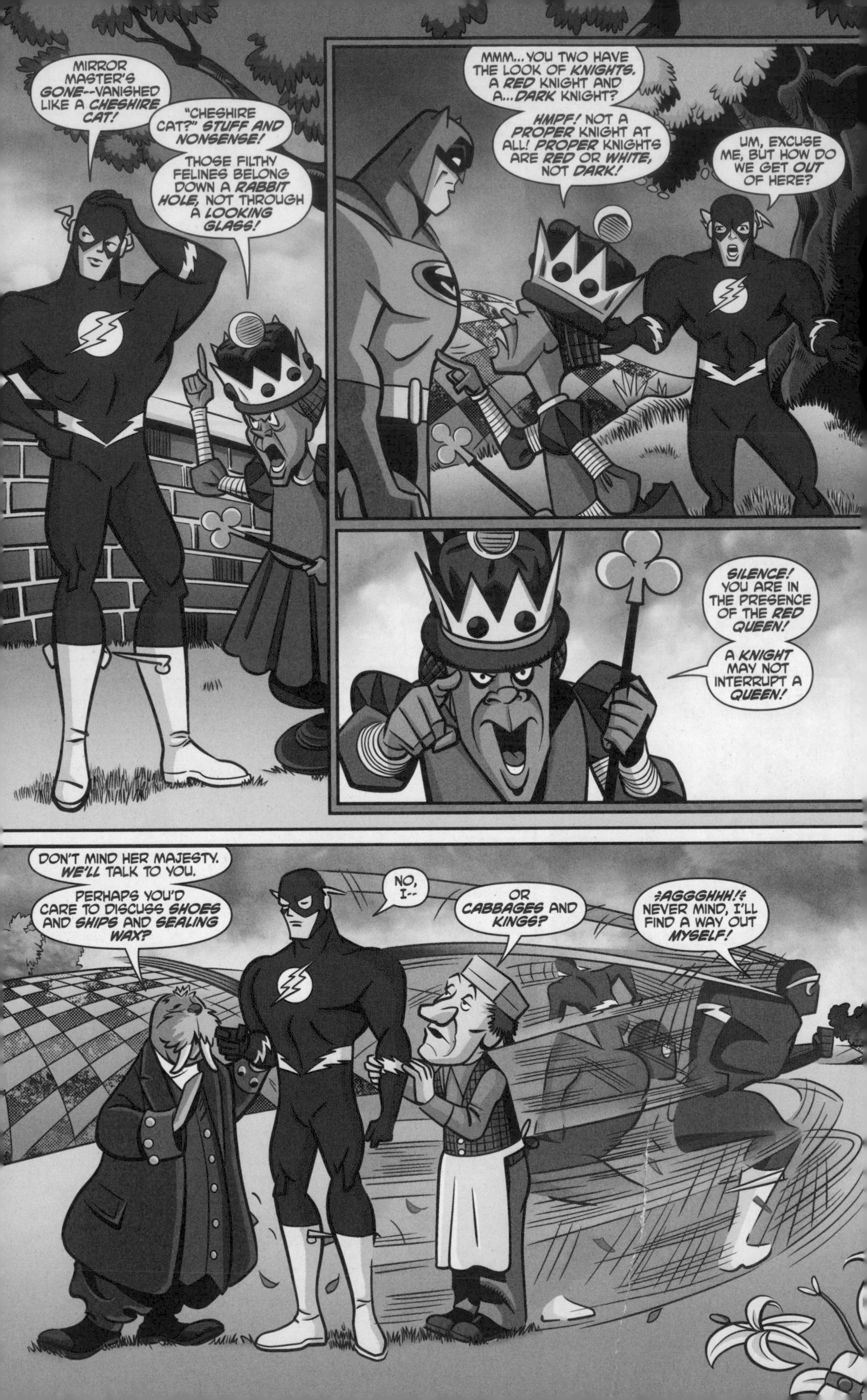
MIRROR MASTER'S GONE--VANISHED LIKE A CHESHIRE CAT!
"CHESHIRE CAT?" STUFF AND NONSENSE!
THOSE FILTHY FELINES BELONG DOWN A RABBIT HOLE, NOT THROUGH A LOOKING GLASS!
MMM... YOU TWO HAVE THE LOOK OF KNIGHTS. A RED KNIGHT AND A... DARK KNIGHT?
HMPF! NOT A PROPER KNIGHT AT ALL! PROPER KNIGHTS ARE RED OR WHITE, NOT DARK!
UM, EXCUSE ME, BUT HOW DO WE GET OUT OF HERE?
SILENCE! YOU ARE IN THE PRESENCE OF THE RED QUEEN!
A KNIGHT MAY NOT INTERRUPT A QUEEN!
DON'T MIND HER MAJESTY. WE'LL TALK TO YOU.
PERHAPS YOU'D CARE TO DISCUSS SHOES AND SHIPS AND SEALING WAX?
NO, I--
OR CABBAGES AND KINGS?
AGGGHHH! NEVER MIND, I'LL FIND A WAY OUT MYSELF!

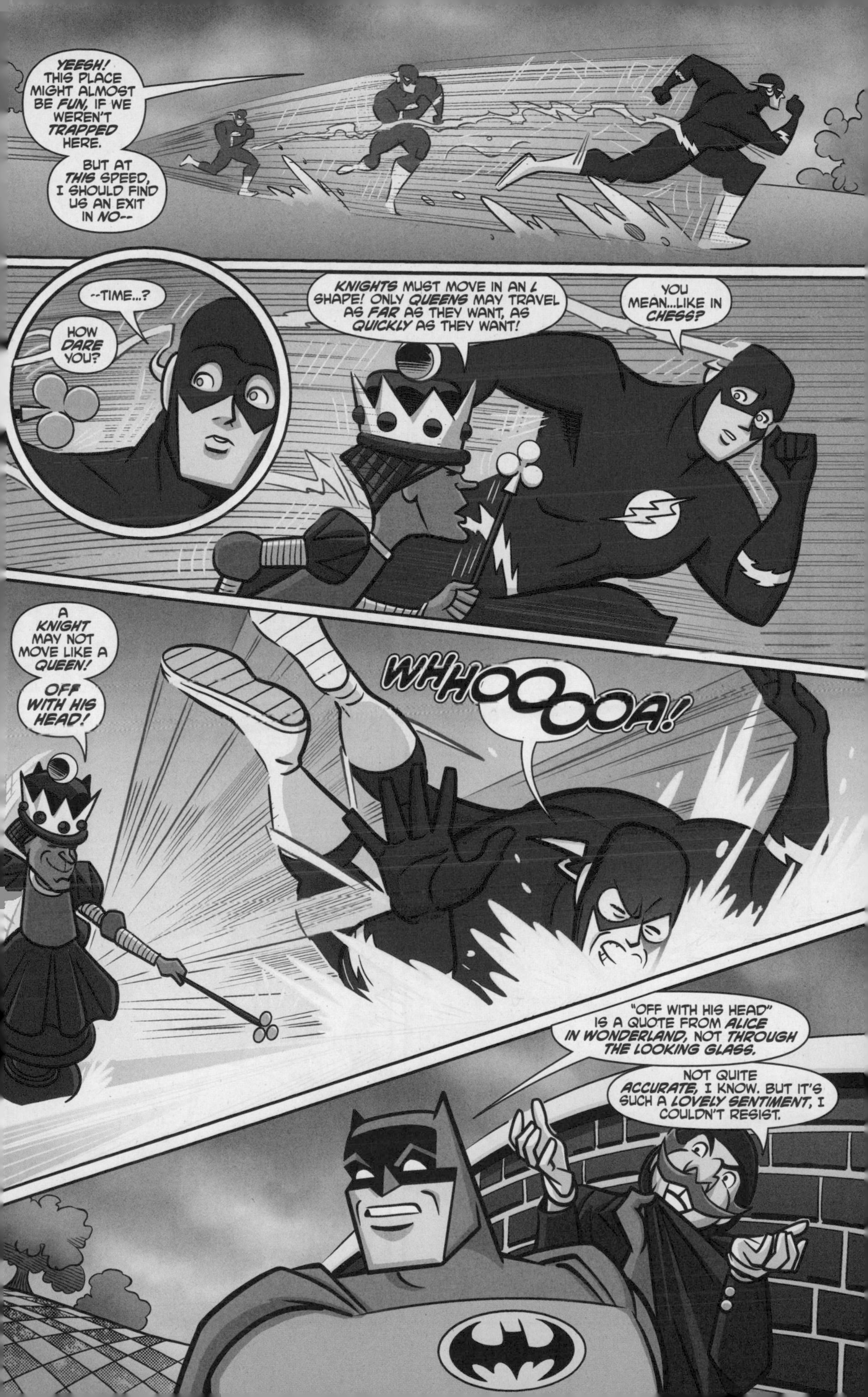
YEESH! THIS PLACE MIGHT ALMOST BE FUN, IF WE WEREN'T TRAPPED HERE.
BUT AT THIS SPEED, I SHOULD FIND US AN EXIT IN NO--
--TIME...?
HOW DARE YOU?
KNIGHTS MUST MOVE IN AN L SHAPE! ONLY QUEENS MAY TRAVEL AS FAR AS THEY WANT, AS QUICKLY AS THEY WANT!
YOU MEAN...LIKE IN CHESS?
A KNIGHT MAY NOT MOVE LIKE A QUEEN!
OFF WITH HIS HEAD!
WHHOOOOOA!
"OFF WITH HIS HEAD" IS A QUOTE FROM ALICE IN WONDERLAND, NOT THROUGH THE LOOKING GLASS.
NOT QUITE ACCURATE, I KNOW. BUT IT'S SUCH A LOVELY SENTIMENT, I COULDN'T RESIST.

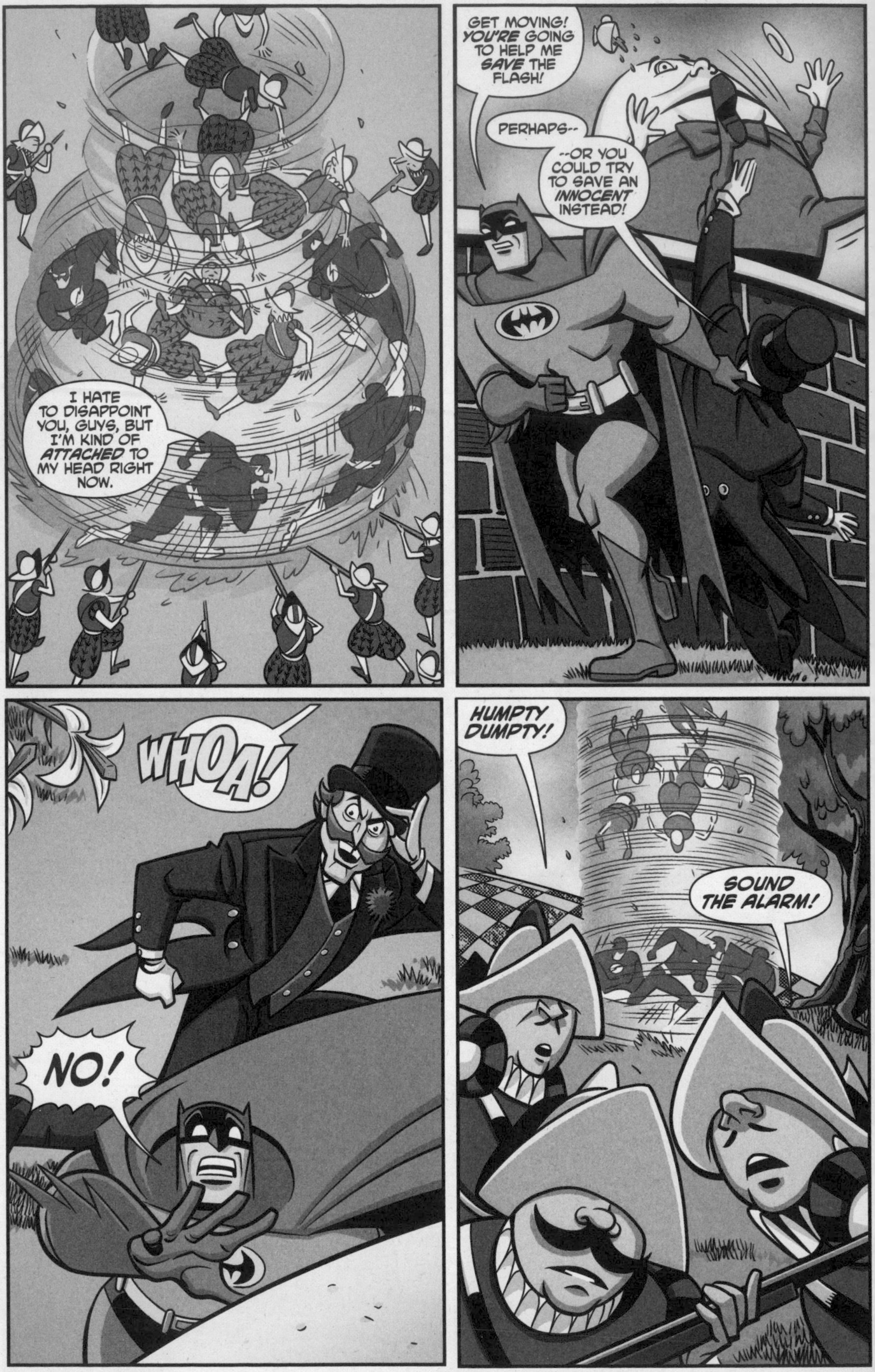
I HATE TO DISAPPOINT YOU, GUYS, BUT I'M KIND OF *ATTACHED* TO MY HEAD RIGHT NOW.
GET MOVING! *YOU'RE* GOING TO HELP ME *SAVE* THE FLASH!
PERHAPS--
--OR YOU COULD TRY TO SAVE AN *INNOCENT* INSTEAD!
WHOA!
NO!
HUMPTY DUMPTY!
SOUND THE ALARM!

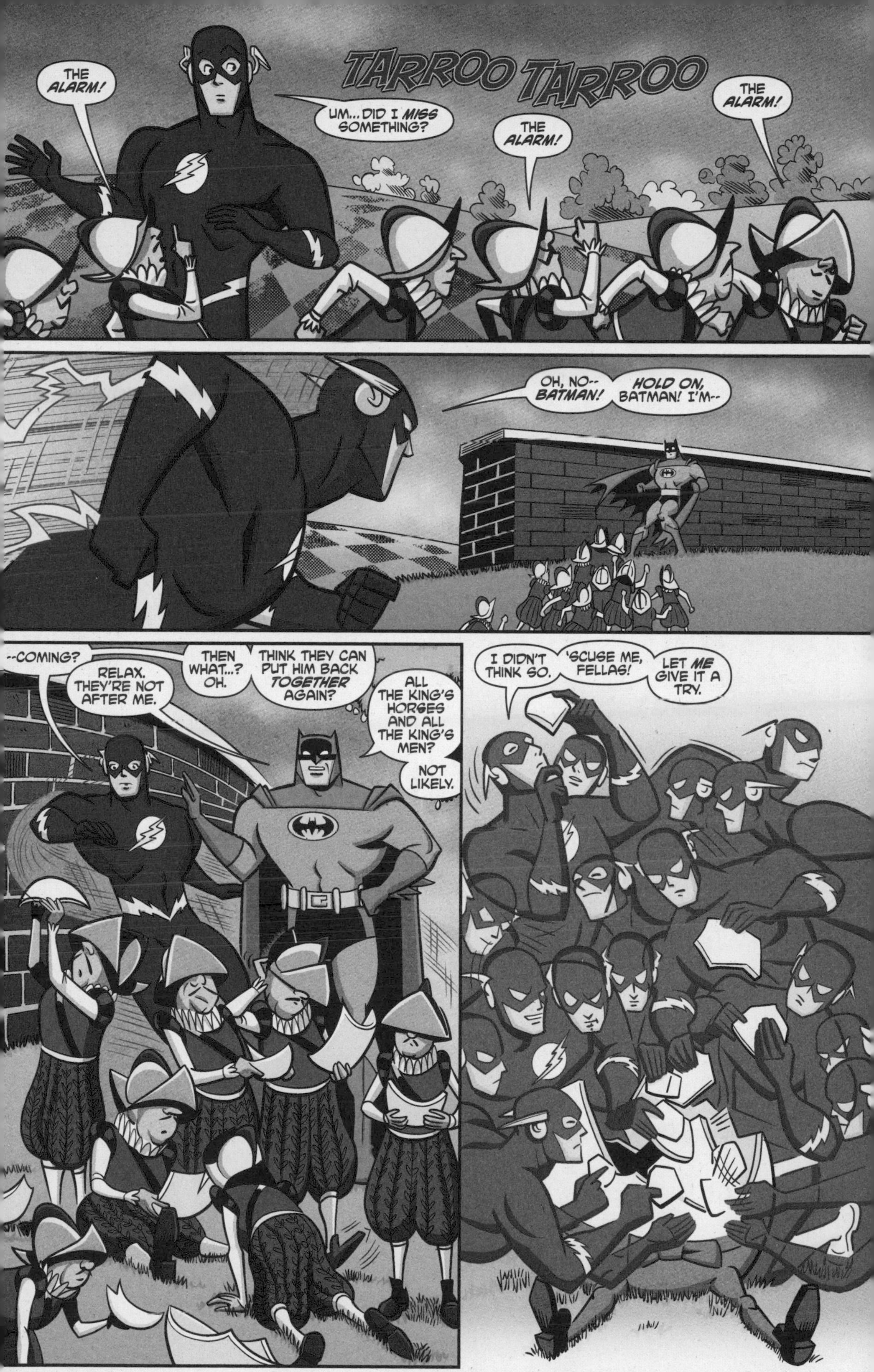
TARROO TARROO
THE ALARM!
UM... DID I MISS SOMETHING?
THE ALARM!
THE ALARM!
OH, NO-- BATMAN!
HOLD ON, BATMAN! I'M--
--COMING?
RELAX. THEY'RE NOT AFTER ME.
THEN WHAT...? OH.
THINK THEY CAN PUT HIM BACK TOGETHER AGAIN?
ALL THE KING'S HORSES AND ALL THE KING'S MEN?
NOT LIKELY.
I DIDN'T THINK SO.
'SCUSE ME, FELLAS!
LET ME GIVE IT A TRY.

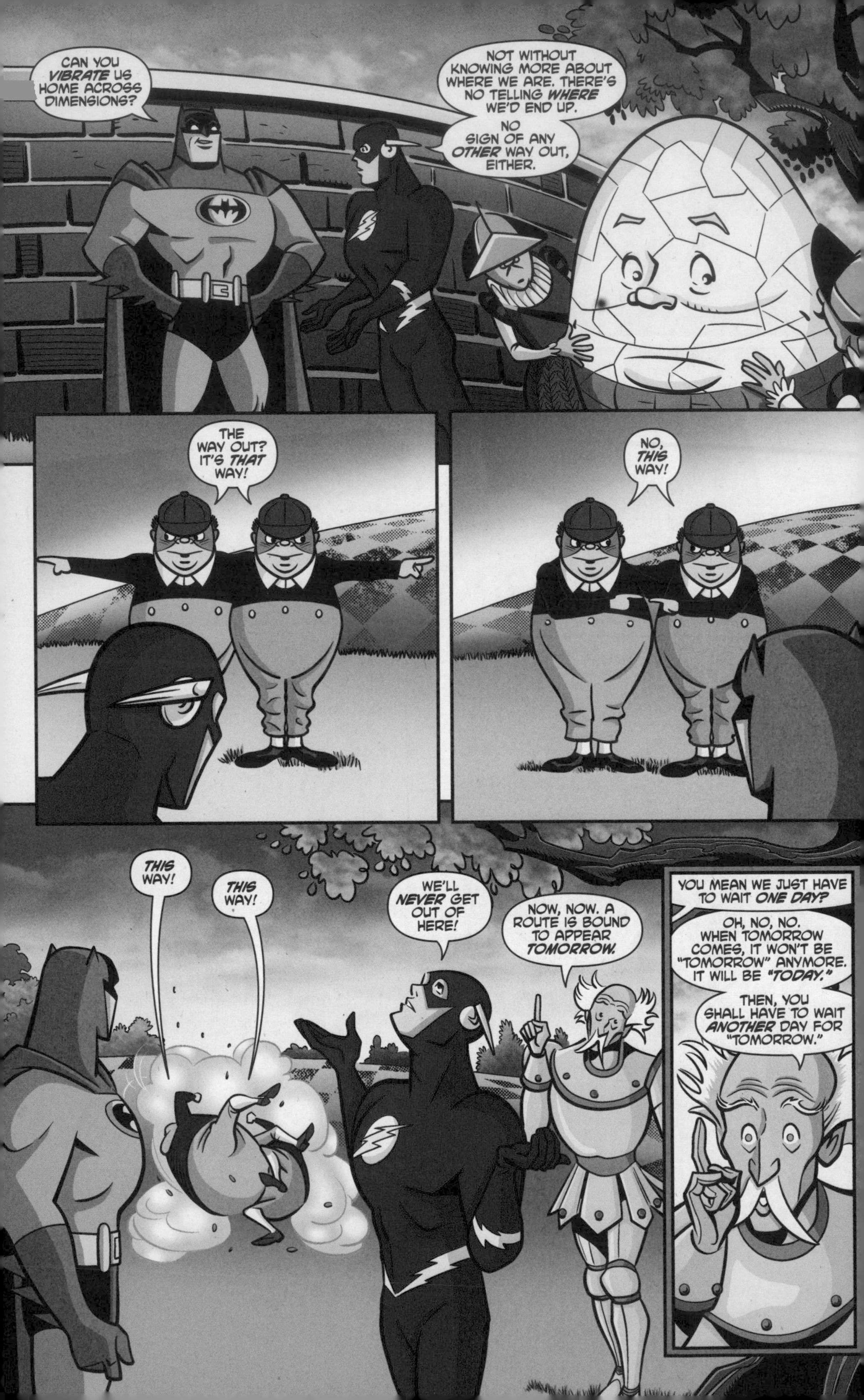
CAN YOU *VIBRATE* US HOME ACROSS DIMENSIONS?
NOT WITHOUT KNOWING MORE ABOUT WHERE WE ARE. THERE'S NO TELLING *WHERE* WE'D END UP.
NO SIGN OF ANY *OTHER* WAY OUT, EITHER.
THE WAY OUT? IT'S *THAT* WAY!
NO, *THIS* WAY!
THIS WAY!
THIS WAY!
WE'LL *NEVER* GET OUT OF HERE!
NOW, NOW. A ROUTE IS BOUND TO APPEAR *TOMORROW.*
YOU MEAN WE JUST HAVE TO WAIT *ONE DAY?*
OH, NO, NO. WHEN TOMORROW COMES, IT WON'T BE "TOMORROW" ANYMORE. IT WILL BE *"TODAY."*
THEN, YOU SHALL HAVE TO WAIT *ANOTHER* DAY FOR "TOMORROW."

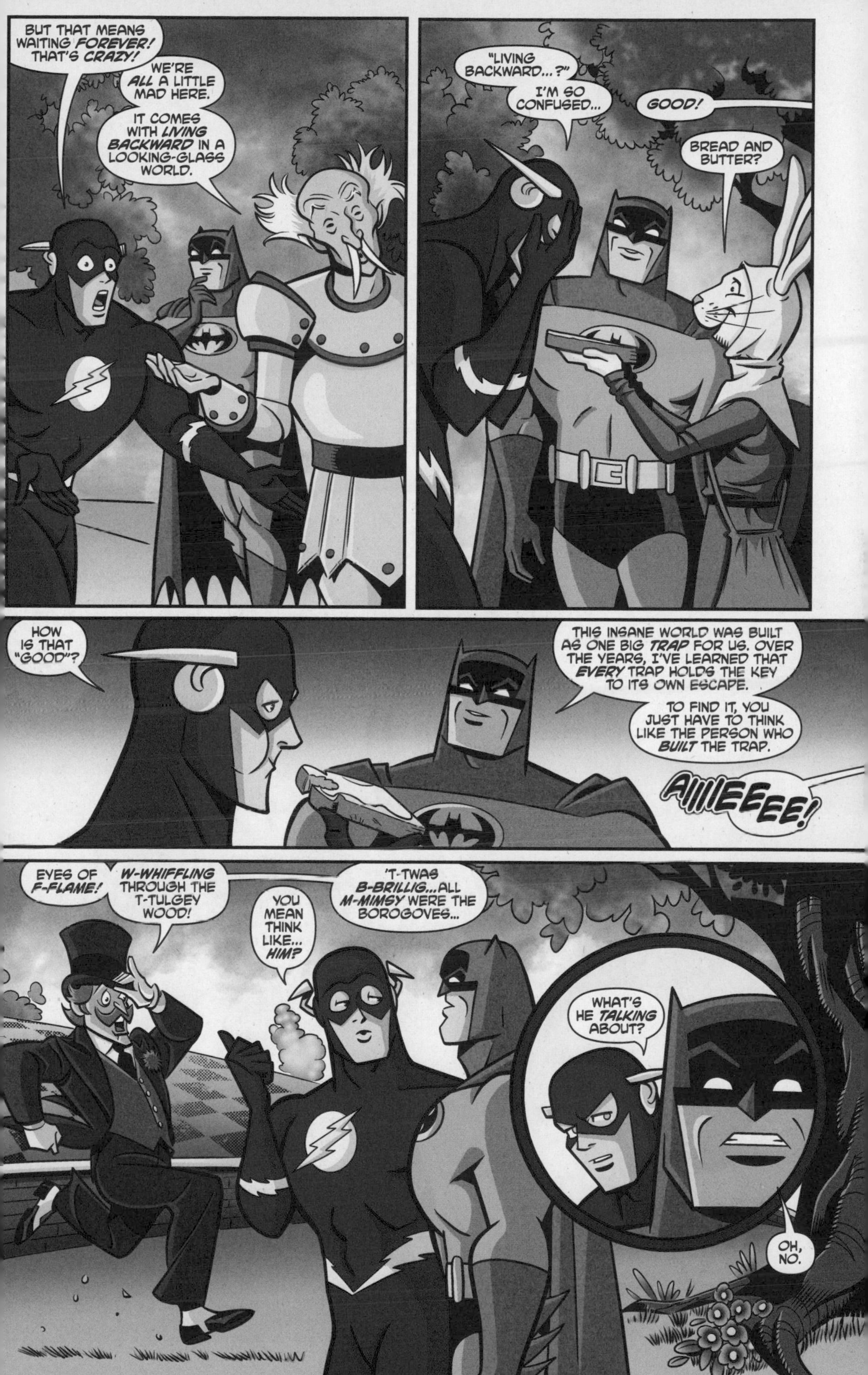
BUT THAT MEANS WAITING *FOREVER!* THAT'S *CRAZY!*
WE'RE *ALL* A LITTLE MAD HERE.
IT COMES WITH *LIVING BACKWARD* IN A LOOKING-GLASS WORLD.
"LIVING BACKWARD...?"
I'M SO CONFUSED...
GOOD!
BREAD AND BUTTER?
HOW IS THAT "GOOD"?
THIS INSANE WORLD WAS BUILT AS ONE BIG *TRAP* FOR US. OVER THE YEARS, I'VE LEARNED THAT *EVERY* TRAP HOLDS THE KEY TO ITS OWN ESCAPE.
TO FIND IT, YOU JUST HAVE TO THINK LIKE THE PERSON WHO *BUILT* THE TRAP.
AIIIEEEEE!
EYES OF *F-FLAME!*
W-WHIFFLING THROUGH THE T-TULGEY WOOD!
YOU MEAN THINK LIKE... *HIM?*
'T-TWAS *B-BRILLIG*...ALL *M-MIMSY* WERE THE BOROGOVES...
WHAT'S HE *TALKING* ABOUT?
OH, NO.

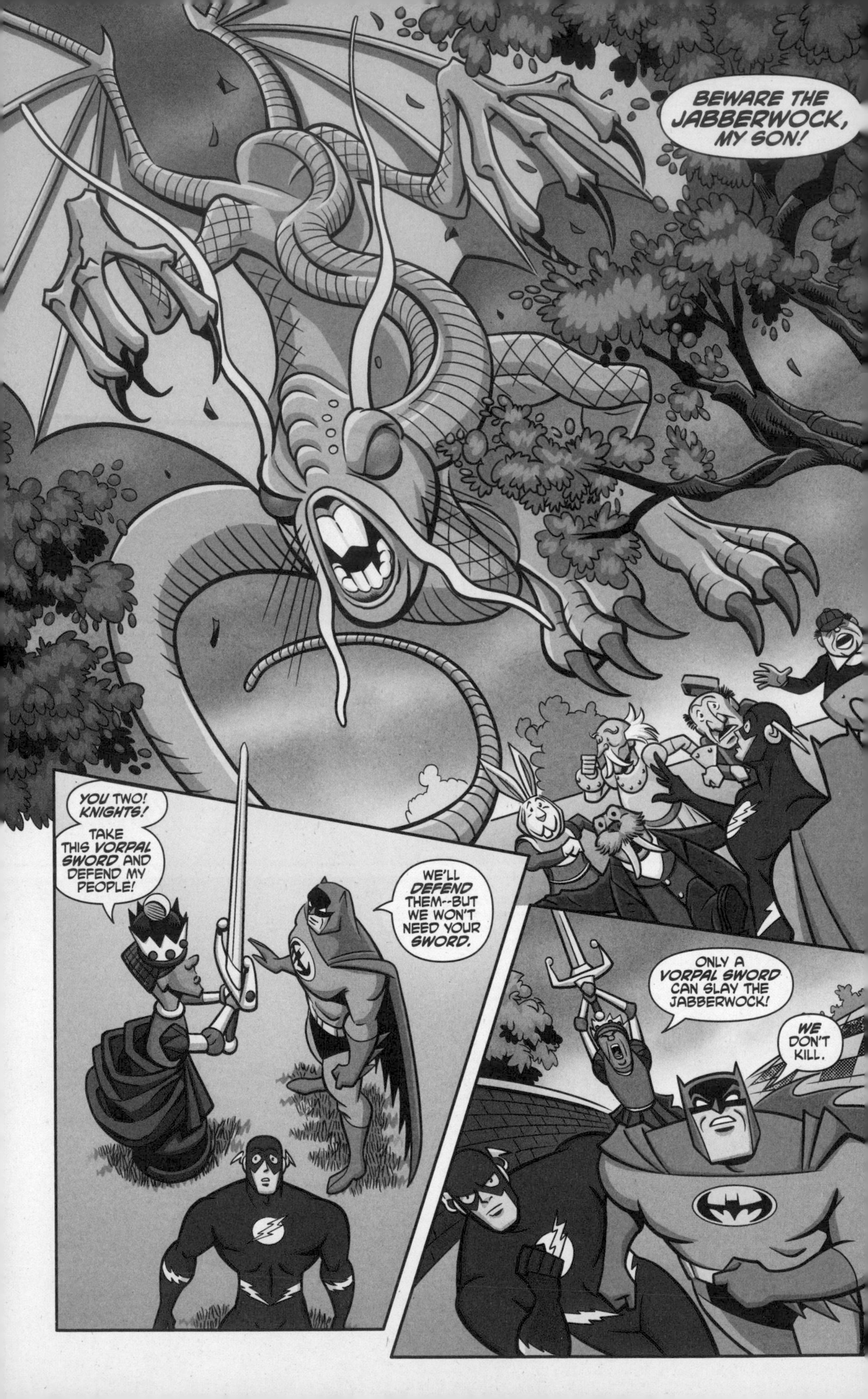
BEWARE THE JABBERWOCK, MY SON!
YOU TWO! KNIGHTS!
TAKE THIS VORPAL SWORD AND DEFEND MY PEOPLE!
WE'LL DEFEND THEM--BUT WE WON'T NEED YOUR SWORD.
ONLY A VORPAL SWORD CAN SLAY THE JABBERWOCK!
WE DON'T KILL.

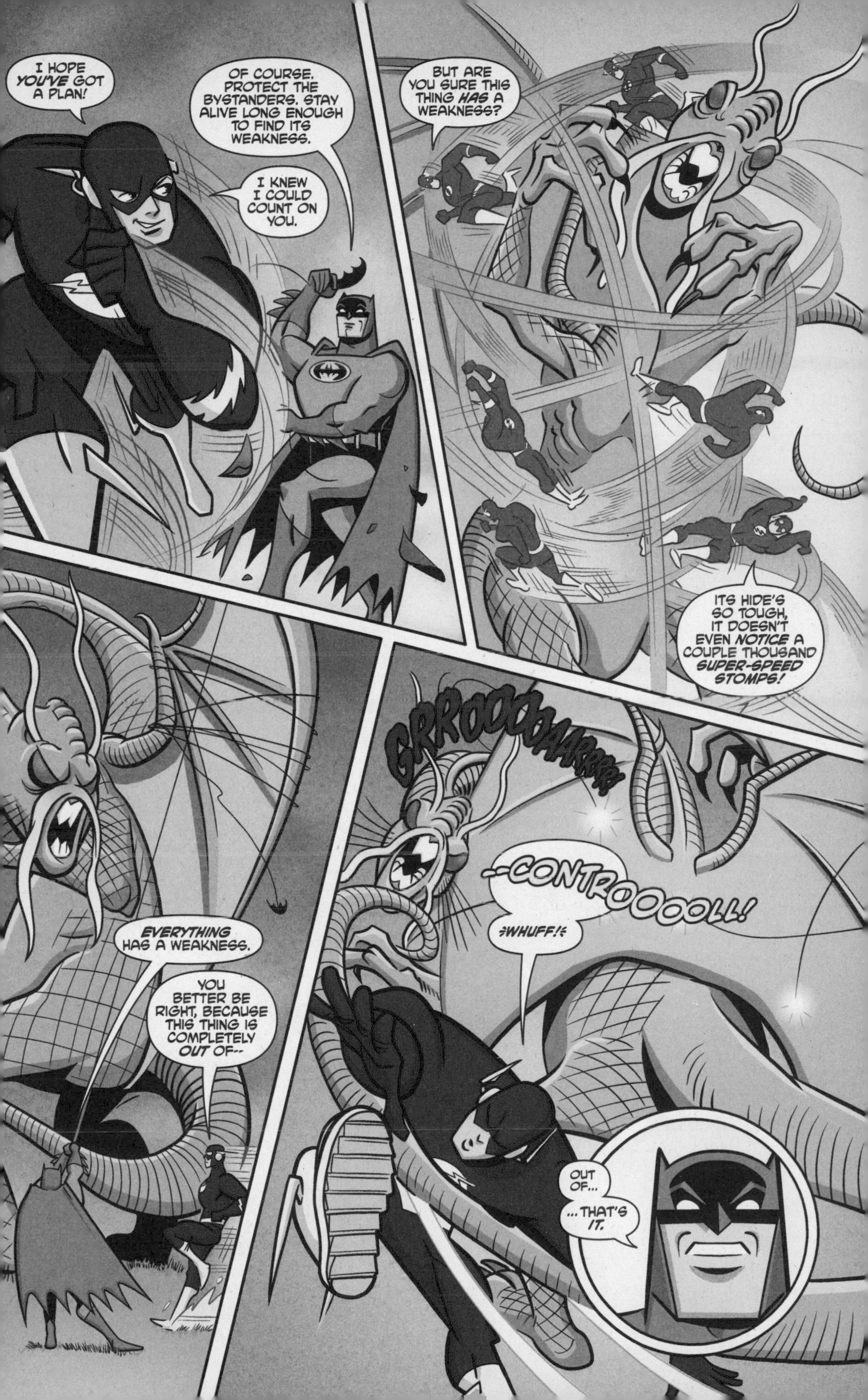
I HOPE *YOU'VE* GOT A PLAN!
OF COURSE. PROTECT THE BYSTANDERS. STAY ALIVE LONG ENOUGH TO FIND ITS WEAKNESS.
I KNEW I COULD COUNT ON YOU.
BUT ARE YOU SURE THIS THING *HAS* A WEAKNESS?
ITS HIDE'S SO TOUGH, IT DOESN'T EVEN *NOTICE* A COUPLE THOUSAND *SUPER-SPEED STOMPS!*
EVERYTHING HAS A WEAKNESS.
YOU BETTER BE RIGHT, BECAUSE THIS THING IS COMPLETELY *OUT* OF--
GRROOOOAARRRR!
--CONTROOOOOLL!
WHUFF!
OUT OF...
...THAT'S *IT.*

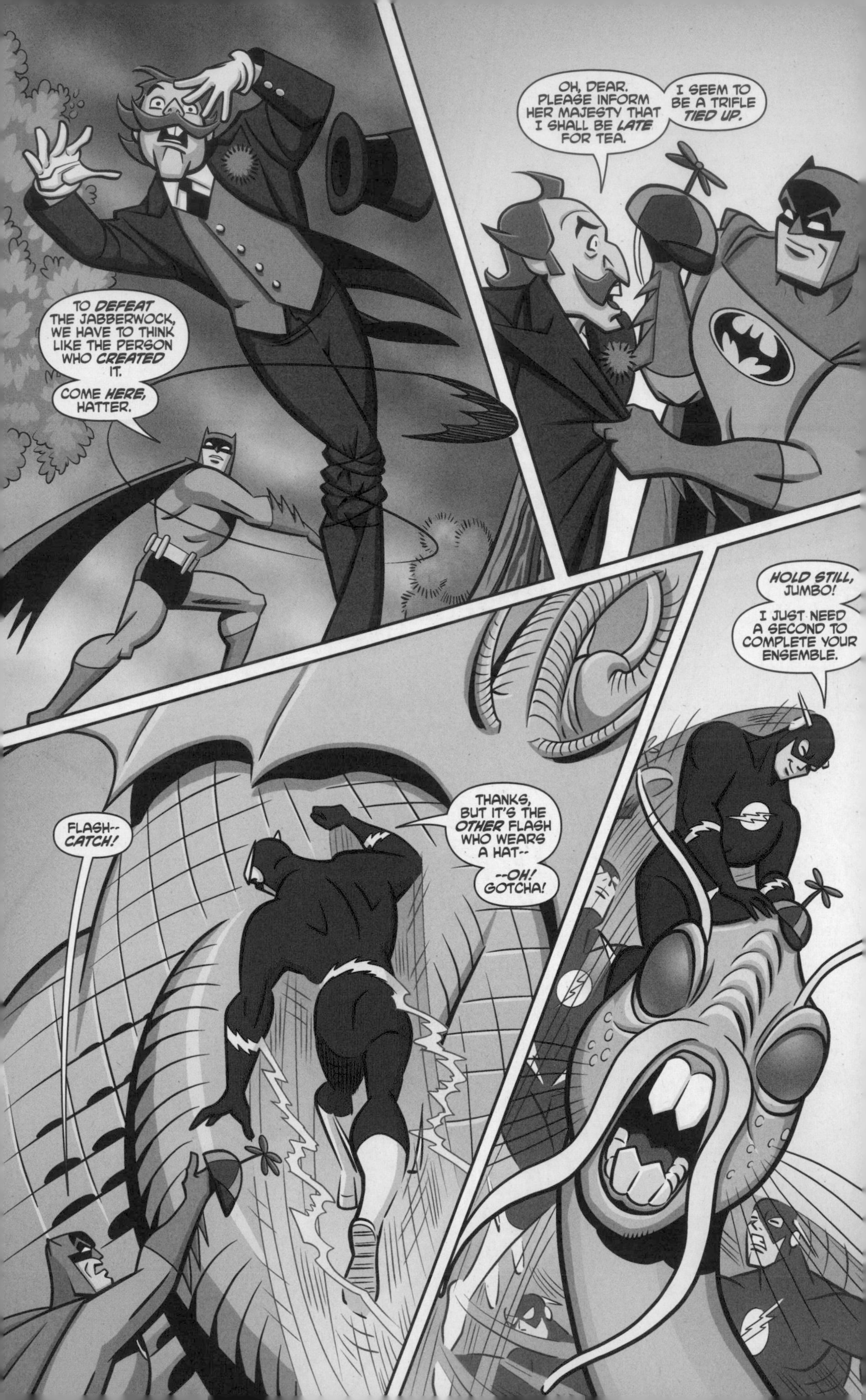
TO DEFEAT THE JABBERWOCK, WE HAVE TO THINK LIKE THE PERSON WHO CREATED IT.
COME HERE, HATTER.
OH, DEAR. PLEASE INFORM HER MAJESTY THAT I SHALL BE LATE FOR TEA.
I SEEM TO BE A TRIFLE TIED UP.
HOLD STILL, JUMBO!
I JUST NEED A SECOND TO COMPLETE YOUR ENSEMBLE.
FLASH-- CATCH!
THANKS, BUT IT'S THE OTHER FLASH WHO WEARS A HAT--
--OH! GOTCHA!

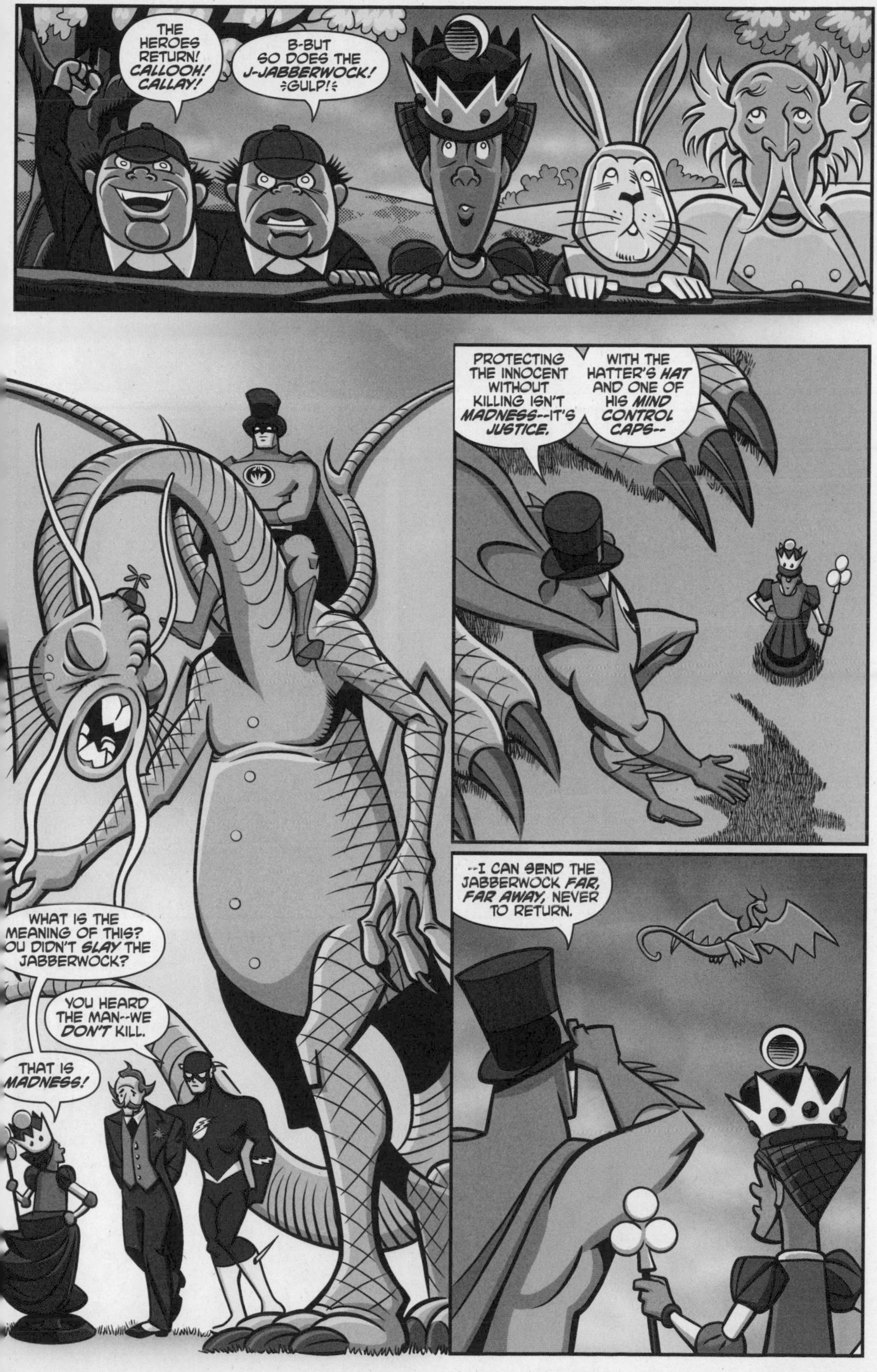
THE HEROES RETURN! CALLOOH! CALLAY!
B-BUT SO DOES THE J-JABBERWOCK! GULP!
WHAT IS THE MEANING OF THIS? YOU DIDN'T SLAY THE JABBERWOCK?
YOU HEARD THE MAN--WE DON'T KILL.
THAT IS MADNESS!
PROTECTING THE INNOCENT WITHOUT KILLING ISN'T MADNESS--IT'S JUSTICE.
WITH THE HATTER'S HAT AND ONE OF HIS MIND CONTROL CAPS--
--I CAN SEND THE JABBERWOCK FAR, FAR AWAY, NEVER TO RETURN.

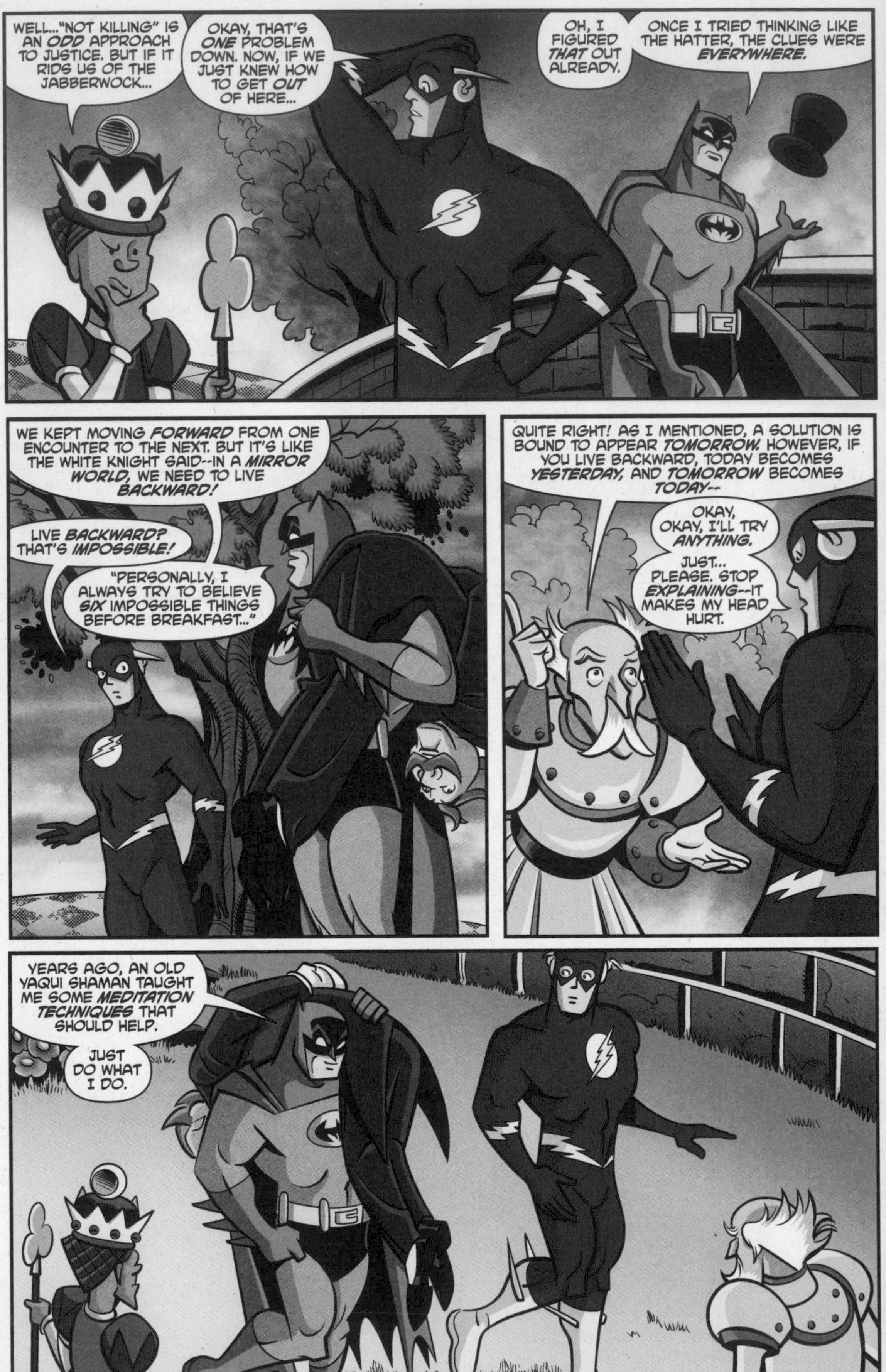
WELL..."NOT KILLING" IS AN ODD APPROACH TO JUSTICE. BUT IF IT RIDS US OF THE JABBERWOCK...
OKAY, THAT'S ONE PROBLEM DOWN. NOW, IF WE JUST KNEW HOW TO GET OUT OF HERE...
OH, I FIGURED THAT OUT ALREADY.
ONCE I TRIED THINKING LIKE THE HATTER, THE CLUES WERE EVERYWHERE.
WE KEPT MOVING FORWARD FROM ONE ENCOUNTER TO THE NEXT. BUT IT'S LIKE THE WHITE KNIGHT SAID--IN A MIRROR WORLD, WE NEED TO LIVE BACKWARD!
LIVE BACKWARD? THAT'S IMPOSSIBLE!
"PERSONALLY, I ALWAYS TRY TO BELIEVE SIX IMPOSSIBLE THINGS BEFORE BREAKFAST..."
QUITE RIGHT! AS I MENTIONED, A SOLUTION IS BOUND TO APPEAR TOMORROW. HOWEVER, IF YOU LIVE BACKWARD, TODAY BECOMES YESTERDAY, AND TOMORROW BECOMES TODAY--
OKAY, OKAY, I'LL TRY ANYTHING.
JUST... PLEASE. STOP EXPLAINING--IT MAKES MY HEAD HURT.
YEARS AGO, AN OLD YAQUI SHAMAN TAUGHT ME SOME MEDITATION TECHNIQUES THAT SHOULD HELP.
JUST DO WHAT I DO.

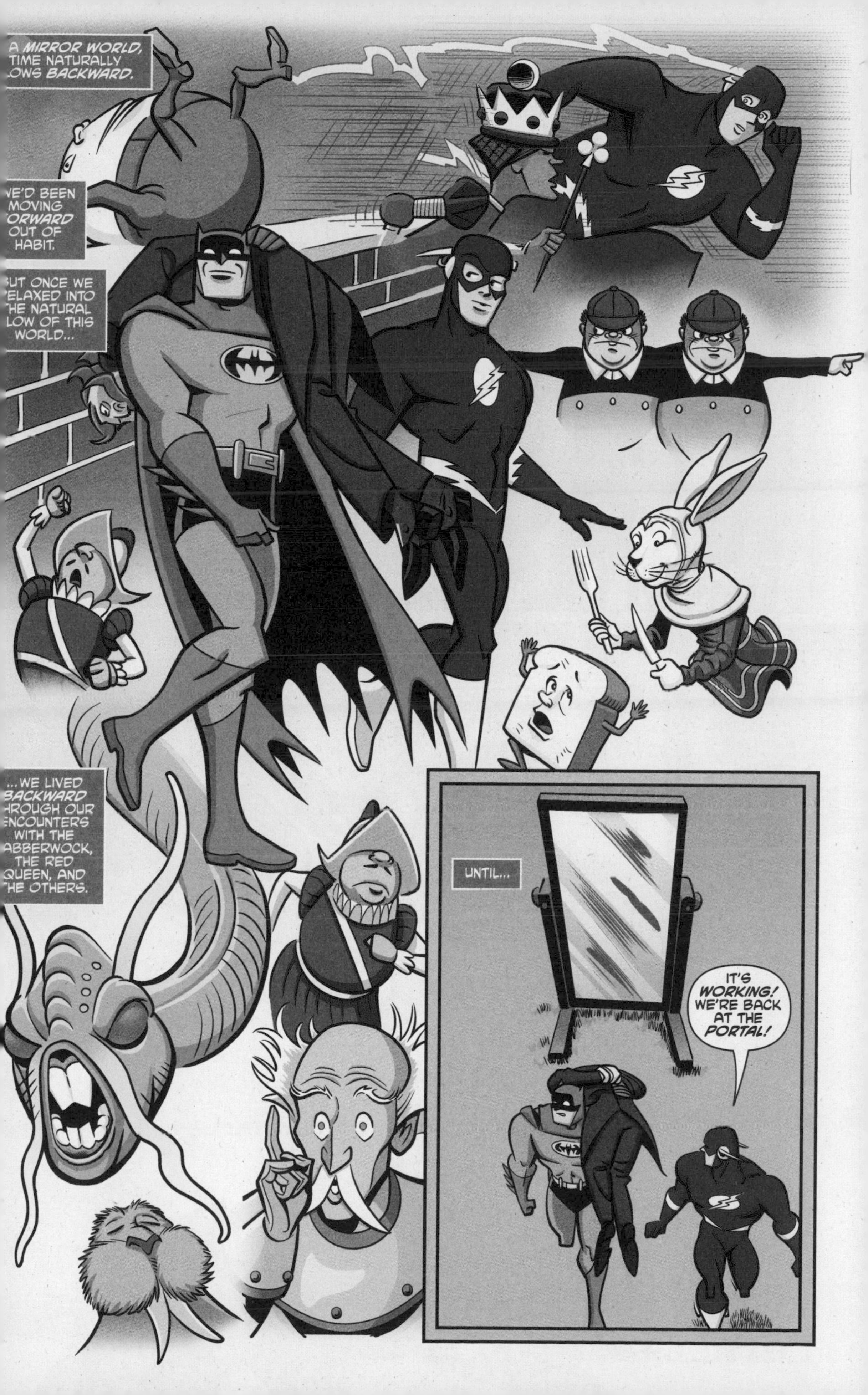
A MIRROR WORLD, TIME NATURALLY LOWS BACKWARD.
WE'D BEEN MOVING FORWARD OUT OF HABIT.
UT ONCE WE ELAXED INTO HE NATURAL LOW OF THIS WORLD...
...WE LIVED BACKWARD HROUGH OUR ENCOUNTERS WITH THE ABBERWOCK, THE RED QUEEN, AND HE OTHERS.
UNTIL...
IT'S WORKING! WE'RE BACK AT THE PORTAL!

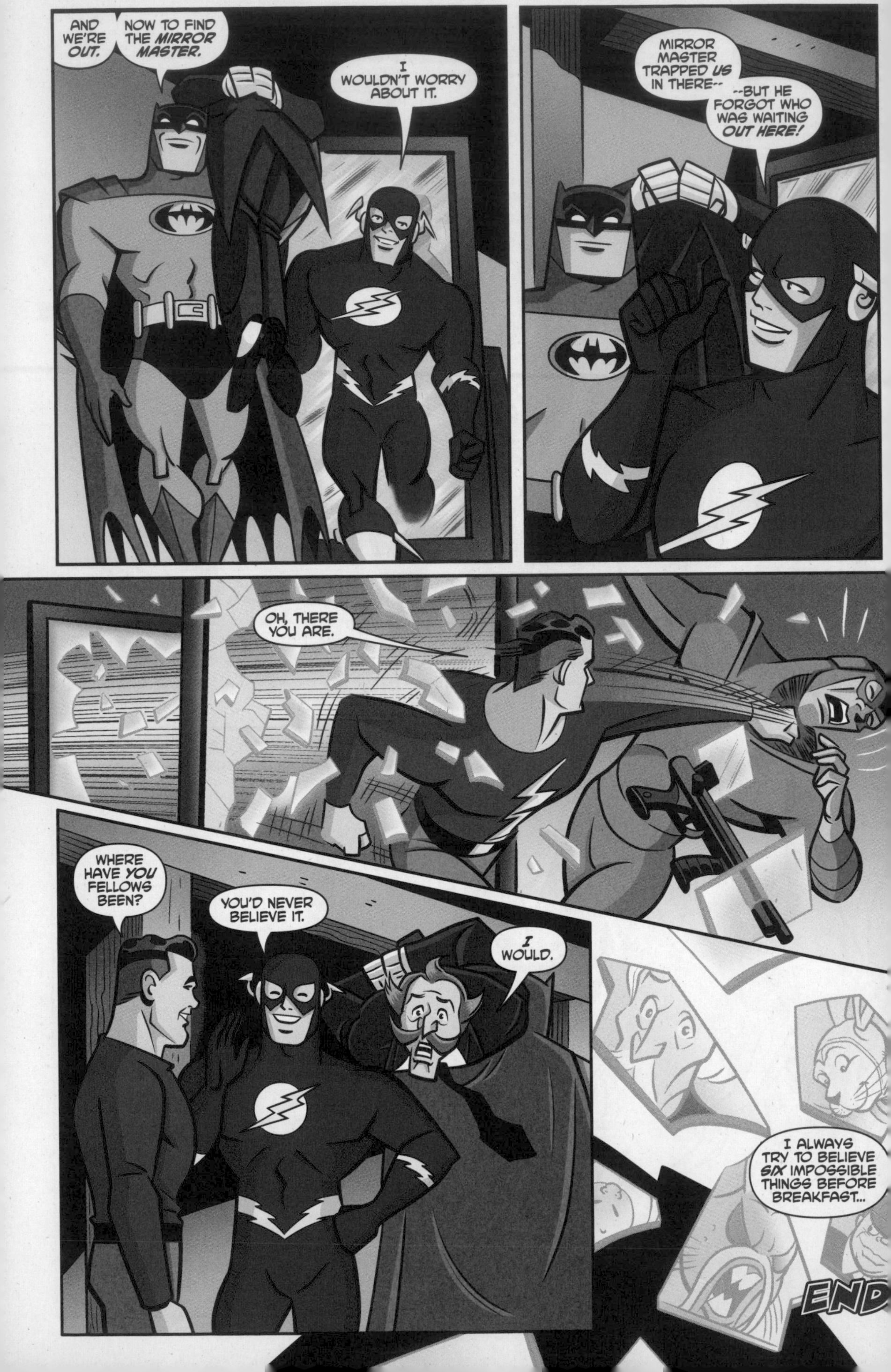
AND WE'RE OUT.
NOW TO FIND THE MIRROR MASTER.
I WOULDN'T WORRY ABOUT IT.
MIRROR MASTER TRAPPED US IN THERE--
--BUT HE FORGOT WHO WAS WAITING OUT HERE!
OH, THERE YOU ARE.
WHERE HAVE YOU FELLOWS BEEN?
YOU'D NEVER BELIEVE IT.
I WOULD.
I ALWAYS TRY TO BELIEVE SIX IMPOSSIBLE THINGS BEFORE BREAKFAST...
END

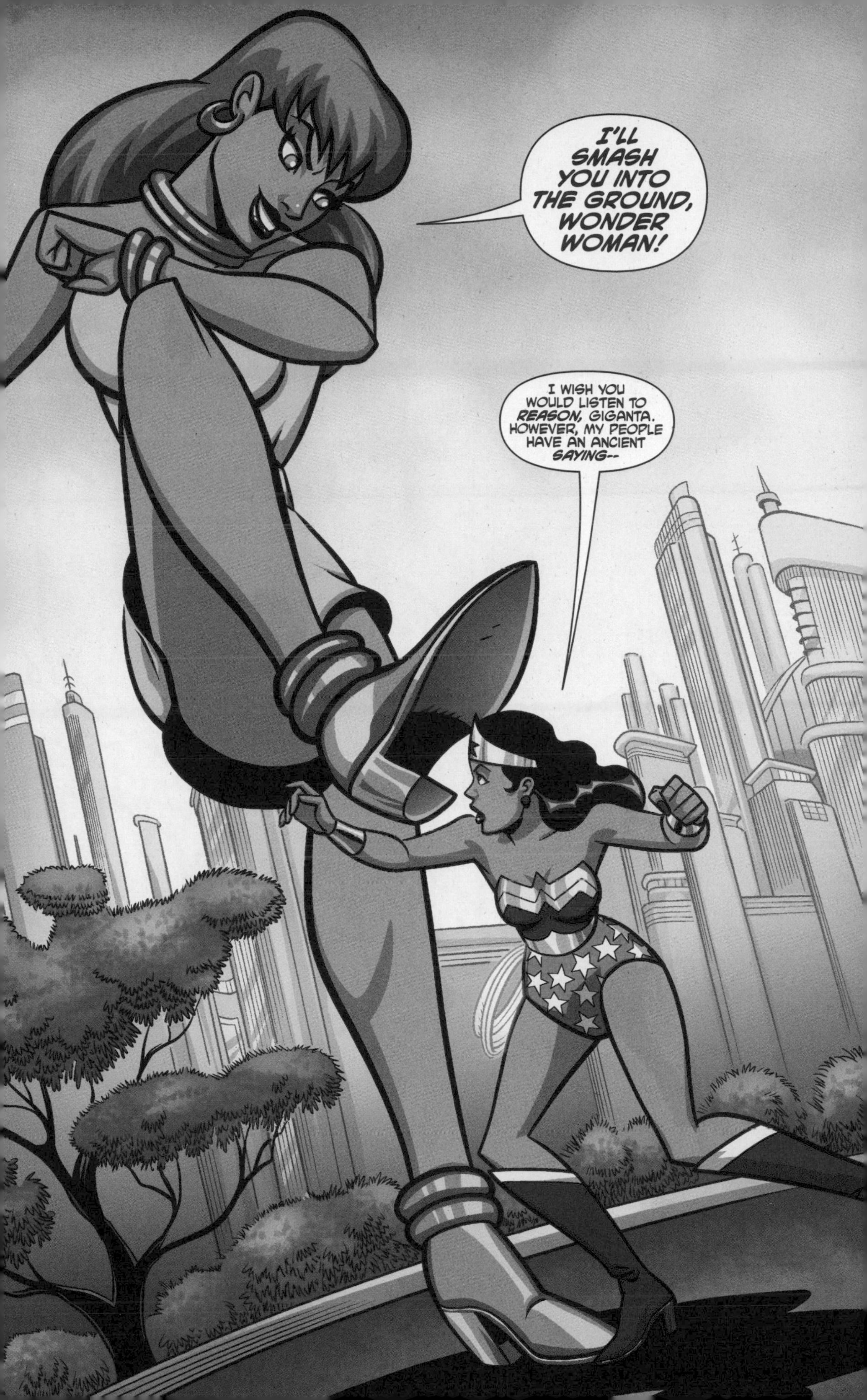
I'LL SMASH YOU INTO THE GROUND, WONDER WOMAN!
I WISH YOU WOULD LISTEN TO REASON, GIGANTA. HOWEVER, MY PEOPLE HAVE AN ANCIENT SAYING--

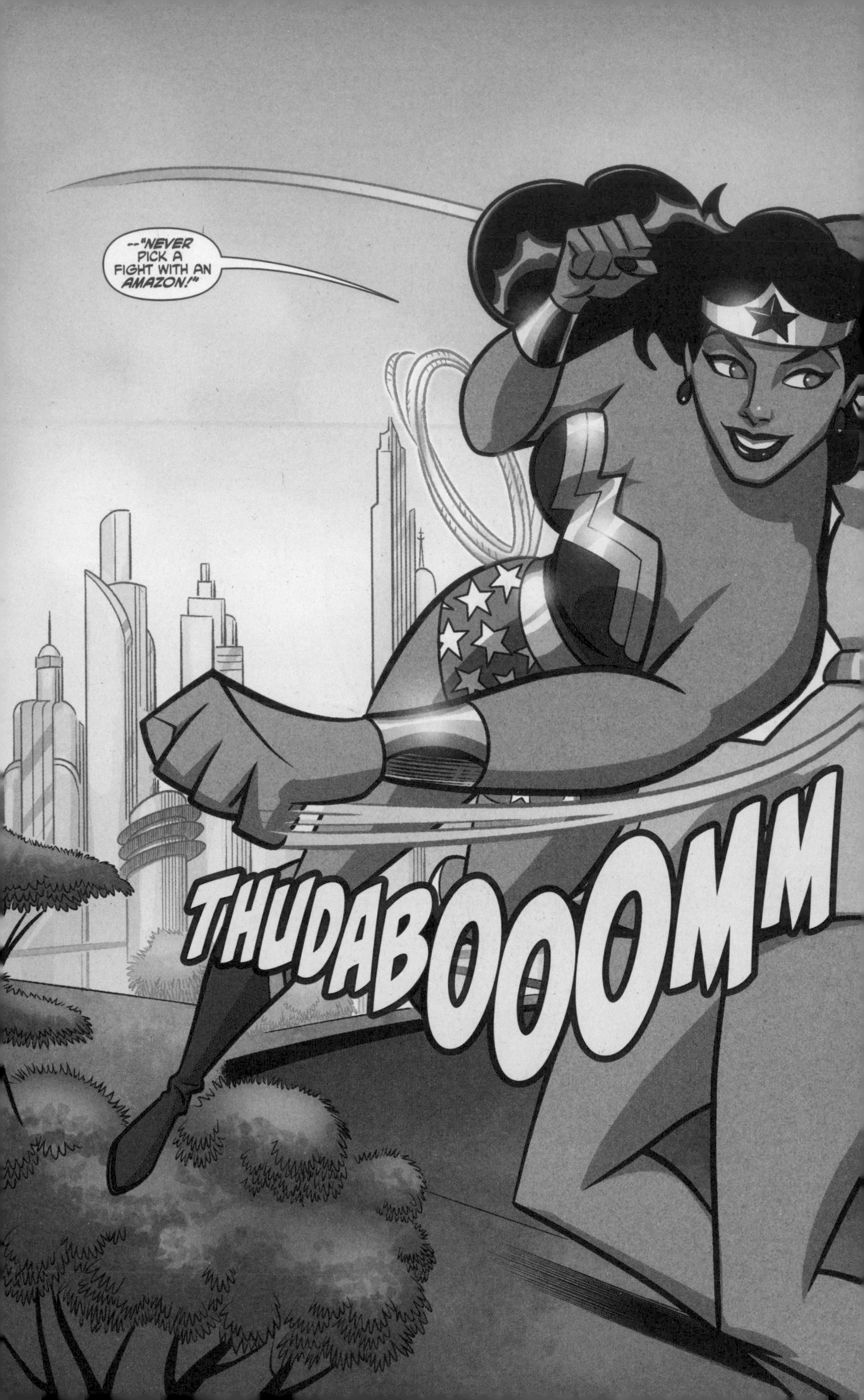
--"NEVER PICK A FIGHT WITH AN AMAZON!"
THUDABOOOMM

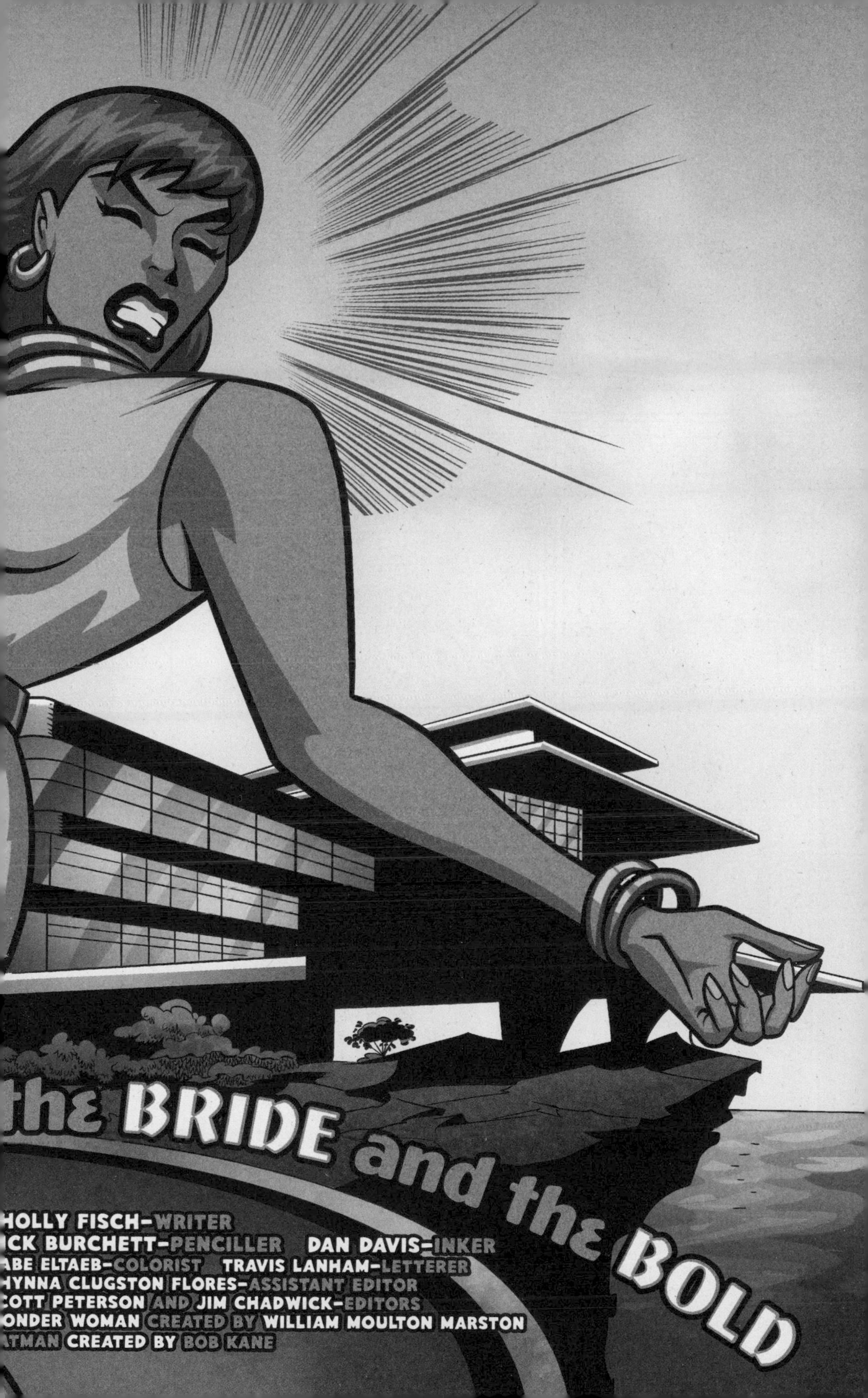
the BRIDE and the BOLD
HOLLY FISCH–WRITER
ICK BURCHETT–PENCILLER DAN DAVIS–INKER
ABE ELTAEB–COLORIST TRAVIS LANHAM–LETTERER
HYNNA CLUGSTON FLORES–ASSISTANT EDITOR
COTT PETERSON AND JIM CHADWICK–EDITORS
ONDER WOMAN CREATED BY WILLIAM MOULTON MARSTON
ATMAN CREATED BY BOB KANE

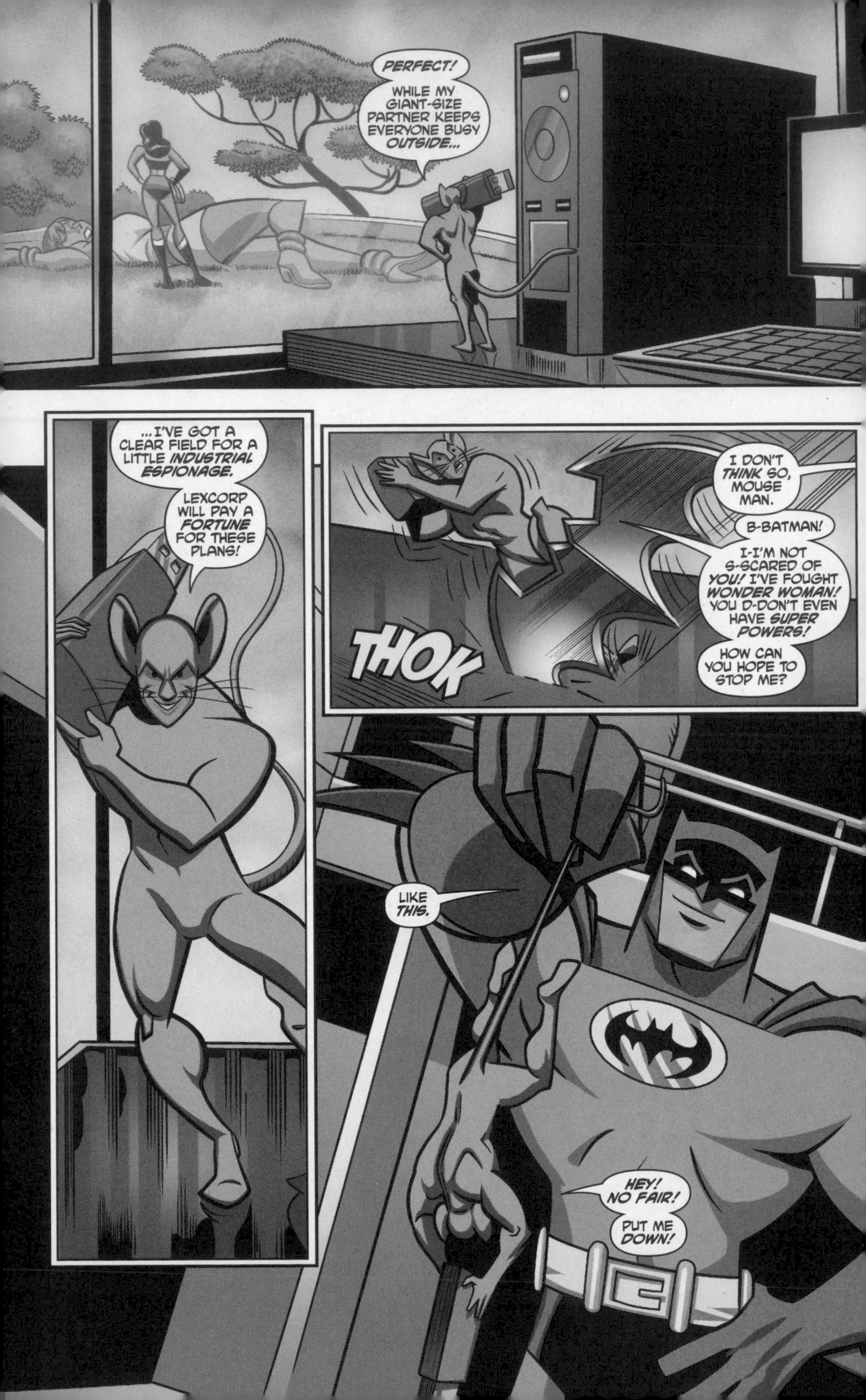
PERFECT!
WHILE MY GIANT-SIZE PARTNER KEEPS EVERYONE BUSY OUTSIDE...
...I'VE GOT A CLEAR FIELD FOR A LITTLE INDUSTRIAL ESPIONAGE.
LEXCORP WILL PAY A FORTUNE FOR THESE PLANS!
THOK
I DON'T THINK SO, MOUSE MAN.
B-BATMAN!
I-I'M NOT S-SCARED OF YOU! I'VE FOUGHT WONDER WOMAN! YOU D-DON'T EVEN HAVE SUPER POWERS!
HOW CAN YOU HOPE TO STOP ME?
LIKE THIS.
HEY! NO FAIR!
PUT ME DOWN!

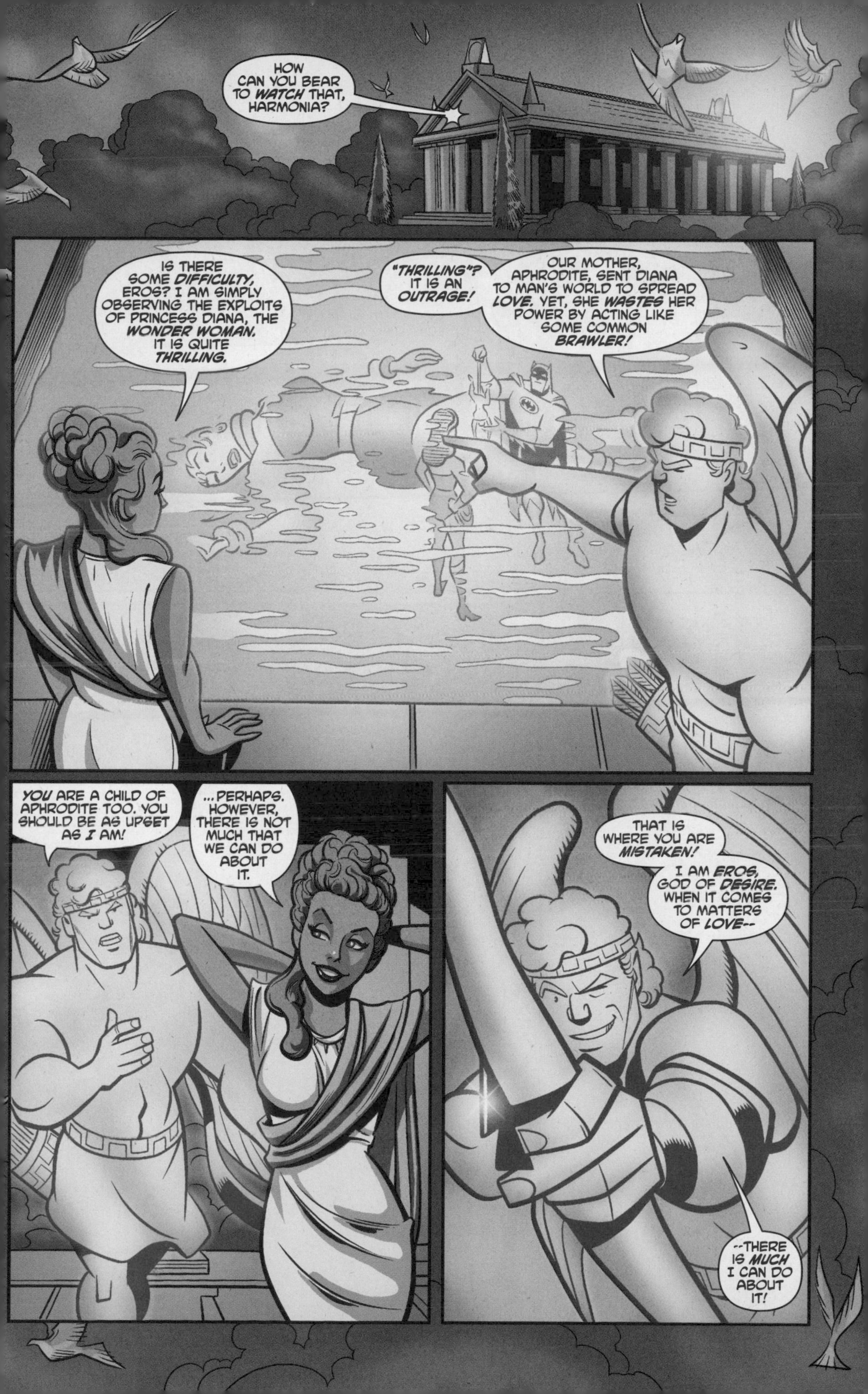
HOW CAN YOU BEAR TO WATCH THAT, HARMONIA?
IS THERE SOME DIFFICULTY, EROS? I AM SIMPLY OBSERVING THE EXPLOITS OF PRINCESS DIANA, THE WONDER WOMAN. IT IS QUITE THRILLING.
"THRILLING"? IT IS AN OUTRAGE!
OUR MOTHER, APHRODITE, SENT DIANA TO MAN'S WORLD TO SPREAD LOVE. YET, SHE WASTES HER POWER BY ACTING LIKE SOME COMMON BRAWLER!
YOU ARE A CHILD OF APHRODITE TOO. YOU SHOULD BE AS UPSET AS I AM!
...PERHAPS. HOWEVER, THERE IS NOT MUCH THAT WE CAN DO ABOUT IT.
THAT IS WHERE YOU ARE MISTAKEN!
I AM EROS, GOD OF DESIRE. WHEN IT COMES TO MATTERS OF LOVE--
--THERE IS MUCH I CAN DO ABOUT IT!

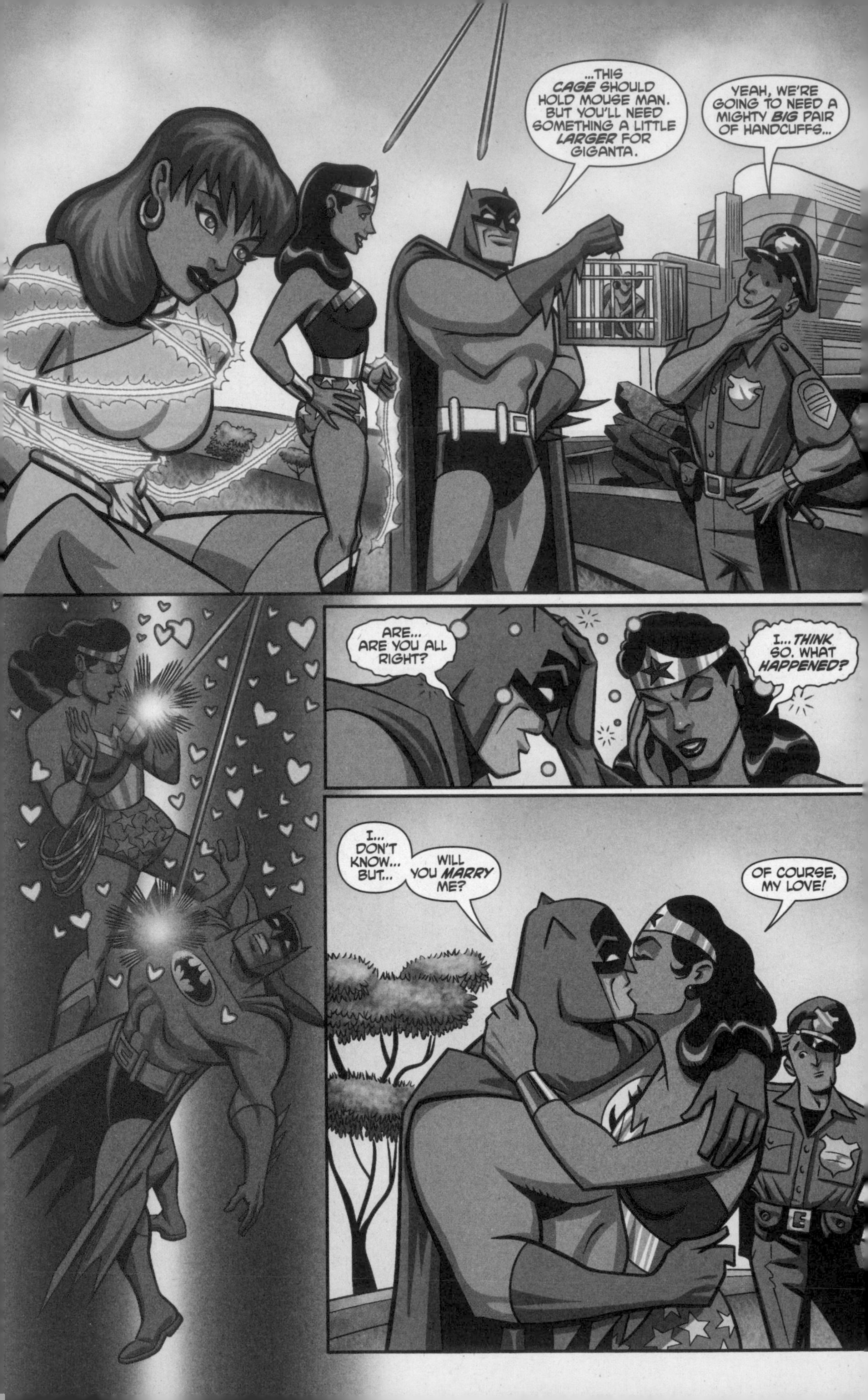
...THIS CAGE SHOULD HOLD MOUSE MAN. BUT YOU'LL NEED SOMETHING A LITTLE LARGER FOR GIGANTA.
YEAH, WE'RE GOING TO NEED A MIGHTY BIG PAIR OF HANDCUFFS...
ARE... ARE YOU ALL RIGHT?
I...THINK SO. WHAT HAPPENED?
I... DON'T KNOW... BUT...
WILL YOU MARRY ME?
OF COURSE, MY LOVE!

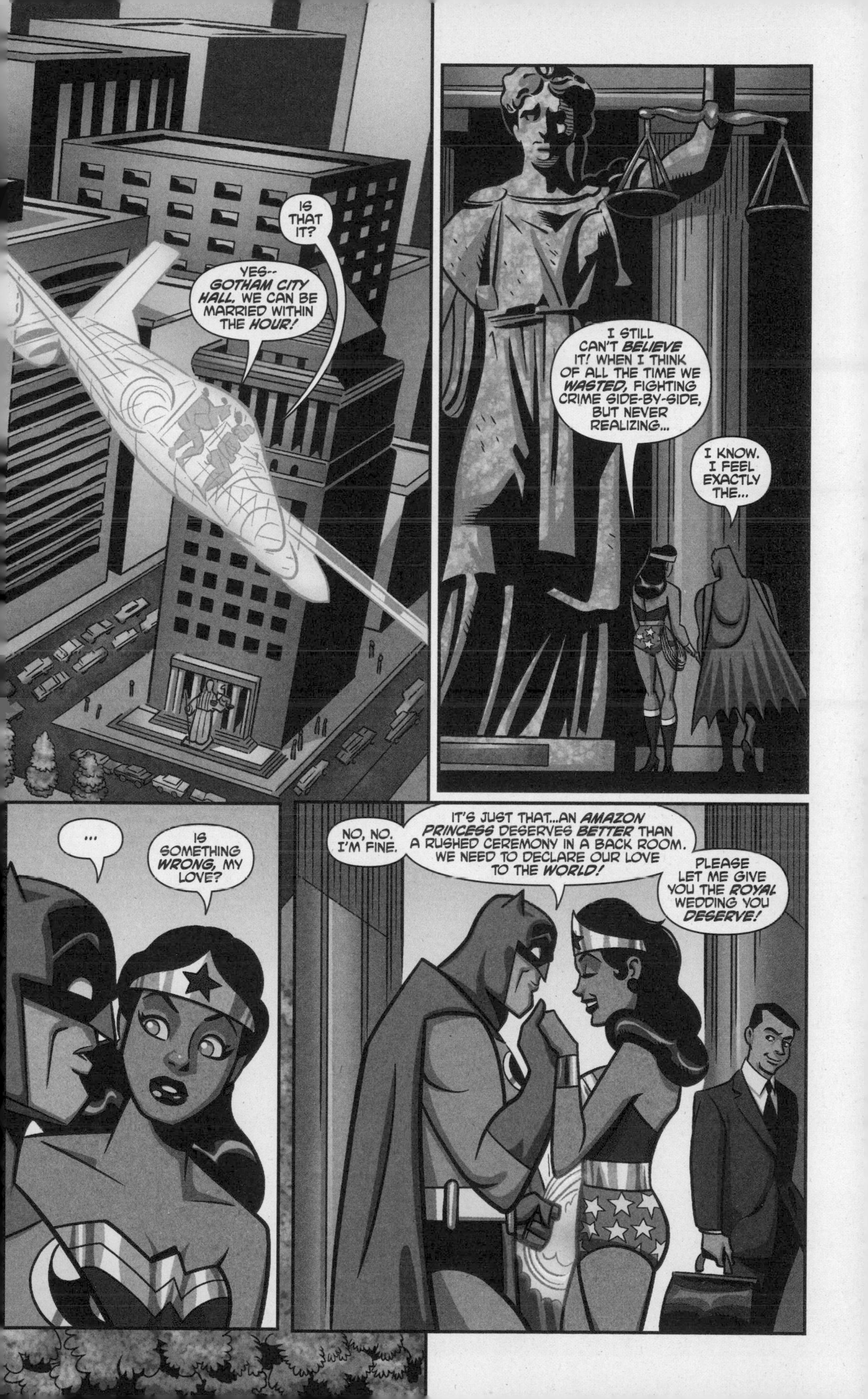
IS THAT IT?
YES-- GOTHAM CITY HALL. WE CAN BE MARRIED WITHIN THE HOUR!
I STILL CAN'T BELIEVE IT! WHEN I THINK OF ALL THE TIME WE WASTED, FIGHTING CRIME SIDE-BY-SIDE, BUT NEVER REALIZING...
I KNOW. I FEEL EXACTLY THE...
...
IS SOMETHING WRONG, MY LOVE?
NO, NO. I'M FINE.
IT'S JUST THAT...AN AMAZON PRINCESS DESERVES BETTER THAN A RUSHED CEREMONY IN A BACK ROOM. WE NEED TO DECLARE OUR LOVE TO THE WORLD!
PLEASE LET ME GIVE YOU THE ROYAL WEDDING YOU DESERVE!

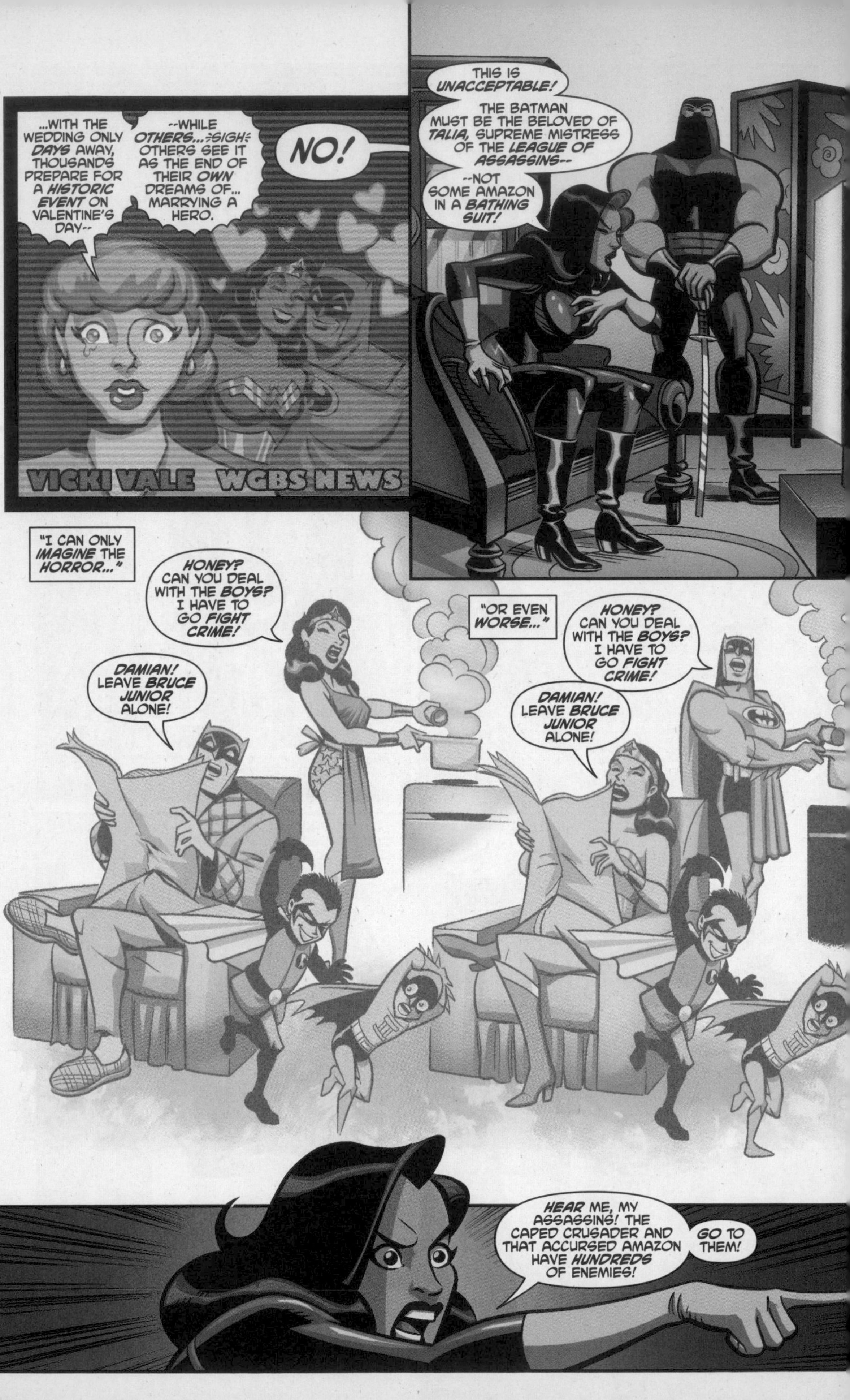
...WITH THE WEDDING ONLY DAYS AWAY, THOUSANDS PREPARE FOR A HISTORIC EVENT ON VALENTINE'S DAY--
--WHILE OTHERS... ~SIGH~ OTHERS SEE IT AS THE END OF THEIR OWN DREAMS OF... MARRYING A HERO.
NO!
VICKI VALE WGBS NEWS
THIS IS UNACCEPTABLE!
THE BATMAN MUST BE THE BELOVED OF TALIA, SUPREME MISTRESS OF THE LEAGUE OF ASSASSINS--
--NOT SOME AMAZON IN A BATHING SUIT!
"I CAN ONLY IMAGINE THE HORROR..."
HONEY? CAN YOU DEAL WITH THE BOYS? I HAVE TO GO FIGHT CRIME!
DAMIAN! LEAVE BRUCE JUNIOR ALONE!
"OR EVEN WORSE..."
HONEY? CAN YOU DEAL WITH THE BOYS? I HAVE TO GO FIGHT CRIME!
DAMIAN! LEAVE BRUCE JUNIOR ALONE!
HEAR ME, MY ASSASSINS! THE CAPED CRUSADER AND THAT ACCURSED AMAZON HAVE HUNDREDS OF ENEMIES!
GO TO THEM!

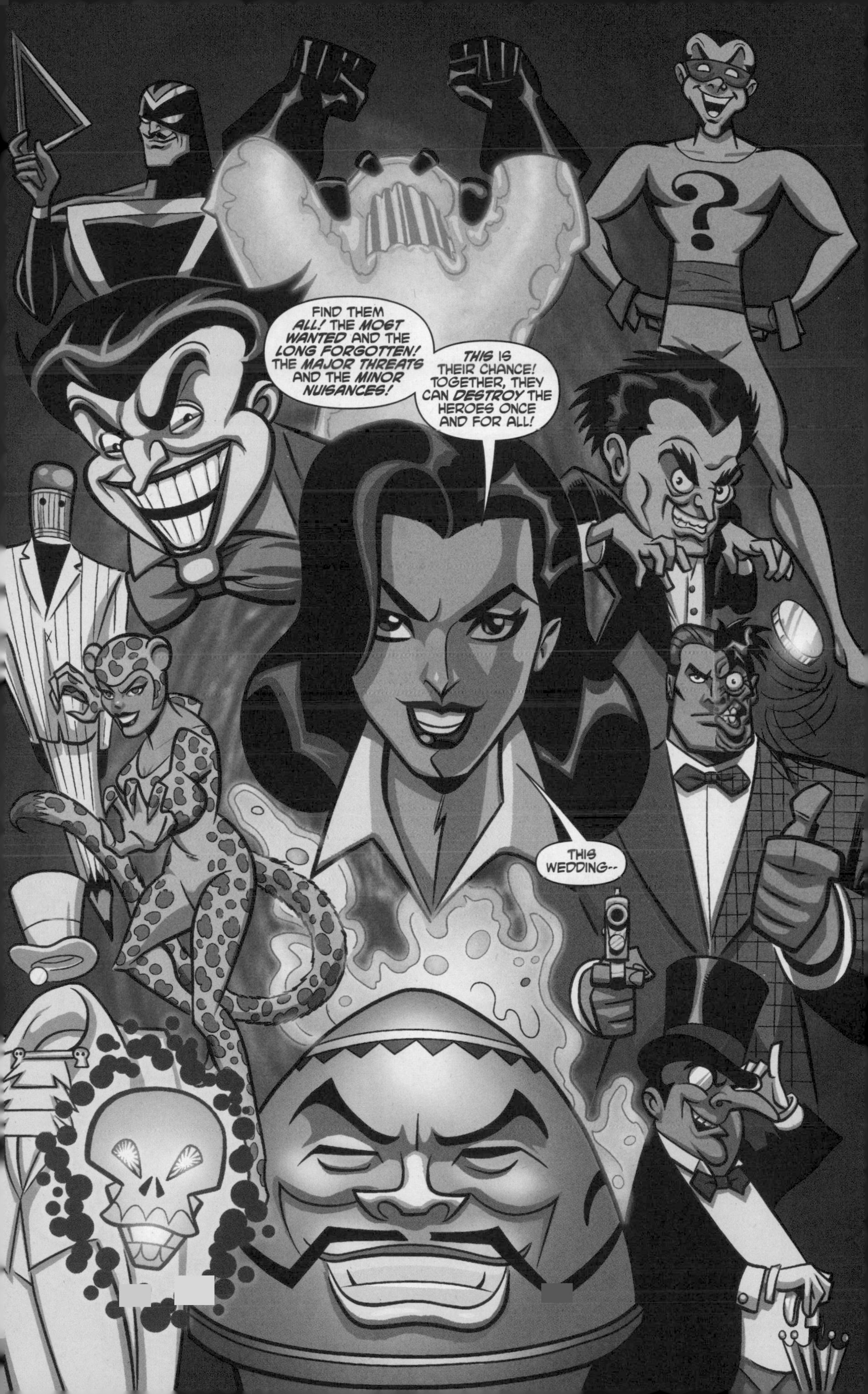
FIND THEM ALL! THE MOST WANTED AND THE LONG FORGOTTEN! THE MAJOR THREATS AND THE MINOR NUISANCES!
THIS IS THEIR CHANCE! TOGETHER, THEY CAN DESTROY THE HEROES ONCE AND FOR ALL!
THIS WEDDING--

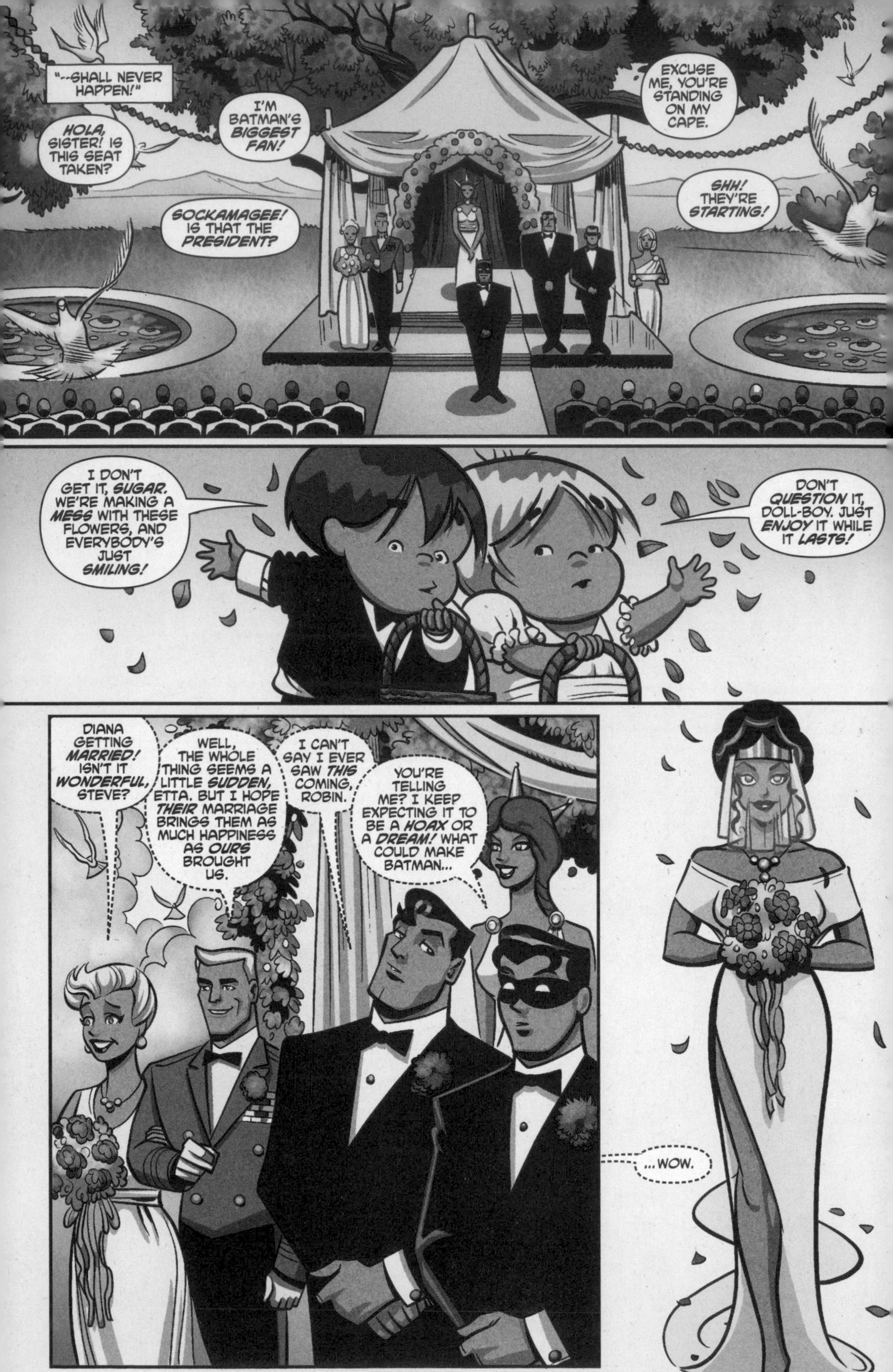
"--SHALL NEVER HAPPEN!"
HOLA, SISTER! IS THIS SEAT TAKEN?
I'M BATMAN'S BIGGEST FAN!
SOCKAMAGEE! IS THAT THE PRESIDENT?
EXCUSE ME, YOU'RE STANDING ON MY CAPE.
SHH! THEY'RE STARTING!
I DON'T GET IT, SUGAR. WE'RE MAKING A MESS WITH THESE FLOWERS, AND EVERYBODY'S JUST SMILING!
DON'T QUESTION IT, DOLL-BOY. JUST ENJOY IT WHILE IT LASTS!
DIANA GETTING MARRIED! ISN'T IT WONDERFUL, STEVE?
WELL, THE WHOLE THING SEEMS A LITTLE SUDDEN, ETTA. BUT I HOPE THEIR MARRIAGE BRINGS THEM AS MUCH HAPPINESS AS OURS BROUGHT US.
I CAN'T SAY I EVER SAW THIS COMING, ROBIN.
YOU'RE TELLING ME? I KEEP EXPECTING IT TO BE A HOAX OR A DREAM! WHAT COULD MAKE BATMAN...
...WOW.

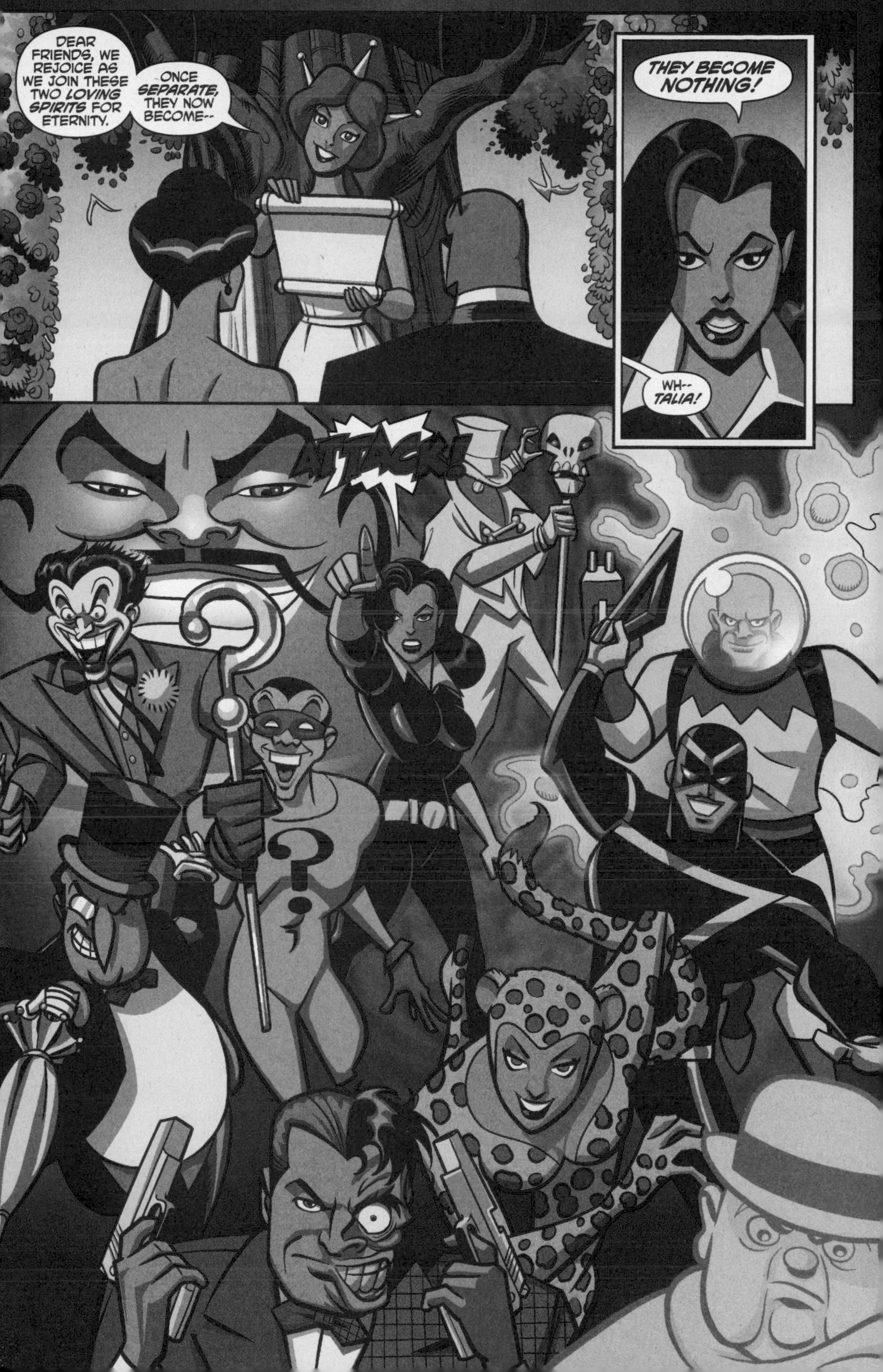
DEAR FRIENDS, WE REJOICE AS WE JOIN THESE TWO *LOVING SPIRITS* FOR ETERNITY.
--ONCE *SEPARATE,* THEY NOW BECOME--
THEY BECOME NOTHING!
WH-- *TALIA!*
ATTACK!

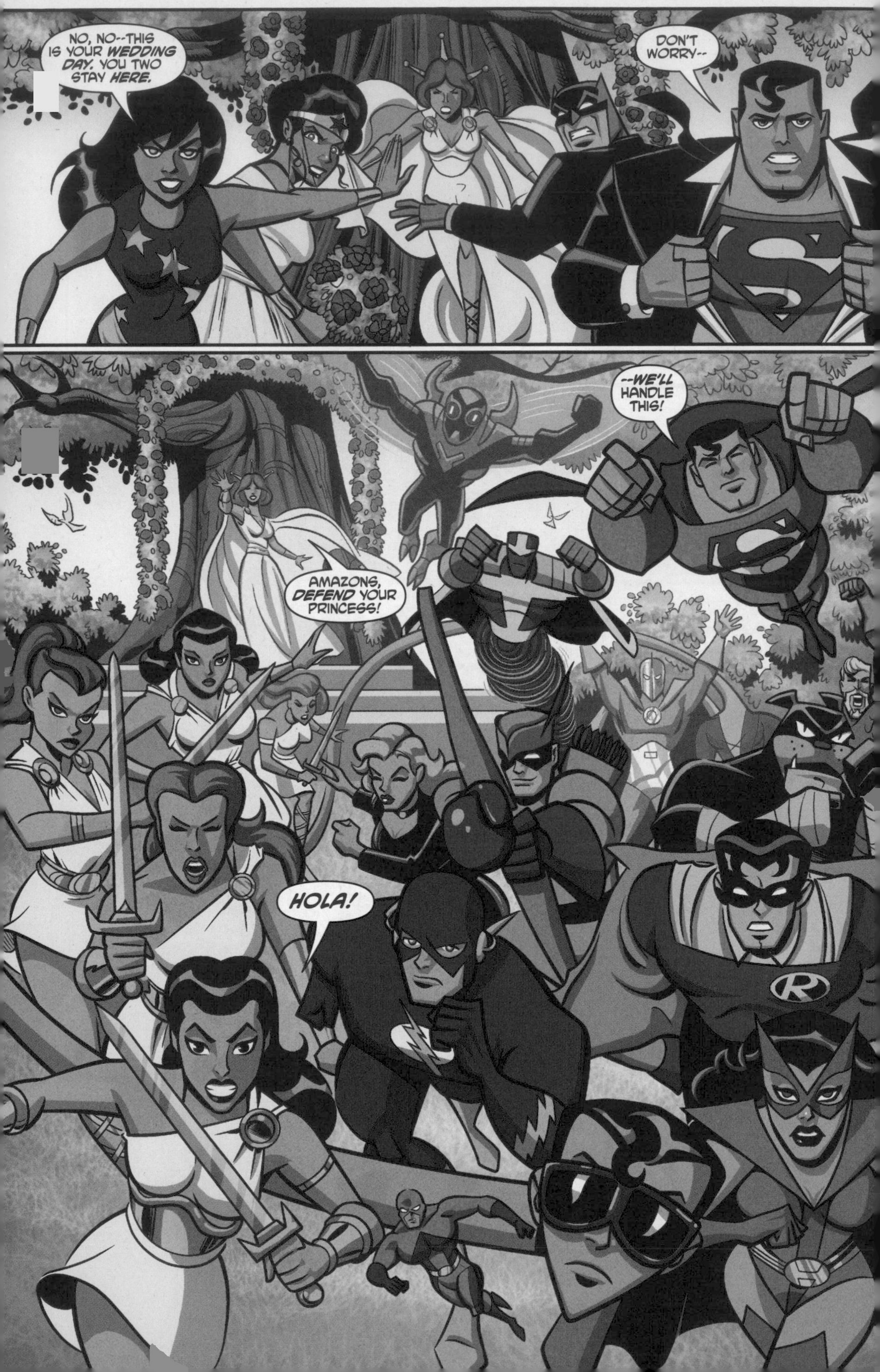
NO, NO--THIS IS YOUR *WEDDING DAY*. YOU TWO STAY *HERE*.
DON'T WORRY--
--*WE'LL* HANDLE THIS!
AMAZONS, *DEFEND* YOUR PRINCESS!
HOLA!

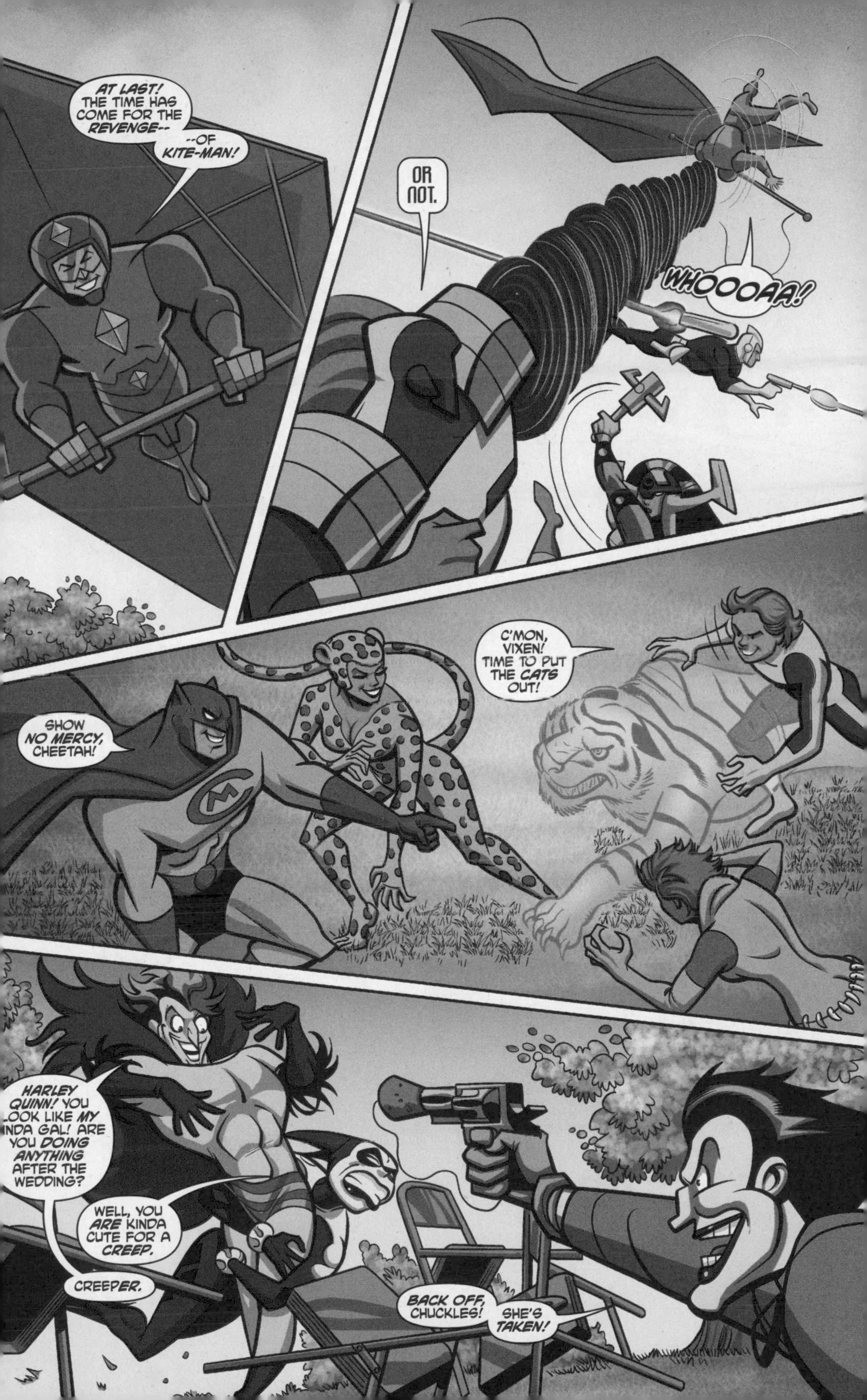

AT LAST! THE TIME HAS COME FOR THE REVENGE--
--OF KITE-MAN!
OR NOT.
WHOOOAA!
SHOW NO MERCY, CHEETAH!
C'MON, VIXEN! TIME TO PUT THE CATS OUT!
HARLEY QUINN! YOU LOOK LIKE MY INDA GAL! ARE YOU DOING ANYTHING AFTER THE WEDDING?
WELL, YOU ARE KINDA CUTE FOR A CREEP.
CREEPER.
BACK OFF, CHUCKLES!
SHE'S TAKEN!

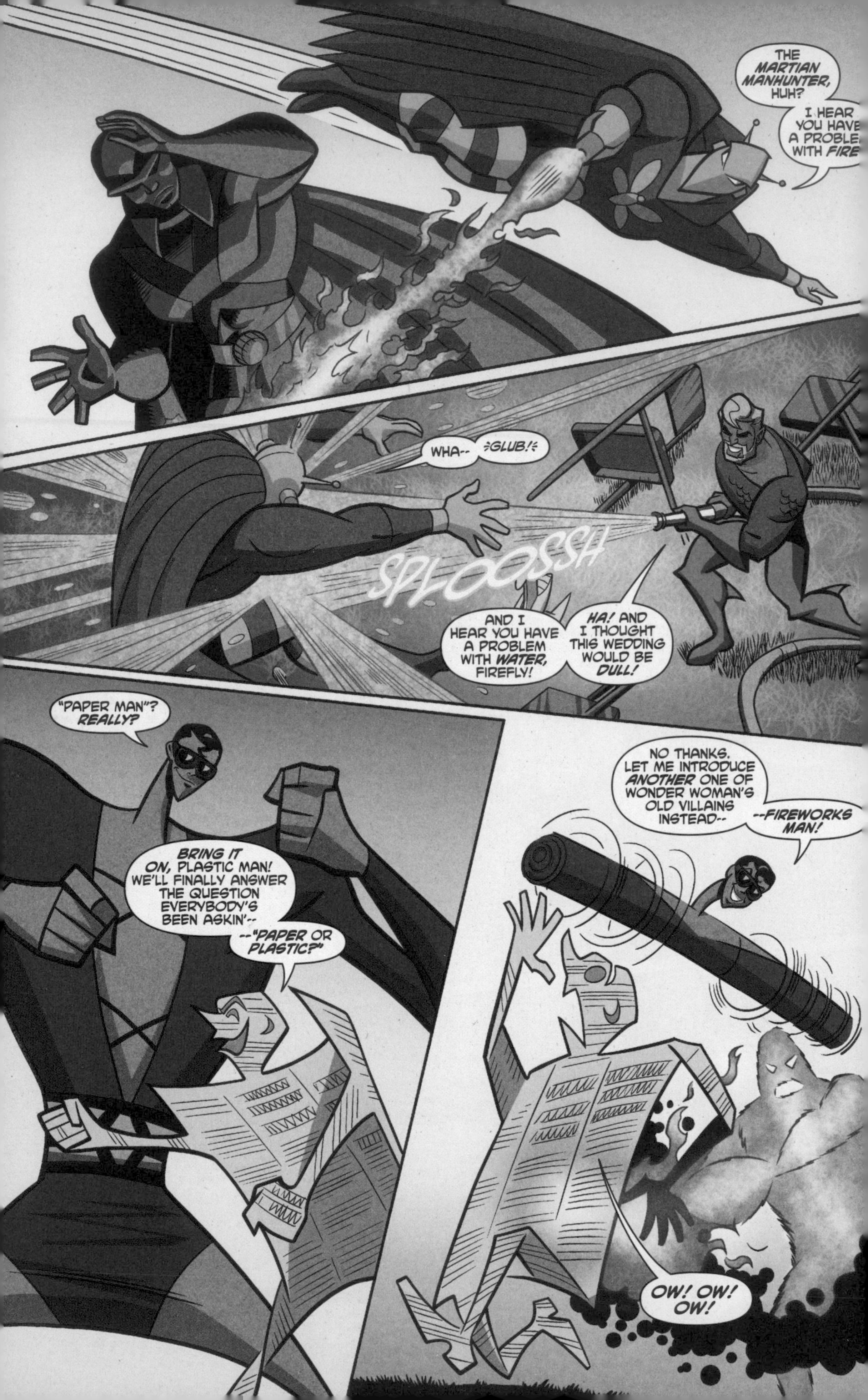
THE MARTIAN MANHUNTER, HUH?
I HEAR YOU HAVE A PROBLE WITH FIRE
WHA--
GLUB!
SPLOOSSH
AND I HEAR YOU HAVE A PROBLEM WITH WATER, FIREFLY!
HA! AND I THOUGHT THIS WEDDING WOULD BE DULL!
"PAPER MAN"? REALLY?
BRING IT ON, PLASTIC MAN! WE'LL FINALLY ANSWER THE QUESTION EVERYBODY'S BEEN ASKIN'--
--"PAPER OR PLASTIC?"
NO THANKS. LET ME INTRODUCE ANOTHER ONE OF WONDER WOMAN'S OLD VILLAINS INSTEAD--
--FIREWORKS MAN!
OW! OW! OW!

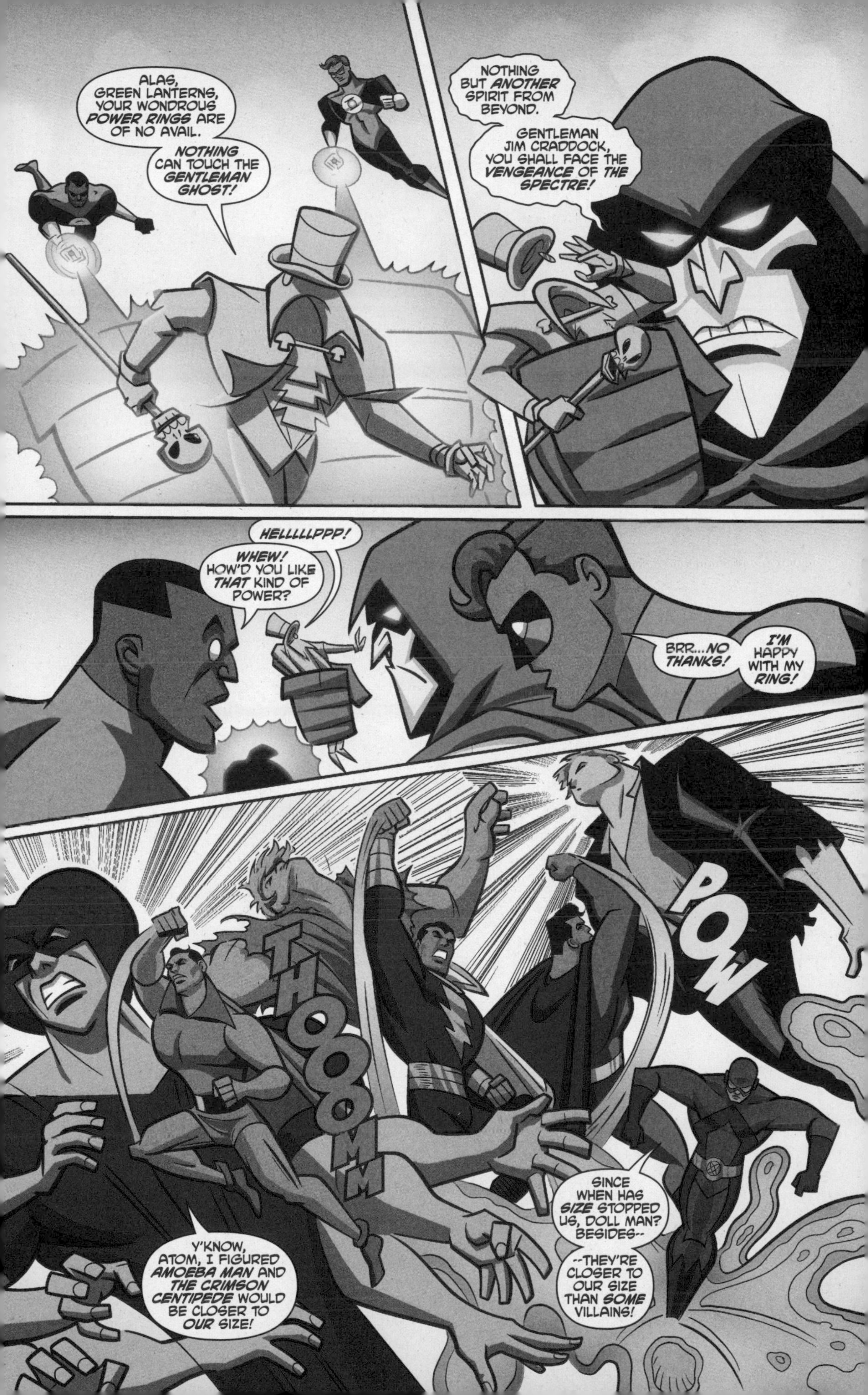

ALAS, GREEN LANTERNS, YOUR WONDROUS POWER RINGS ARE OF NO AVAIL.
NOTHING CAN TOUCH THE GENTLEMAN GHOST!
NOTHING BUT ANOTHER SPIRIT FROM BEYOND.
GENTLEMAN JIM CRADDOCK, YOU SHALL FACE THE VENGEANCE OF THE SPECTRE!
HELLLLLLPPP!
WHEW! HOW'D YOU LIKE THAT KIND OF POWER?
BRR...NO THANKS!
I'M HAPPY WITH MY RING!
THOOOMMM
POW
Y'KNOW, ATOM, I FIGURED AMOEBA MAN AND THE CRIMSON CENTIPEDE WOULD BE CLOSER TO OUR SIZE!
SINCE WHEN HAS SIZE STOPPED US, DOLL MAN? BESIDES--
--THEY'RE CLOSER TO OUR SIZE THAN SOME VILLAINS!

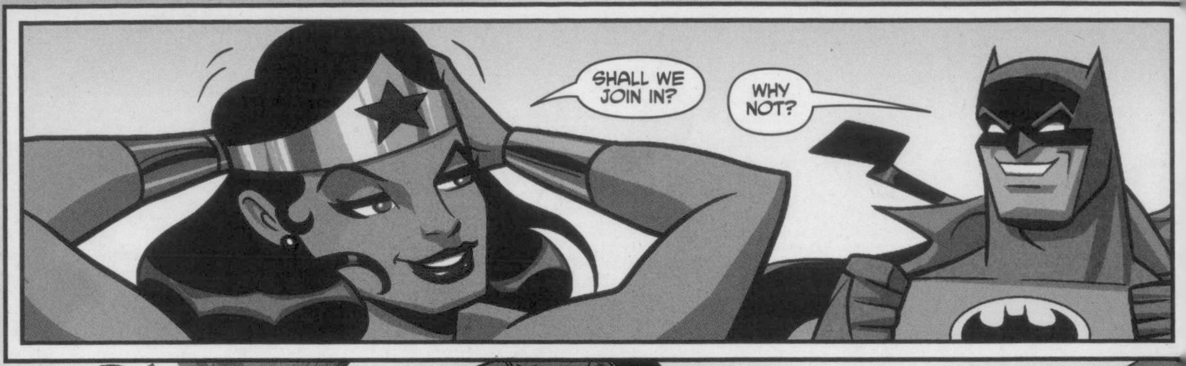
SHALL WE JOIN IN?
WHY NOT?

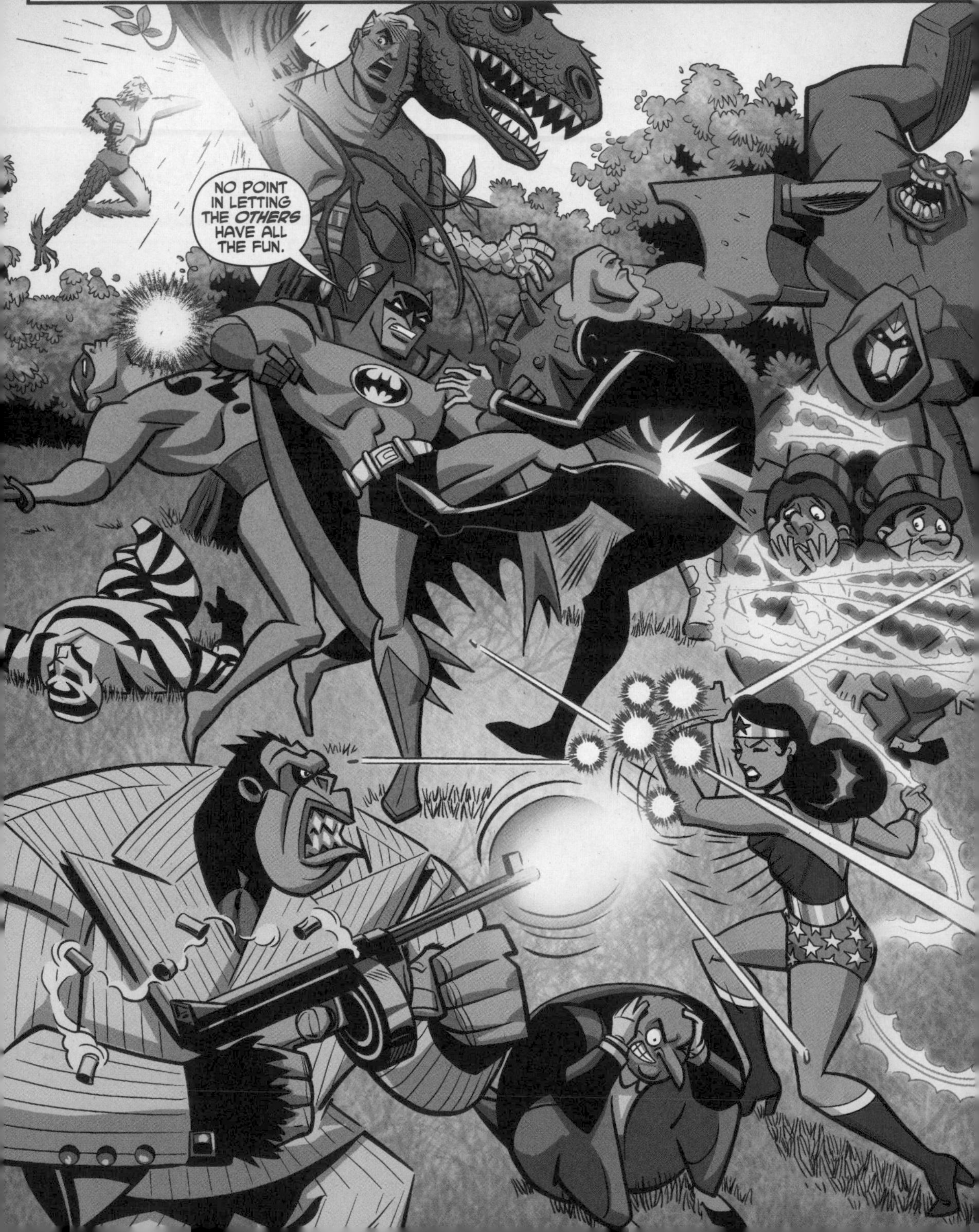
NO POINT IN LETTING THE OTHERS HAVE ALL THE FUN.

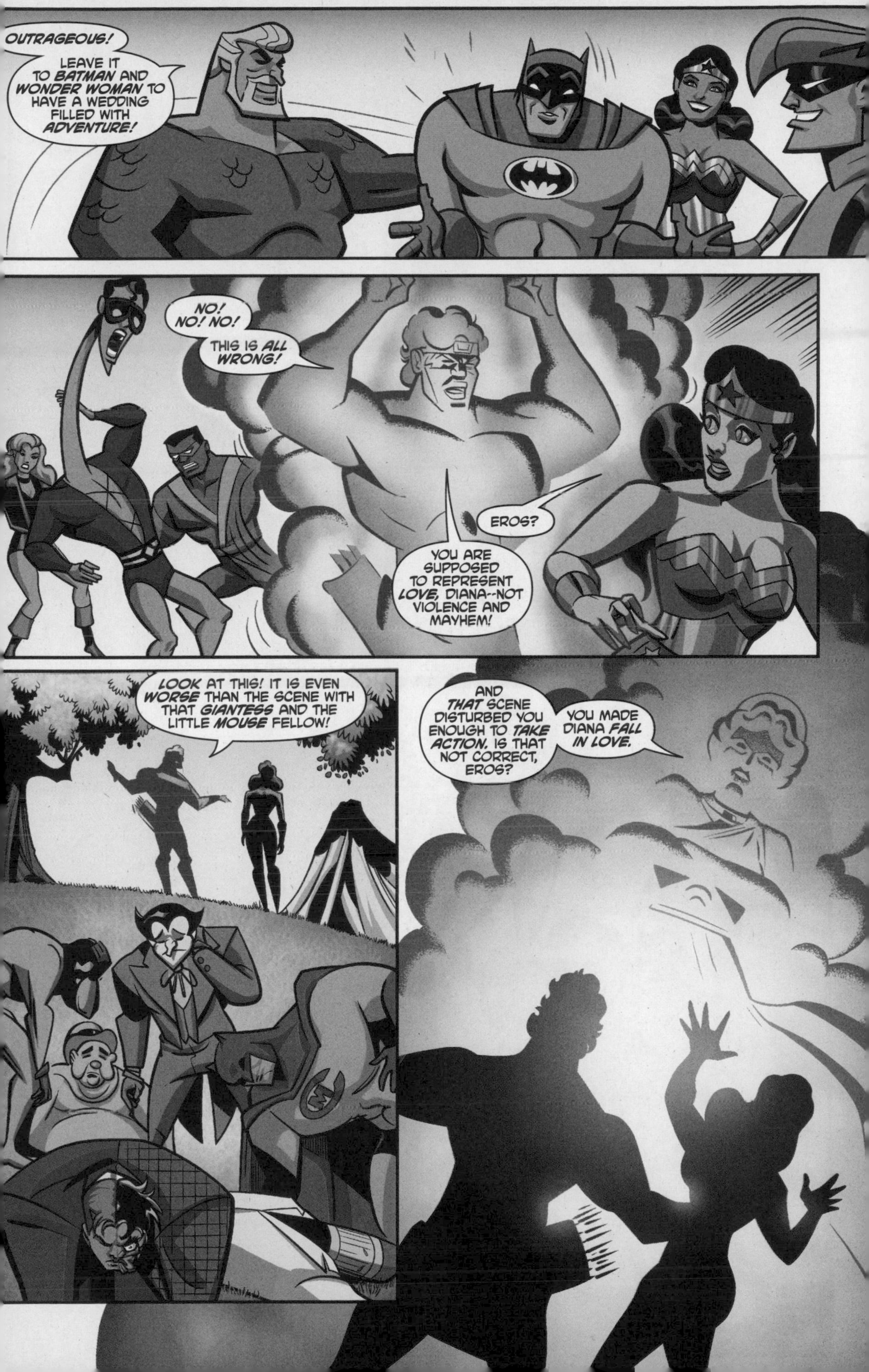
OUTRAGEOUS!
LEAVE IT TO BATMAN AND WONDER WOMAN TO HAVE A WEDDING FILLED WITH ADVENTURE!
NO! NO! NO!
THIS IS ALL WRONG!
EROS?
YOU ARE SUPPOSED TO REPRESENT LOVE, DIANA--NOT VIOLENCE AND MAYHEM!
LOOK AT THIS! IT IS EVEN WORSE THAN THE SCENE WITH THAT GIANTESS AND THE LITTLE MOUSE FELLOW!
AND THAT SCENE DISTURBED YOU ENOUGH TO TAKE ACTION. IS THAT NOT CORRECT, EROS?
YOU MADE DIANA FALL IN LOVE.

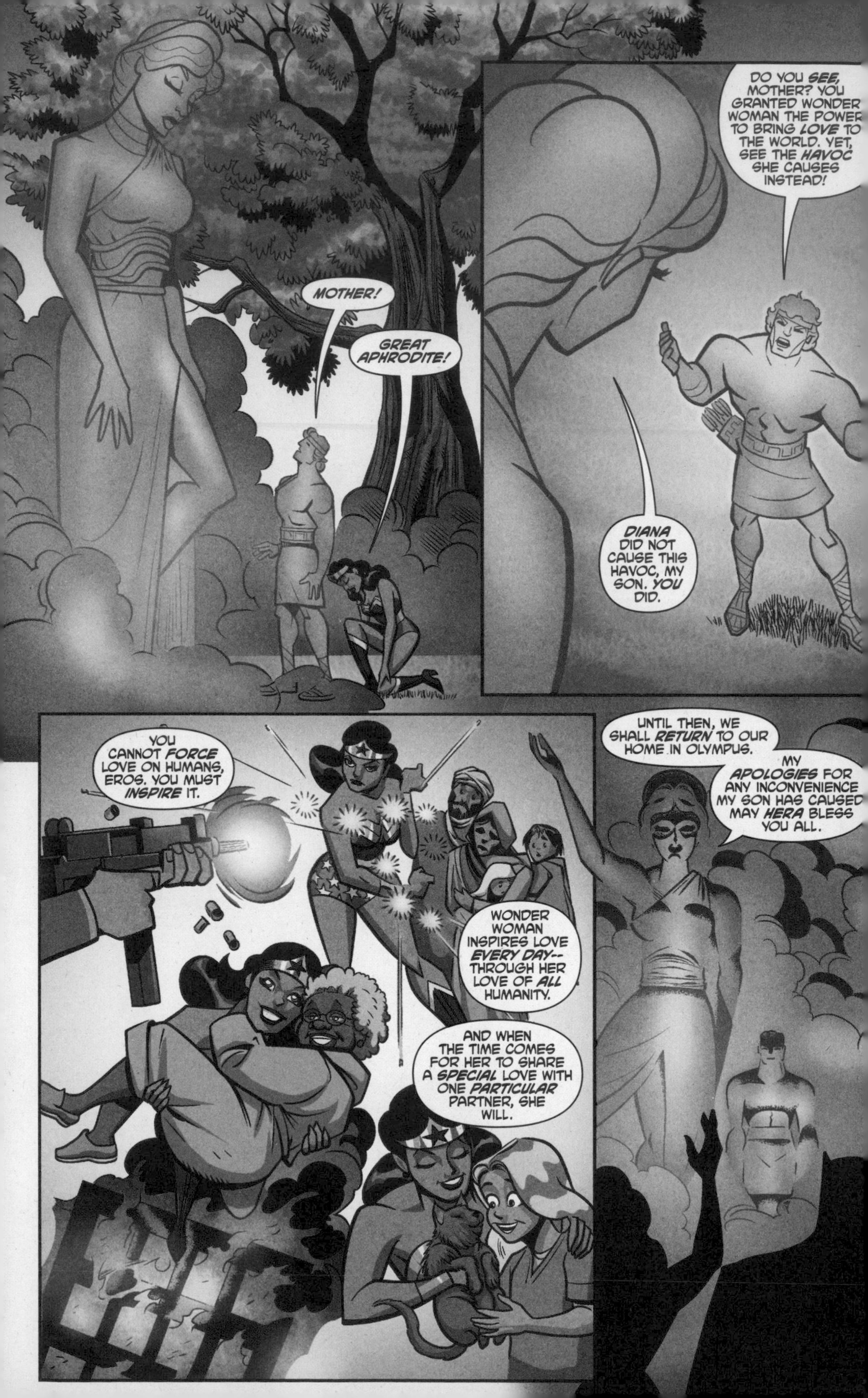
MOTHER!
GREAT APHRODITE!
DO YOU SEE, MOTHER? YOU GRANTED WONDER WOMAN THE POWER TO BRING LOVE TO THE WORLD. YET, SEE THE HAVOC SHE CAUSES INSTEAD!
DIANA DID NOT CAUSE THIS HAVOC, MY SON. YOU DID.
YOU CANNOT FORCE LOVE ON HUMANS, EROS. YOU MUST INSPIRE IT.
WONDER WOMAN INSPIRES LOVE EVERY DAY-- THROUGH HER LOVE OF ALL HUMANITY.
AND WHEN THE TIME COMES FOR HER TO SHARE A SPECIAL LOVE WITH ONE PARTICULAR PARTNER, SHE WILL.
UNTIL THEN, WE SHALL RETURN TO OUR HOME IN OLYMPUS.
MY APOLOGIES FOR ANY INCONVENIENCE MY SON HAS CAUSED. MAY HERA BLESS YOU ALL.

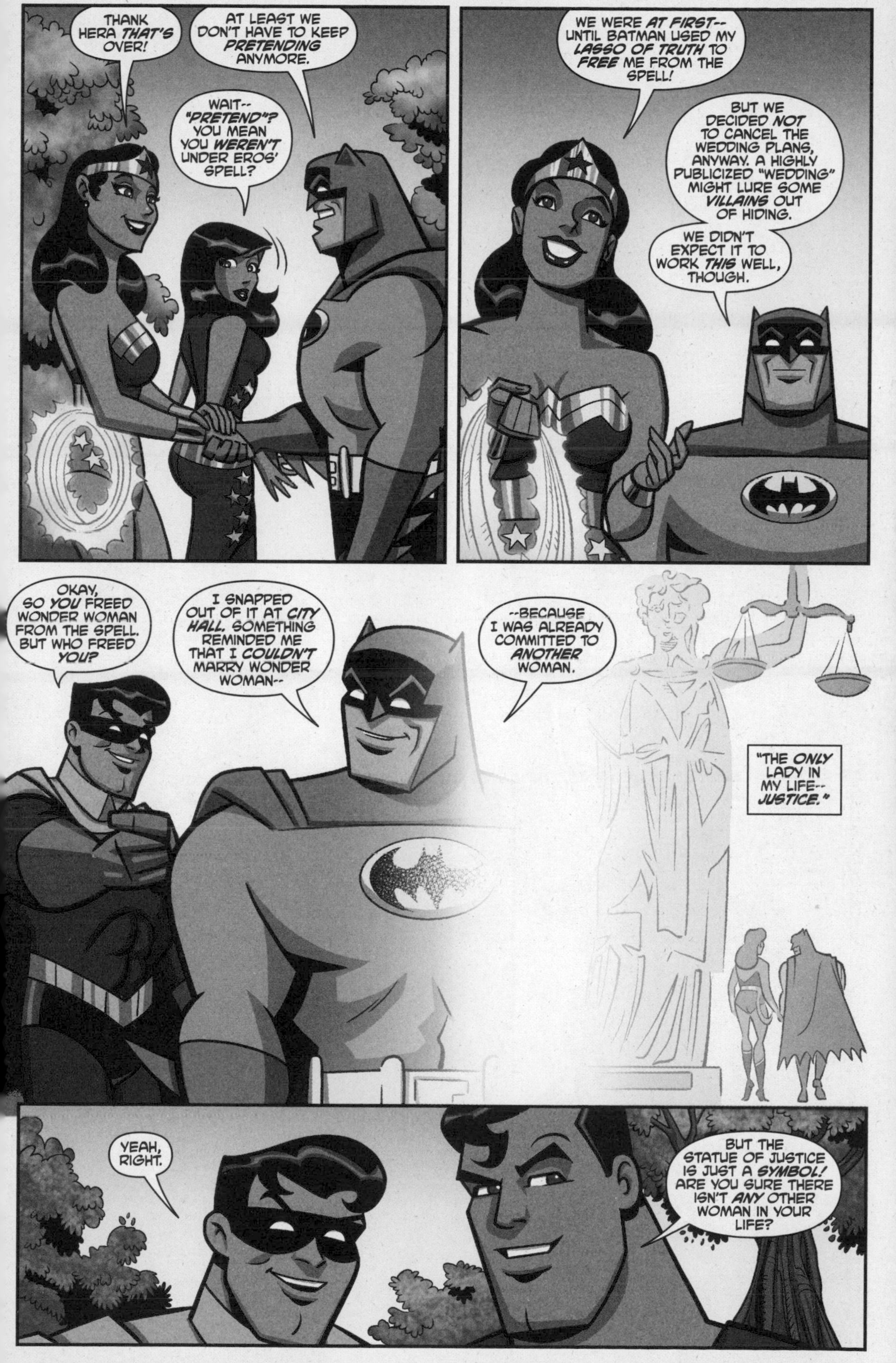
THANK HERA THAT'S OVER!
AT LEAST WE DON'T HAVE TO KEEP PRETENDING ANYMORE.
WAIT-- "PRETEND"? YOU MEAN YOU WEREN'T UNDER EROS' SPELL?
WE WERE AT FIRST-- UNTIL BATMAN USED MY LASSO OF TRUTH TO FREE ME FROM THE SPELL!
BUT WE DECIDED NOT TO CANCEL THE WEDDING PLANS, ANYWAY. A HIGHLY PUBLICIZED "WEDDING" MIGHT LURE SOME VILLAINS OUT OF HIDING.
WE DIDN'T EXPECT IT TO WORK THIS WELL, THOUGH.
OKAY, SO YOU FREED WONDER WOMAN FROM THE SPELL. BUT WHO FREED YOU?
I SNAPPED OUT OF IT AT CITY HALL. SOMETHING REMINDED ME THAT I COULDN'T MARRY WONDER WOMAN--
--BECAUSE I WAS ALREADY COMMITTED TO ANOTHER WOMAN.
"THE ONLY LADY IN MY LIFE-- JUSTICE."
YEAH, RIGHT.
BUT THE STATUE OF JUSTICE IS JUST A SYMBOL! ARE YOU SURE THERE ISN'T ANY OTHER WOMAN IN YOUR LIFE?

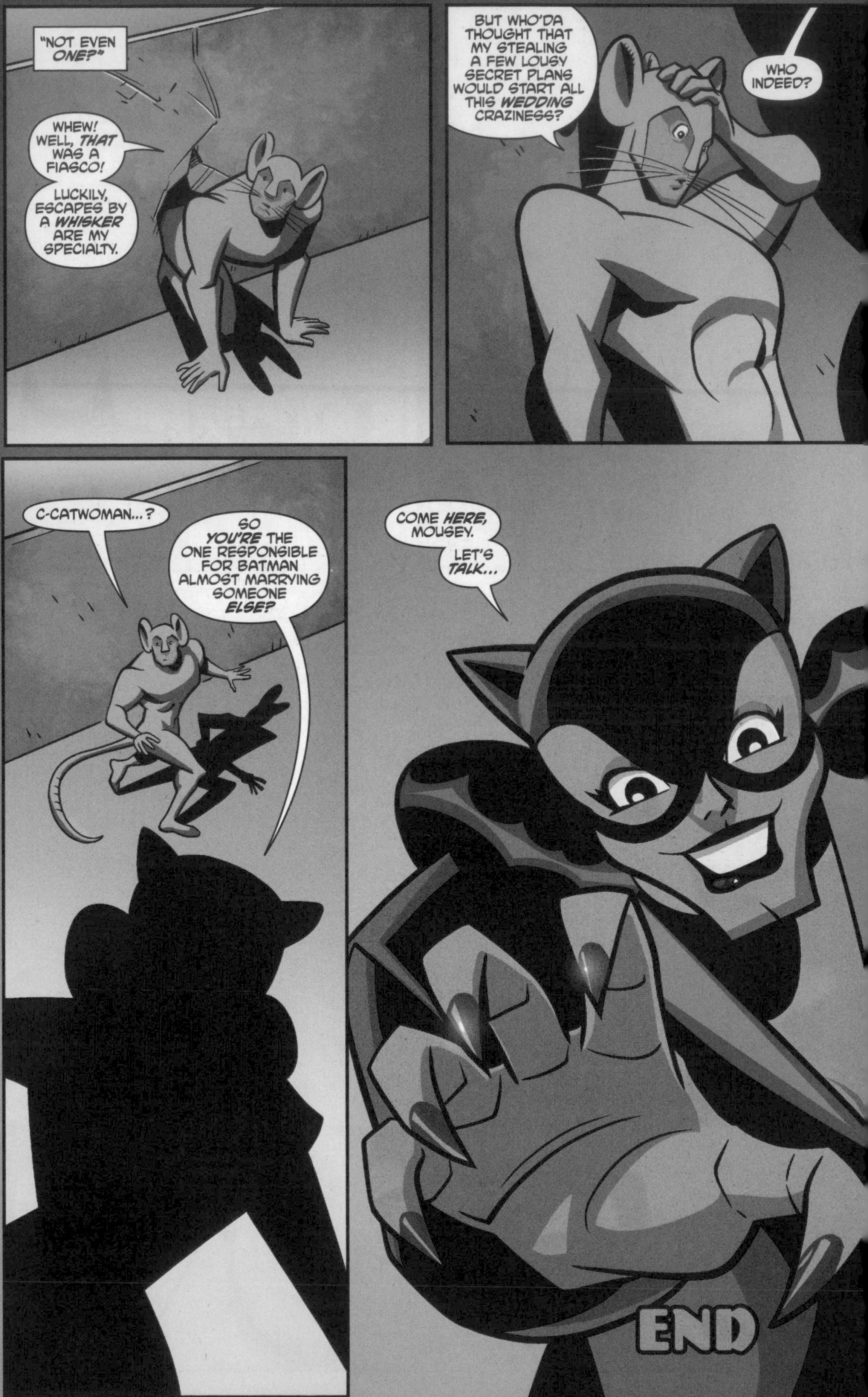
"NOT EVEN ONE?"
WHEW! WELL, THAT WAS A FIASCO!
LUCKILY, ESCAPES BY A WHISKER ARE MY SPECIALTY.
BUT WHO'DA THOUGHT THAT MY STEALING A FEW LOUSY SECRET PLANS WOULD START ALL THIS WEDDING CRAZINESS?
WHO INDEED?
C-CATWOMAN...?
SO YOU'RE THE ONE RESPONSIBLE FOR BATMAN ALMOST MARRYING SOMEONE ELSE?
COME HERE, MOUSEY.
LET'S TALK...
END

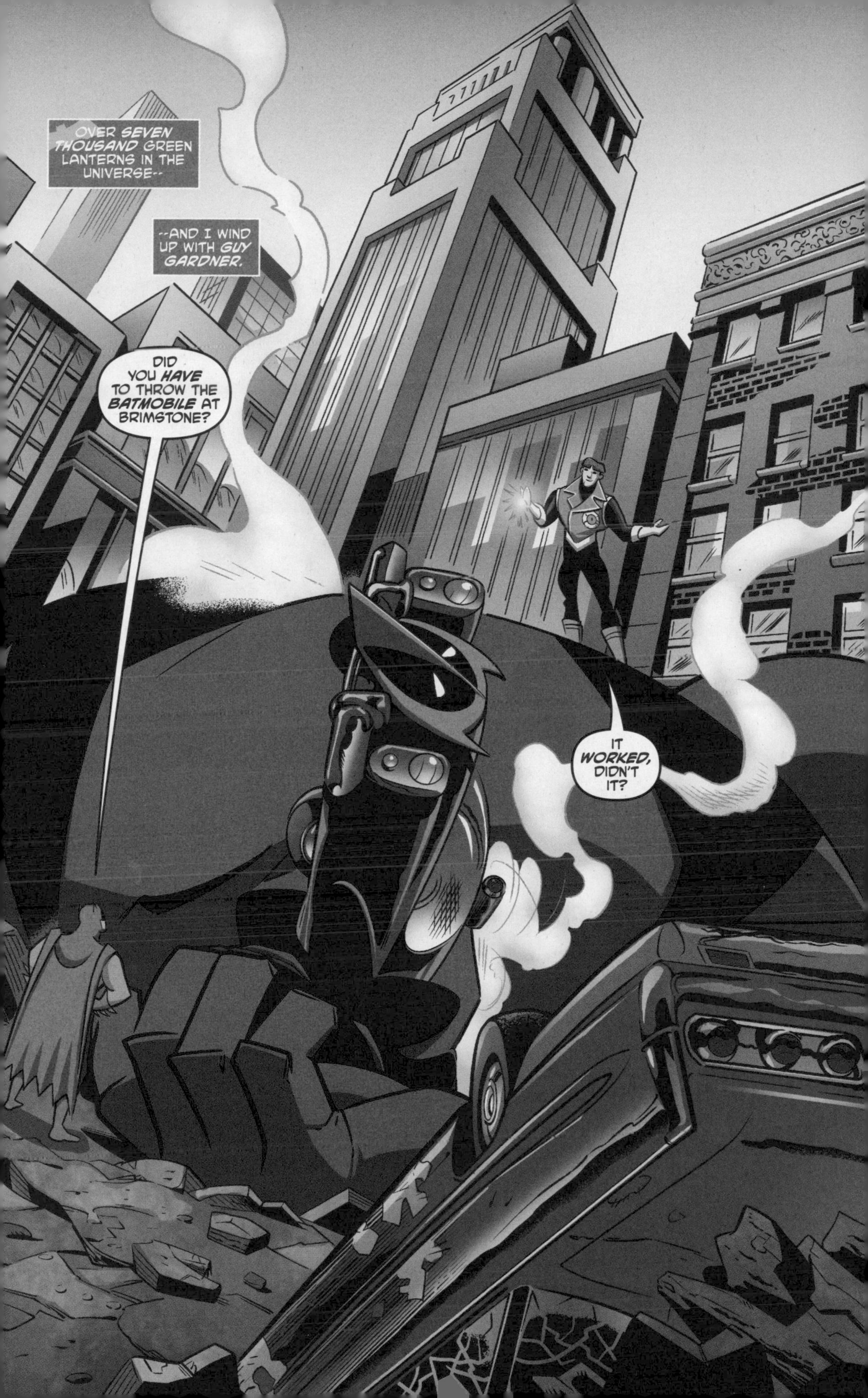
OVER SEVEN THOUSAND GREEN LANTERNS IN THE UNIVERSE--
--AND I WIND UP WITH GUY GARDNER.
DID YOU HAVE TO THROW THE BATMOBILE AT BRIMSTONE?
IT WORKED, DIDN'T IT?

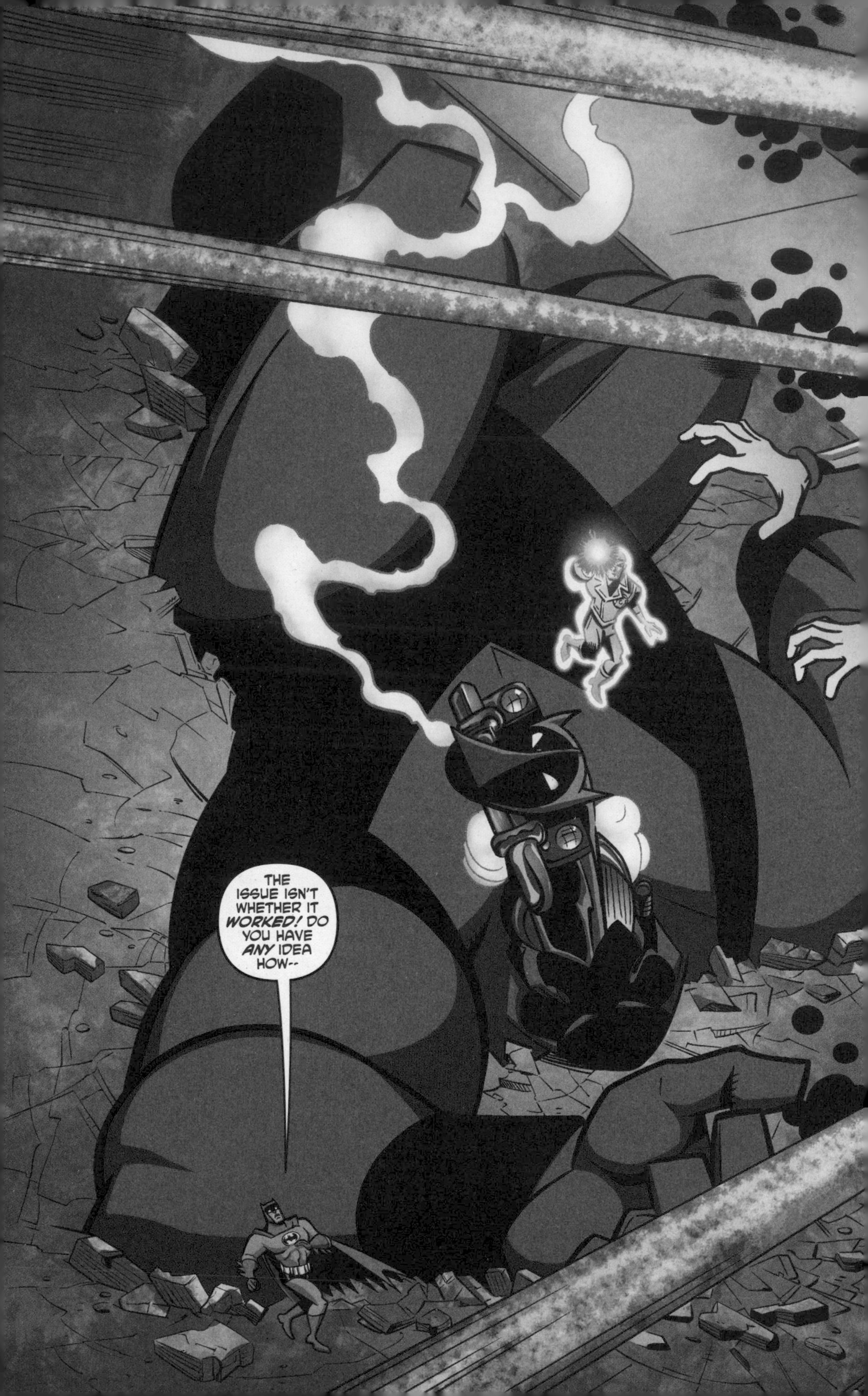
THE ISSUE ISN'T WHETHER IT *WORKED!* DO YOU HAVE *ANY* IDEA HOW--

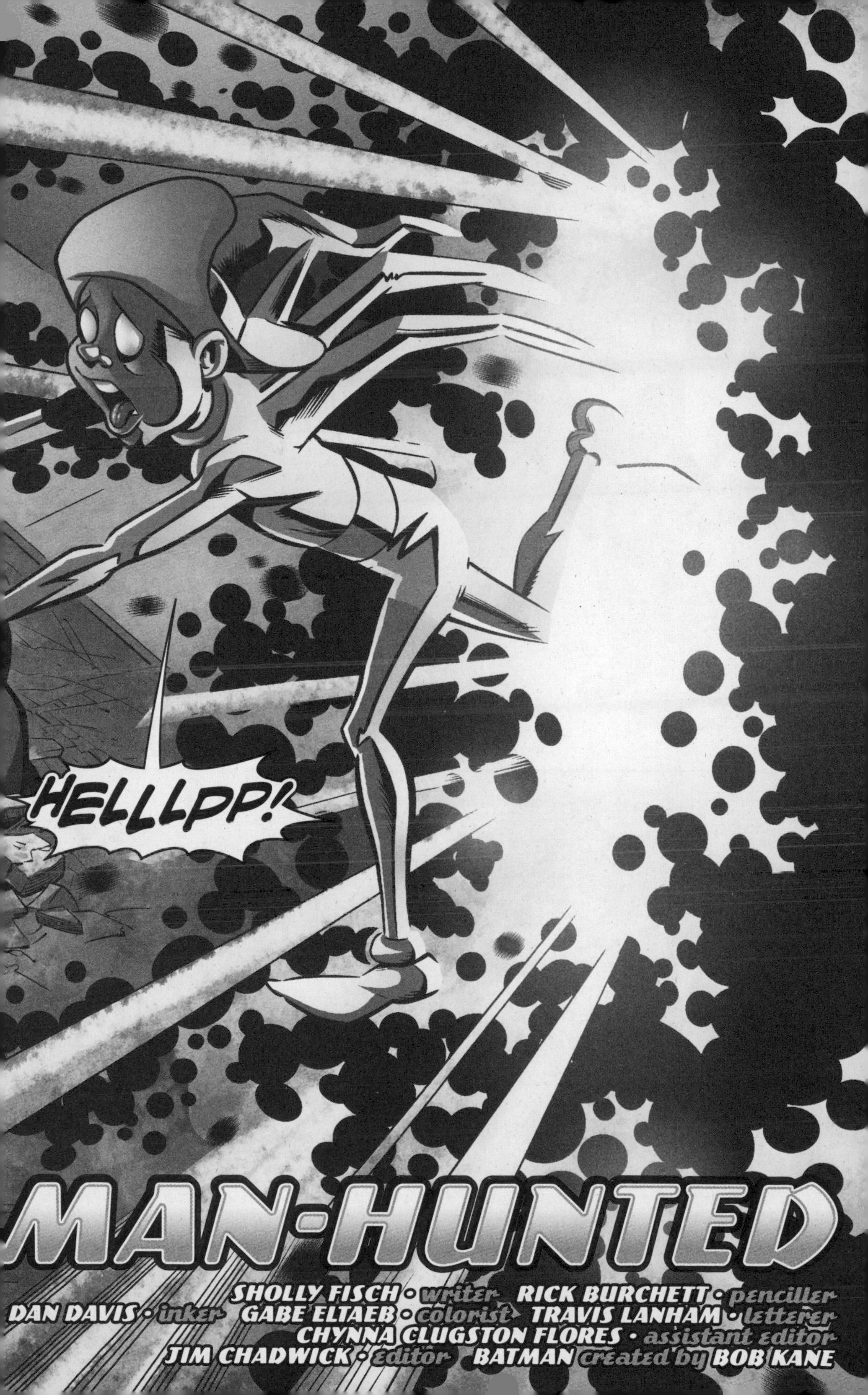
HELLLPP!
MAN-HUNTED
SHOLLY FISCH • writer RICK BURCHETT • penciller
DAN DAVIS • inker GABE ELTAEB • colorist TRAVIS LANHAM • letterer
CHYNNA CLUGSTON FLORES • assistant editor
JIM CHADWICK • editor BATMAN created by BOB KANE

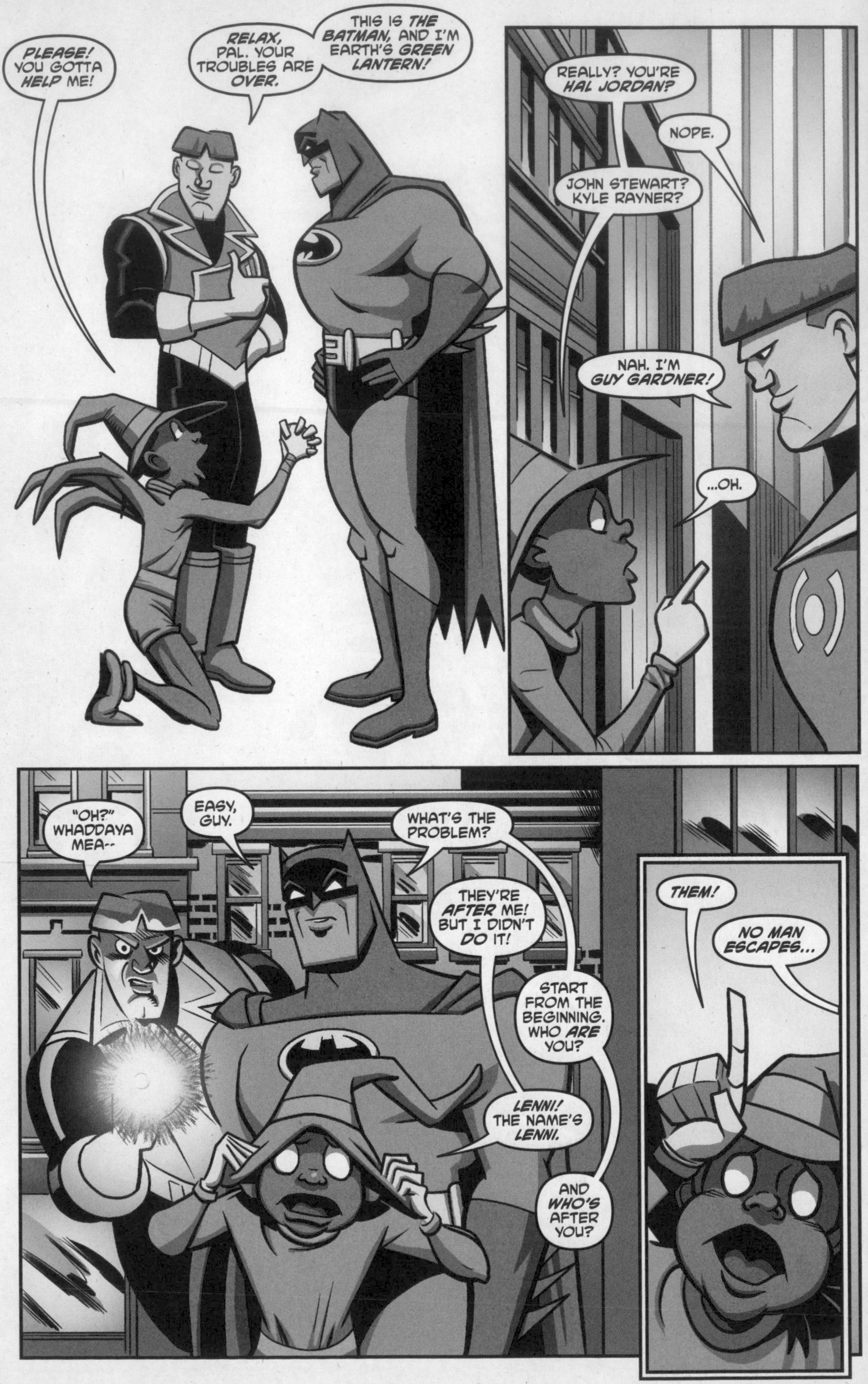
PLEASE! YOU GOTTA HELP ME!
RELAX, PAL. YOUR TROUBLES ARE OVER.
THIS IS THE BATMAN, AND I'M EARTH'S GREEN LANTERN!
REALLY? YOU'RE HAL JORDAN?
NOPE.
JOHN STEWART? KYLE RAYNER?
NAH. I'M GUY GARDNER!
...OH.
"OH?" WHADDAYA MEA--
EASY, GUY.
WHAT'S THE PROBLEM?
THEY'RE AFTER ME! BUT I DIDN'T DO IT!
START FROM THE BEGINNING. WHO ARE YOU?
LENNI! THE NAME'S LENNI.
AND WHO'S AFTER YOU?
THEM!
NO MAN ESCAPES...

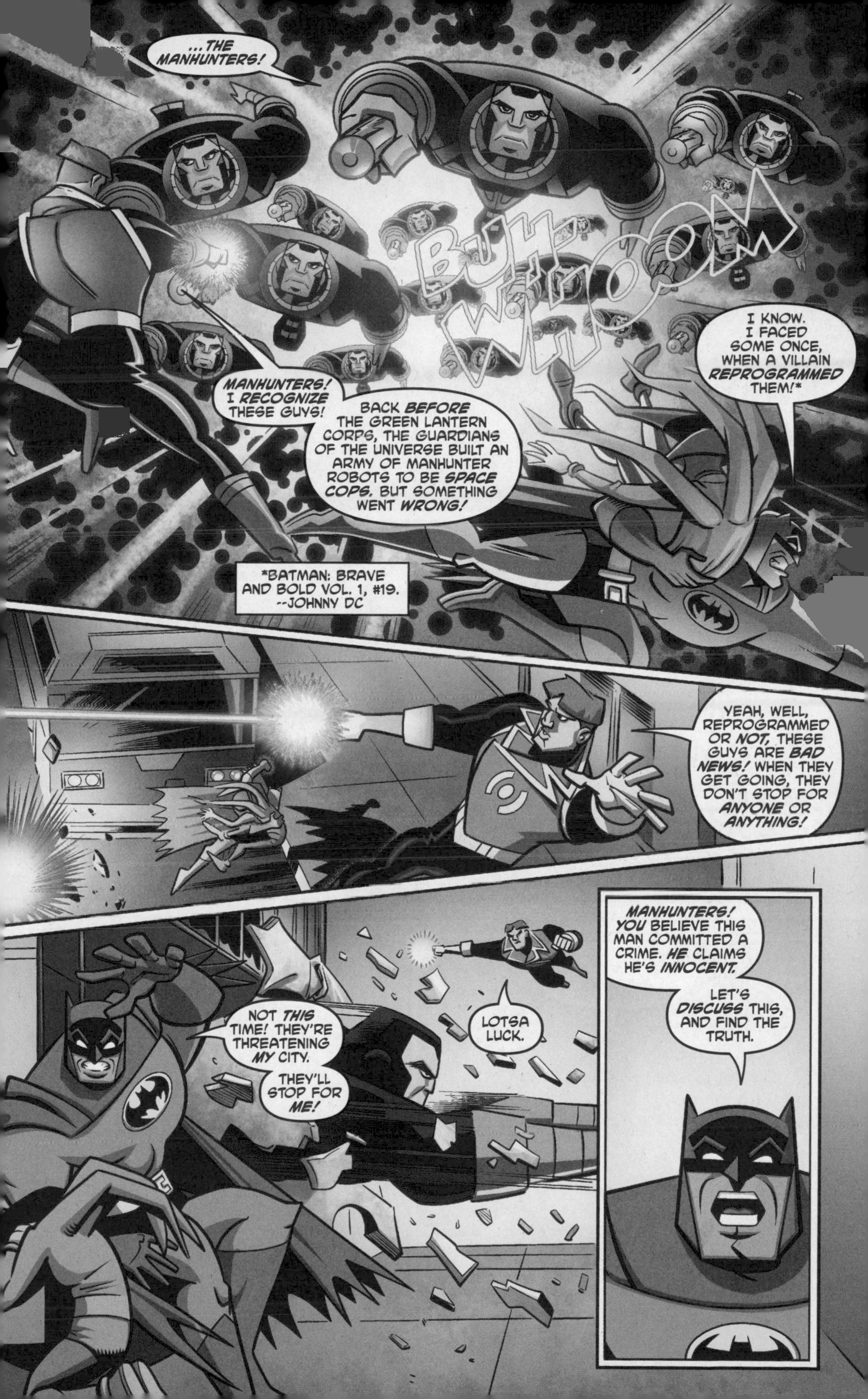
...THE MANHUNTERS!
BUH-WHOOM
MANHUNTERS! I RECOGNIZE THESE GUYS!
BACK BEFORE THE GREEN LANTERN CORPS, THE GUARDIANS OF THE UNIVERSE BUILT AN ARMY OF MANHUNTER ROBOTS TO BE SPACE COPS. BUT SOMETHING WENT WRONG!
I KNOW. I FACED SOME ONCE, WHEN A VILLAIN REPROGRAMMED THEM!*
*BATMAN: BRAVE AND BOLD VOL. 1, #19. --JOHNNY DC
YEAH, WELL, REPROGRAMMED OR NOT, THESE GUYS ARE BAD NEWS! WHEN THEY GET GOING, THEY DON'T STOP FOR ANYONE OR ANYTHING!
NOT THIS TIME! THEY'RE THREATENING MY CITY.
THEY'LL STOP FOR ME!
LOTSA LUCK.
MANHUNTERS! YOU BELIEVE THIS MAN COMMITTED A CRIME. HE CLAIMS HE'S INNOCENT.
LET'S DISCUSS THIS, AND FIND THE TRUTH.

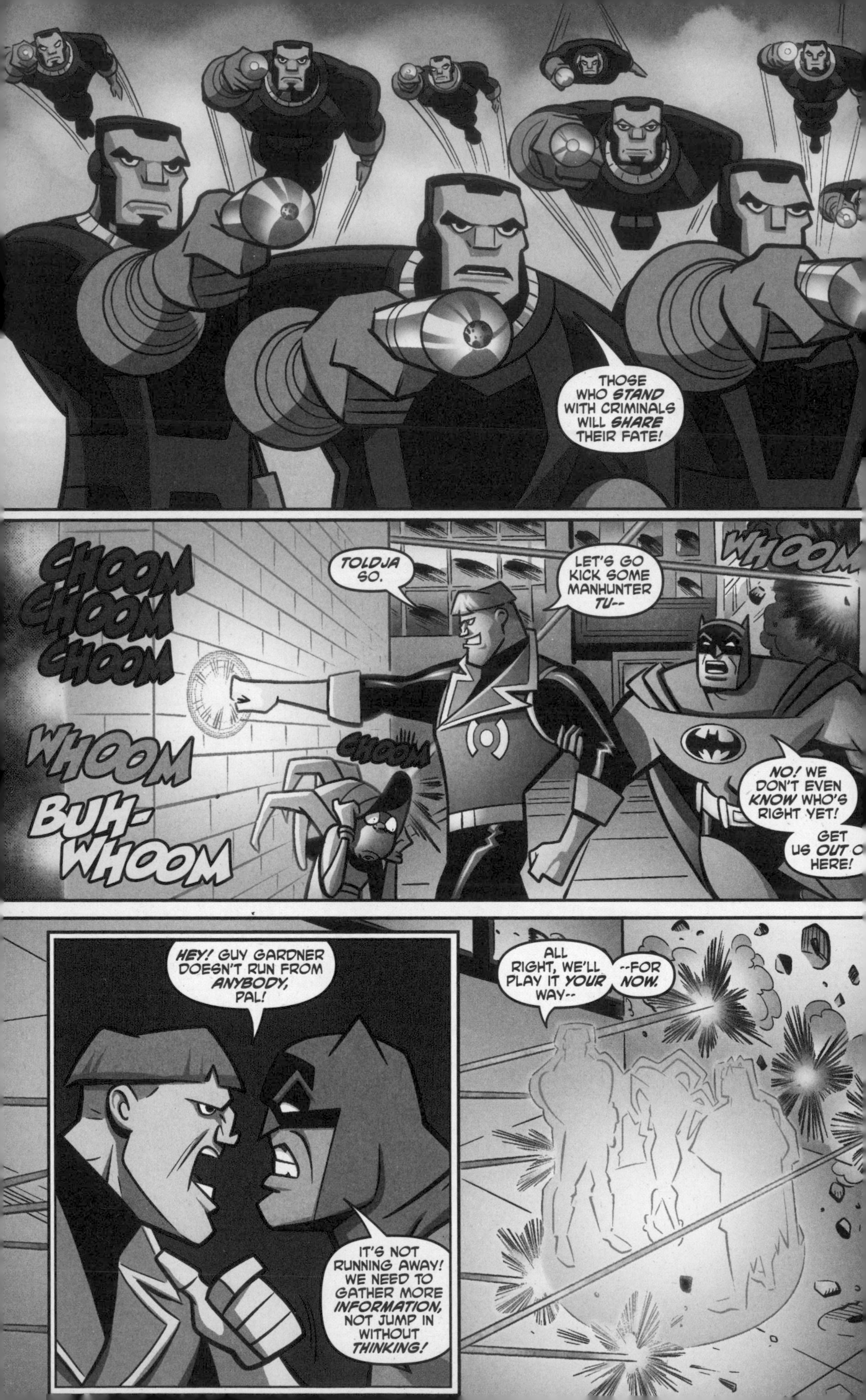
THOSE WHO STAND WITH CRIMINALS WILL SHARE THEIR FATE!
CHOOM CHOOM CHOOM
WHOOM
BUH-WHOOM
TOLDJA SO.
LET'S GO KICK SOME MANHUNTER TU--
WHOOM
CHOOM
NO! WE DON'T EVEN KNOW WHO'S RIGHT YET!
GET US OUT O HERE!
HEY! GUY GARDNER DOESN'T RUN FROM ANYBODY, PAL!
IT'S NOT RUNNING AWAY! WE NEED TO GATHER MORE INFORMATION, NOT JUMP IN WITHOUT THINKING!
ALL RIGHT, WE'LL PLAY IT YOUR WAY--
--FOR NOW.

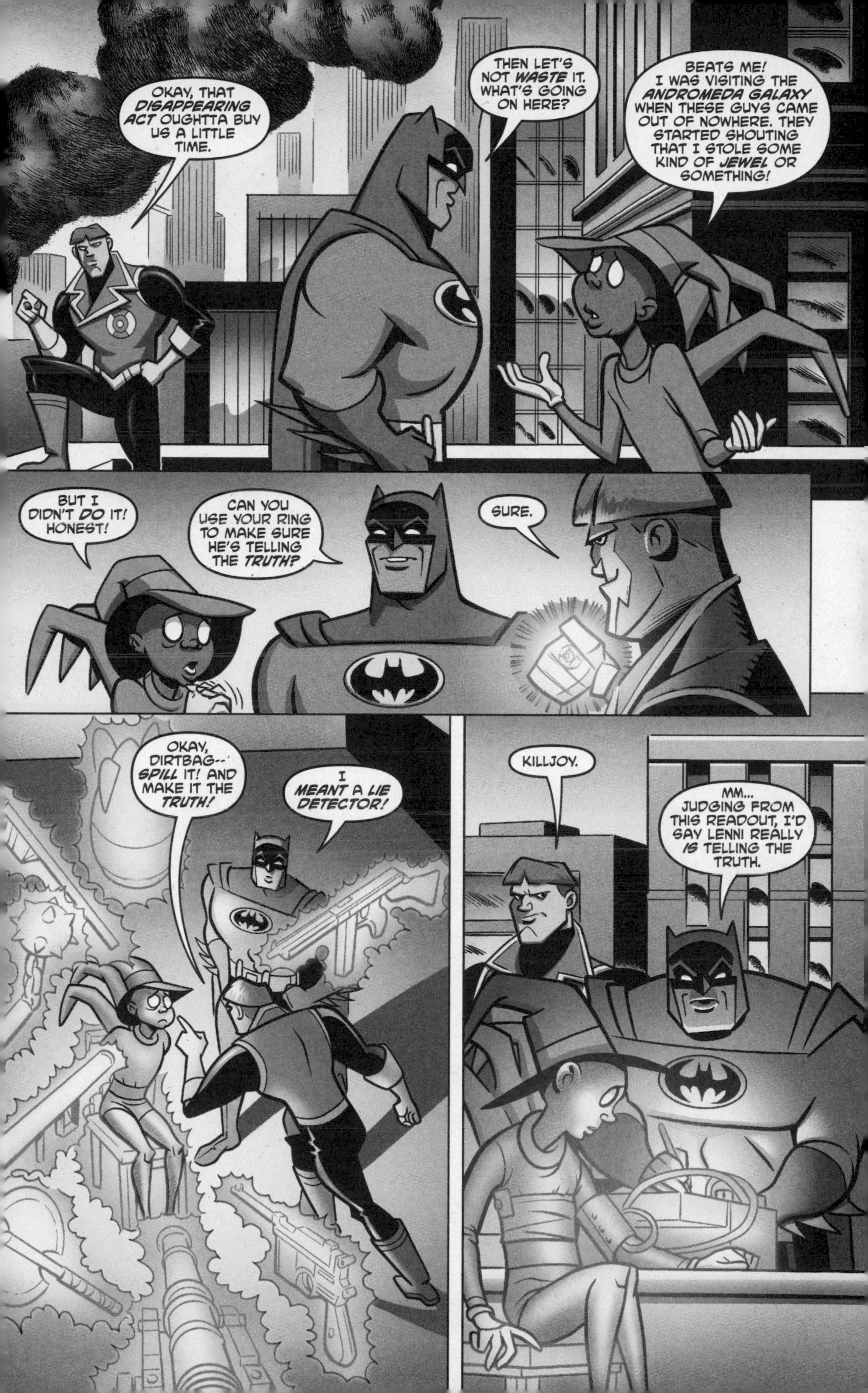
OKAY, THAT DISAPPEARING ACT OUGHTTA BUY US A LITTLE TIME.
THEN LET'S NOT WASTE IT. WHAT'S GOING ON HERE?
BEATS ME! I WAS VISITING THE ANDROMEDA GALAXY WHEN THESE GUYS CAME OUT OF NOWHERE. THEY STARTED SHOUTING THAT I STOLE SOME KIND OF JEWEL OR SOMETHING!
BUT I DIDN'T DO IT! HONEST!
CAN YOU USE YOUR RING TO MAKE SURE HE'S TELLING THE TRUTH?
SURE.
OKAY, DIRTBAG-- SPILL IT! AND MAKE IT THE TRUTH!
I MEANT A LIE DETECTOR!
KILLJOY.
MM... JUDGING FROM THIS READOUT, I'D SAY LENNI REALLY IS TELLING THE TRUTH.

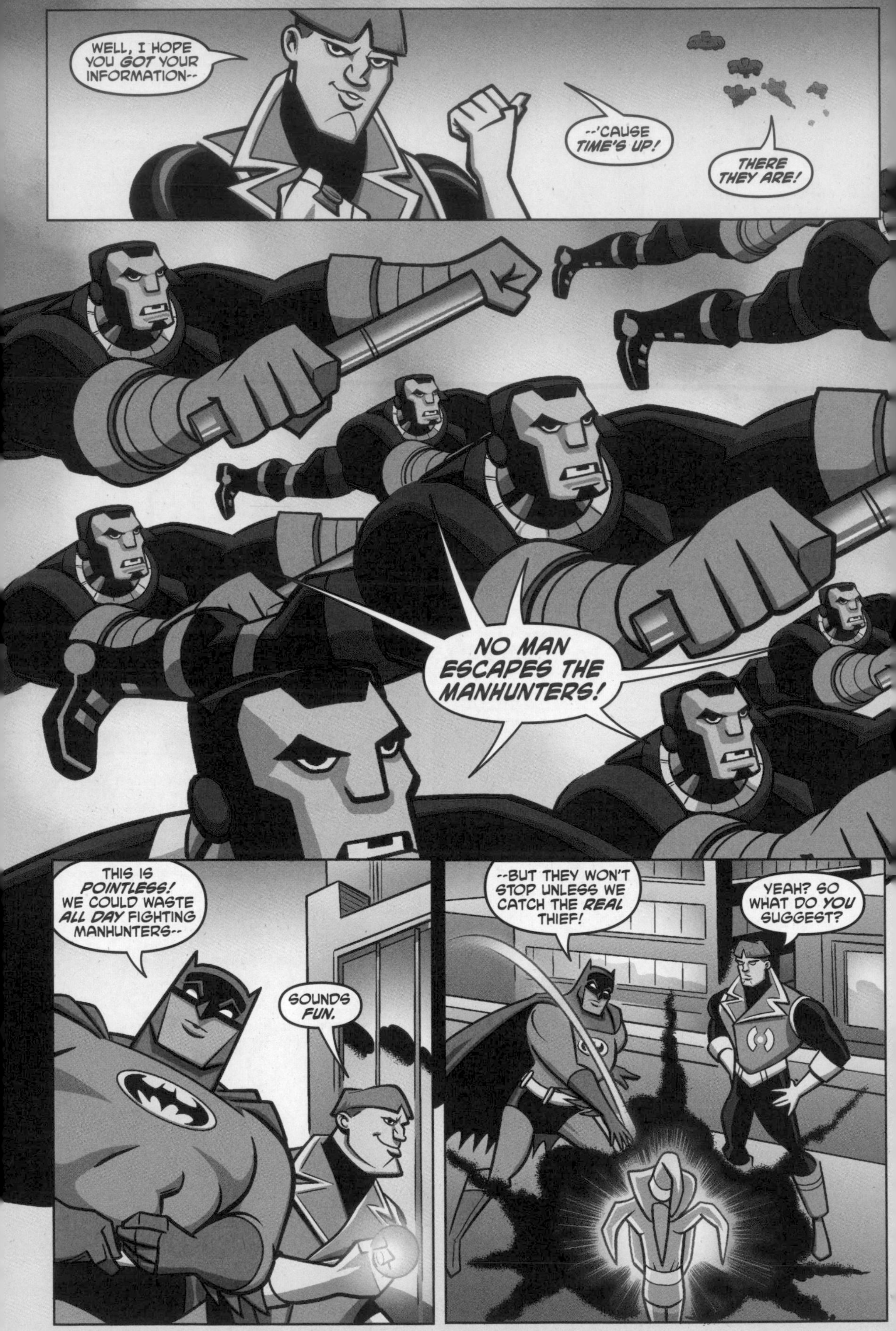
WELL, I HOPE YOU GOT YOUR INFORMATION--
--'CAUSE TIME'S UP!
THERE THEY ARE!
NO MAN ESCAPES THE MANHUNTERS!
THIS IS POINTLESS! WE COULD WASTE ALL DAY FIGHTING MANHUNTERS--
SOUNDS FUN.
--BUT THEY WON'T STOP UNLESS WE CATCH THE REAL THIEF!
YEAH? SO WHAT DO YOU SUGGEST?

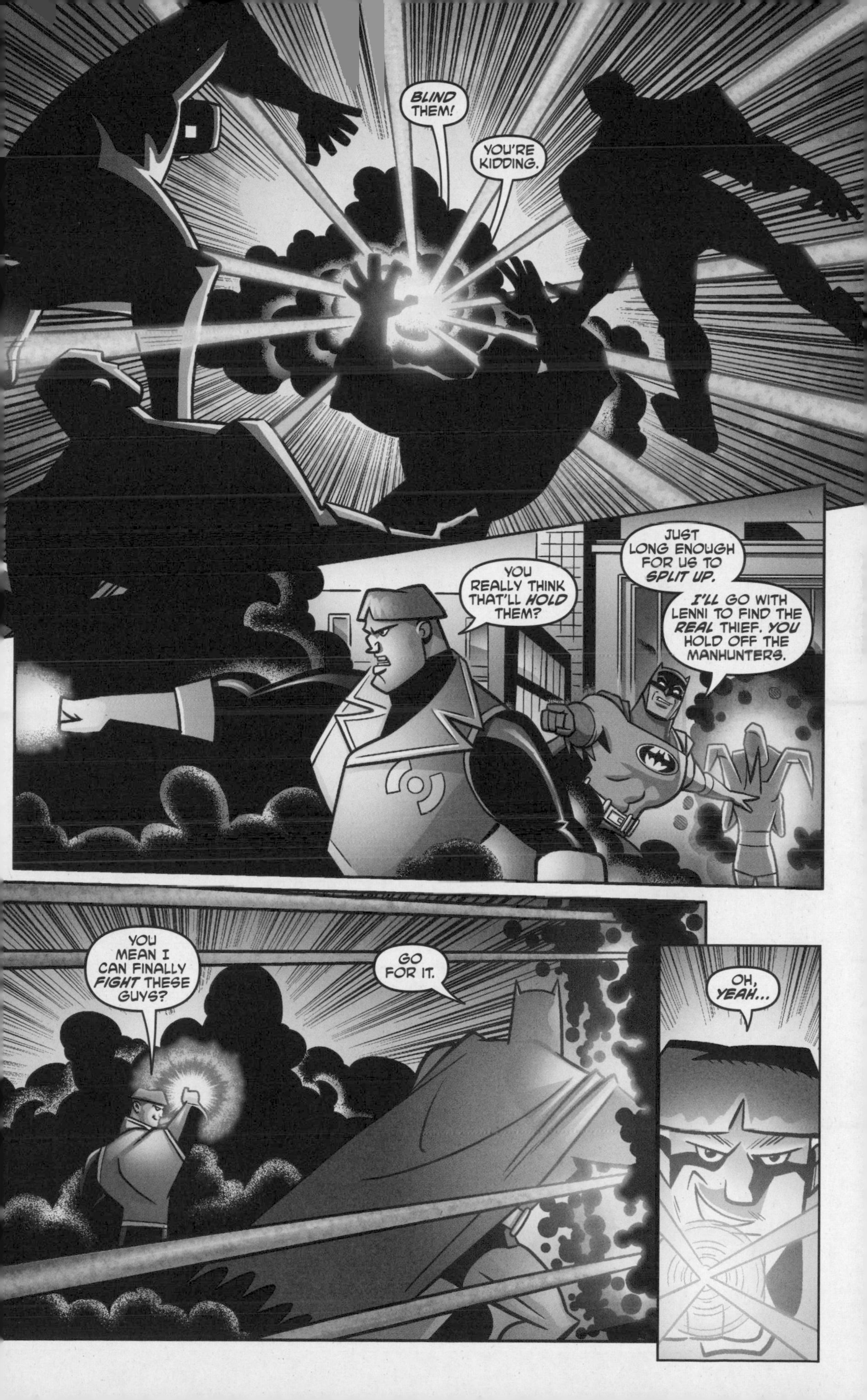
BLIND THEM!
YOU'RE KIDDING.
YOU REALLY THINK THAT'LL HOLD THEM?
JUST LONG ENOUGH FOR US TO SPLIT UP.
I'LL GO WITH LENNI TO FIND THE REAL THIEF. YOU HOLD OFF THE MANHUNTERS.
YOU MEAN I CAN FINALLY FIGHT THESE GUYS?
GO FOR IT.
OH, YEAH...

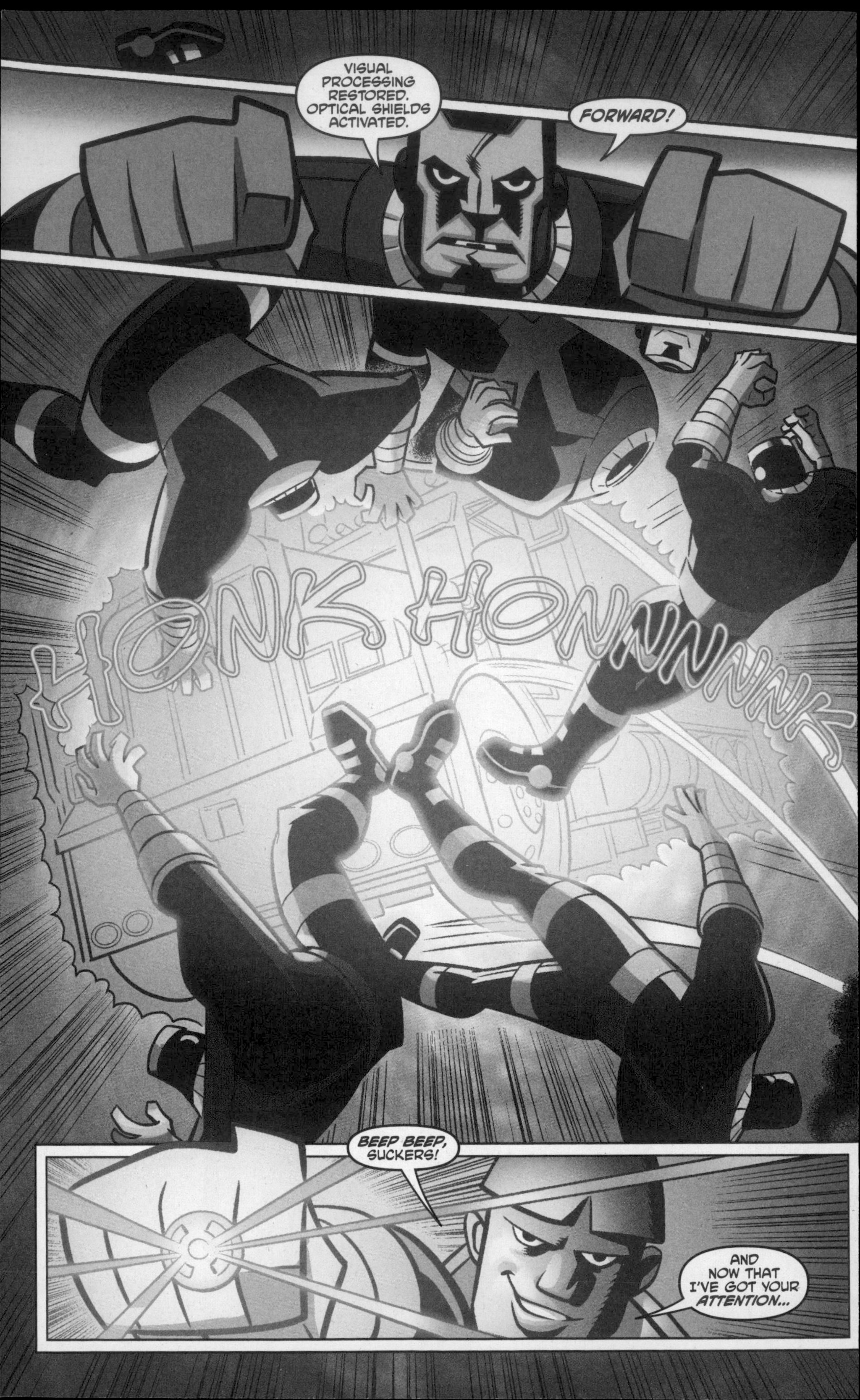
VISUAL PROCESSING RESTORED. OPTICAL SHIELDS ACTIVATED.
FORWARD!
HONK HONNNNNNK
BEEP BEEP, SUCKERS!
AND NOW THAT I'VE GOT YOUR ATTENTION...

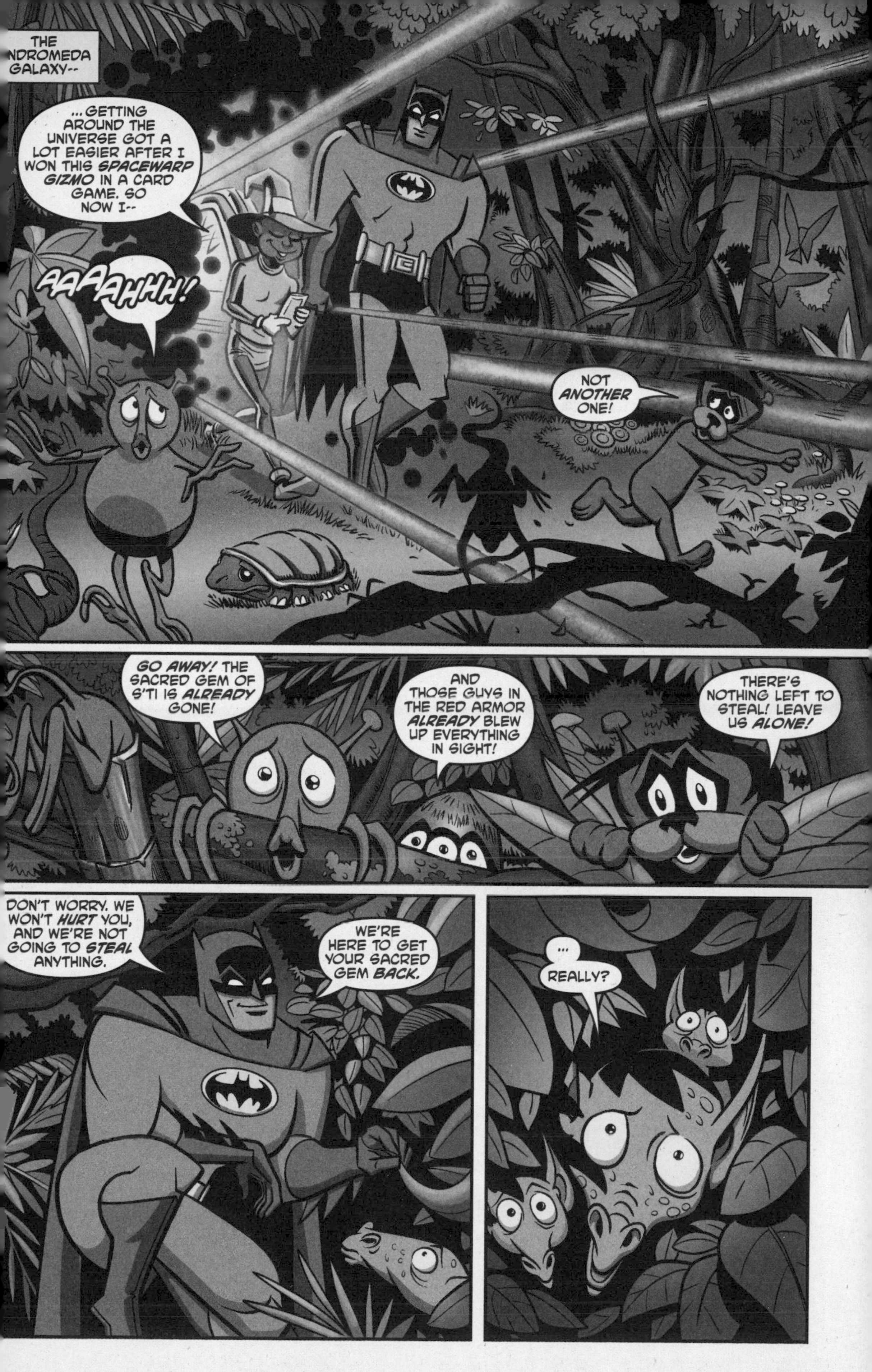
THE
NDROMEDA
GALAXY--
...GETTING AROUND THE UNIVERSE GOT A LOT EASIER AFTER I WON THIS SPACEWARP GIZMO IN A CARD GAME. SO NOW I--
AAAAHHH!
NOT ANOTHER ONE!
GO AWAY! THE SACRED GEM OF S'TI IS ALREADY GONE!
AND THOSE GUYS IN THE RED ARMOR ALREADY BLEW UP EVERYTHING IN SIGHT!
THERE'S NOTHING LEFT TO STEAL! LEAVE US ALONE!
DON'T WORRY. WE WON'T HURT YOU, AND WE'RE NOT GOING TO STEAL ANYTHING.
WE'RE HERE TO GET YOUR SACRED GEM BACK.
...
REALLY?

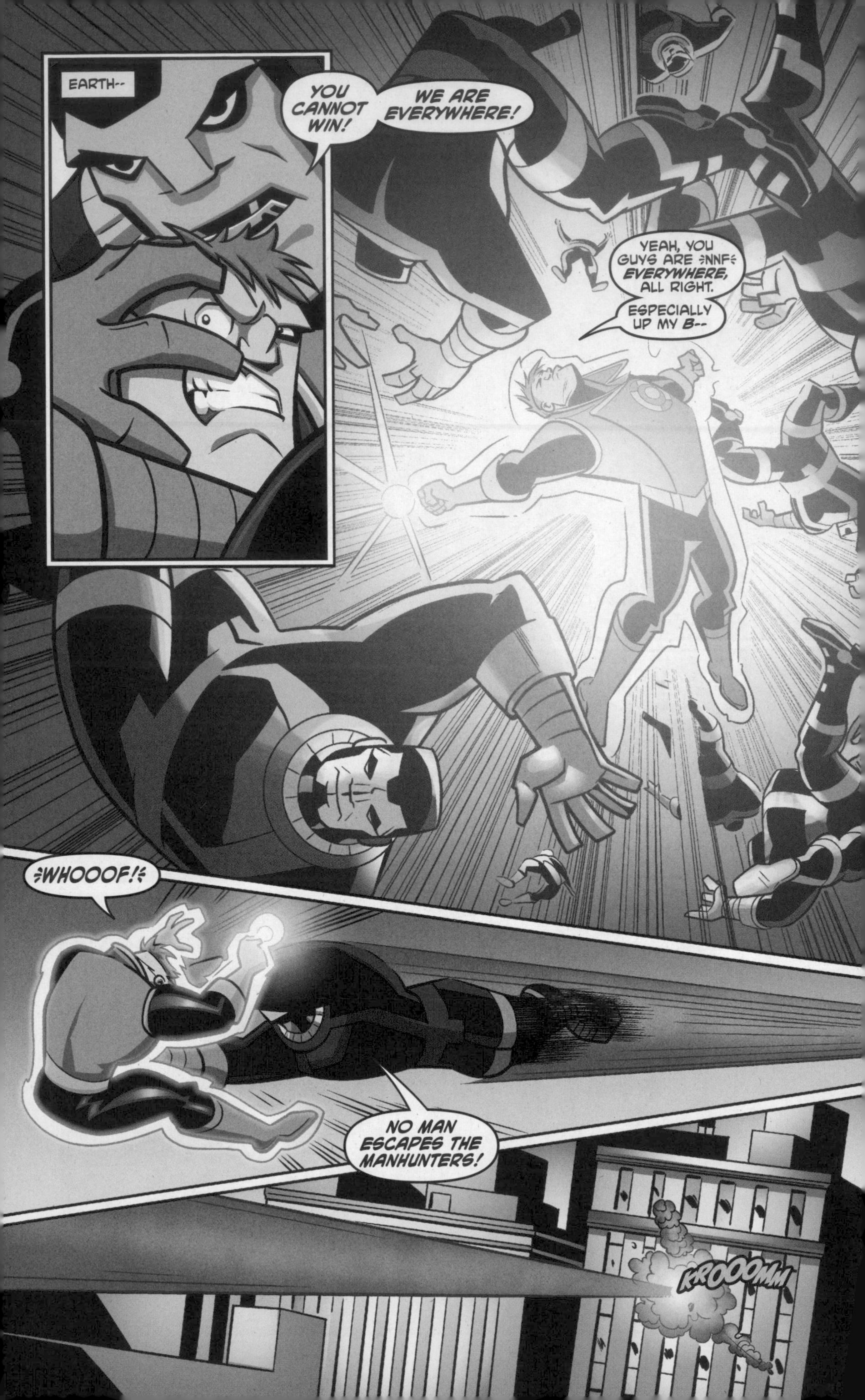
EARTH--
YOU CANNOT WIN!
WE ARE EVERYWHERE!
YEAH, YOU GUYS ARE =NNF= EVERYWHERE, ALL RIGHT.
ESPECIALLY UP MY B--
=WHOOOF!=
NO MAN ESCAPES THE MANHUNTERS!
KROOOMM

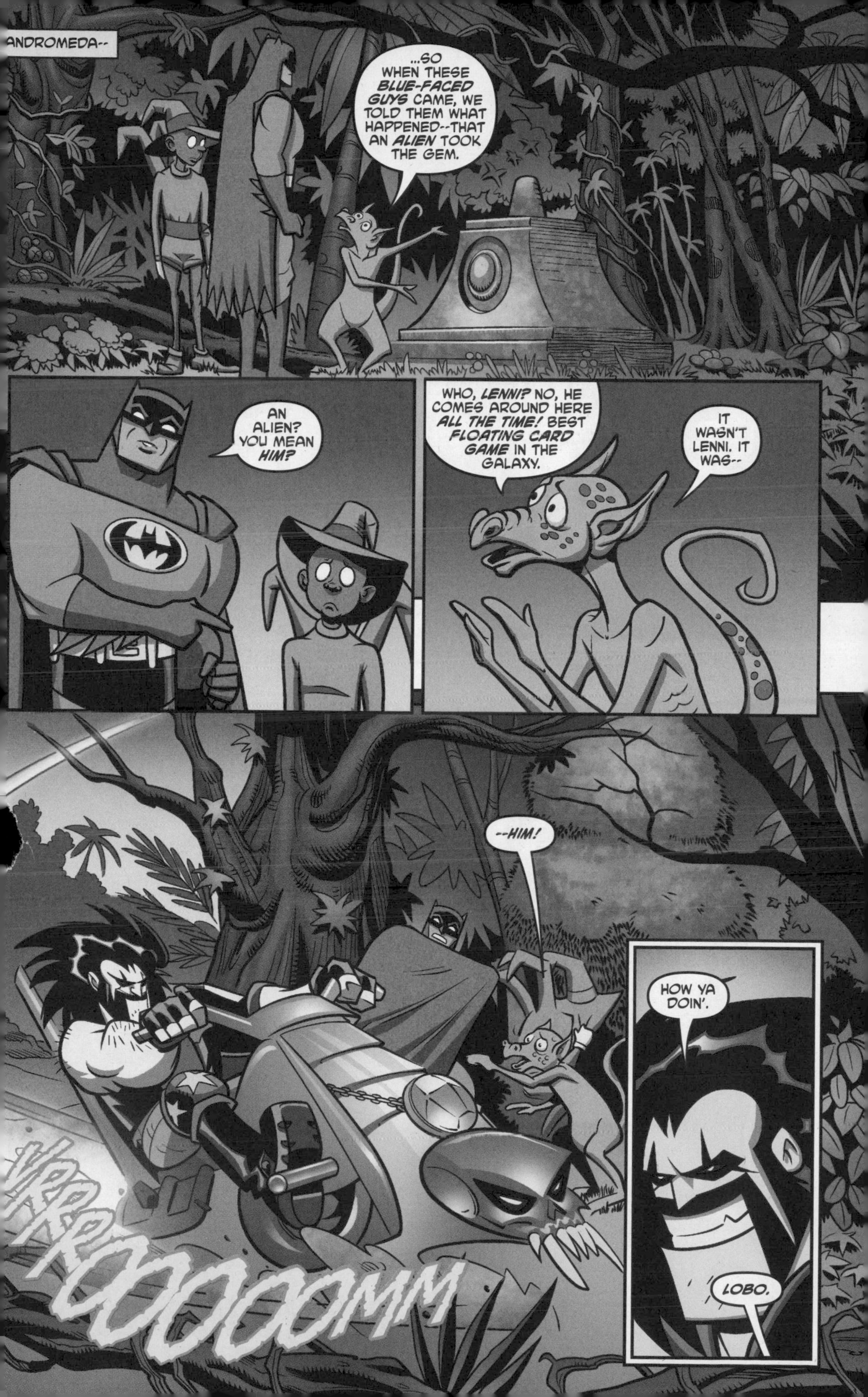
ANDROMEDA--
...SO WHEN THESE BLUE-FACED GUYS CAME, WE TOLD THEM WHAT HAPPENED--THAT AN ALIEN TOOK THE GEM.
AN ALIEN? YOU MEAN HIM?
WHO, LENNI? NO, HE COMES AROUND HERE ALL THE TIME! BEST FLOATING CARD GAME IN THE GALAXY.
IT WASN'T LENNI. IT WAS--
--HIM!
VRRROOOOOMM
HOW YA DOIN'.
LOBO.

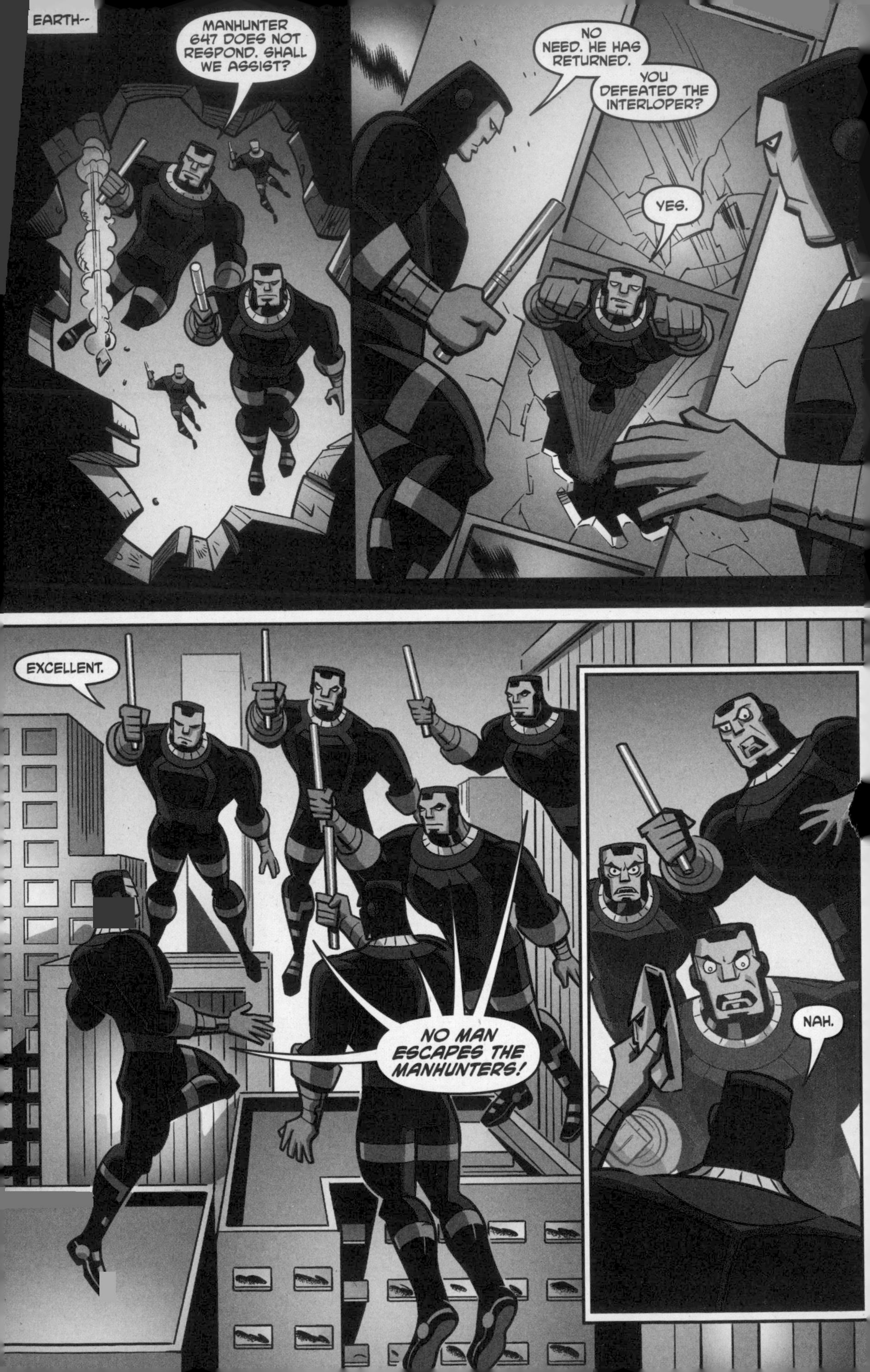
EARTH--
MANHUNTER 647 DOES NOT RESPOND. SHALL WE ASSIST?
NO NEED. HE HAS RETURNED.
YOU DEFEATED THE INTERLOPER?
YES.
EXCELLENT.
NO MAN ESCAPES THE MANHUNTERS!
NAH.

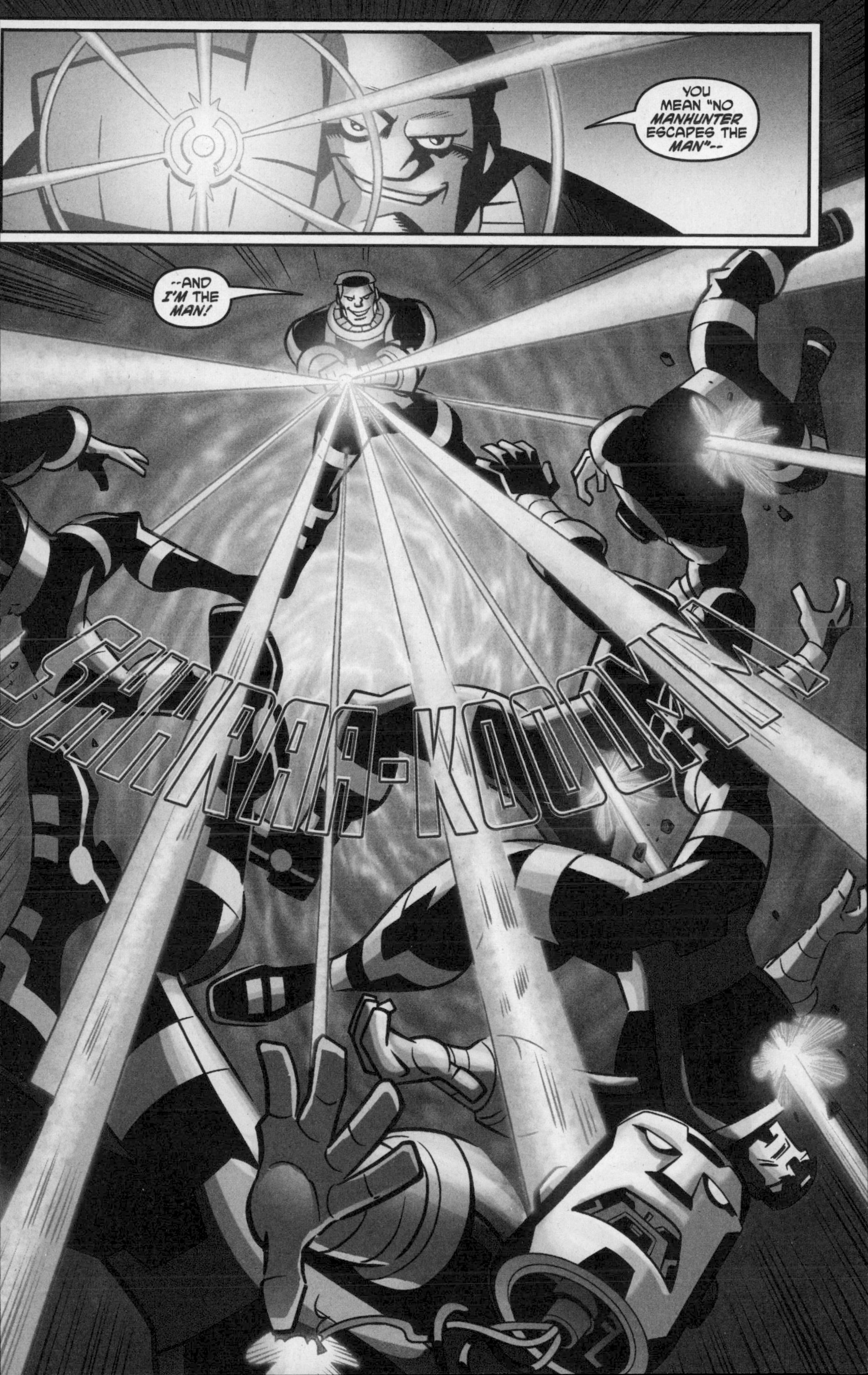
YOU MEAN "NO *MANHUNTER* ESCAPES THE *MAN*"--
--AND *I'M* THE *MAN!*
SHRRA-KOOM!

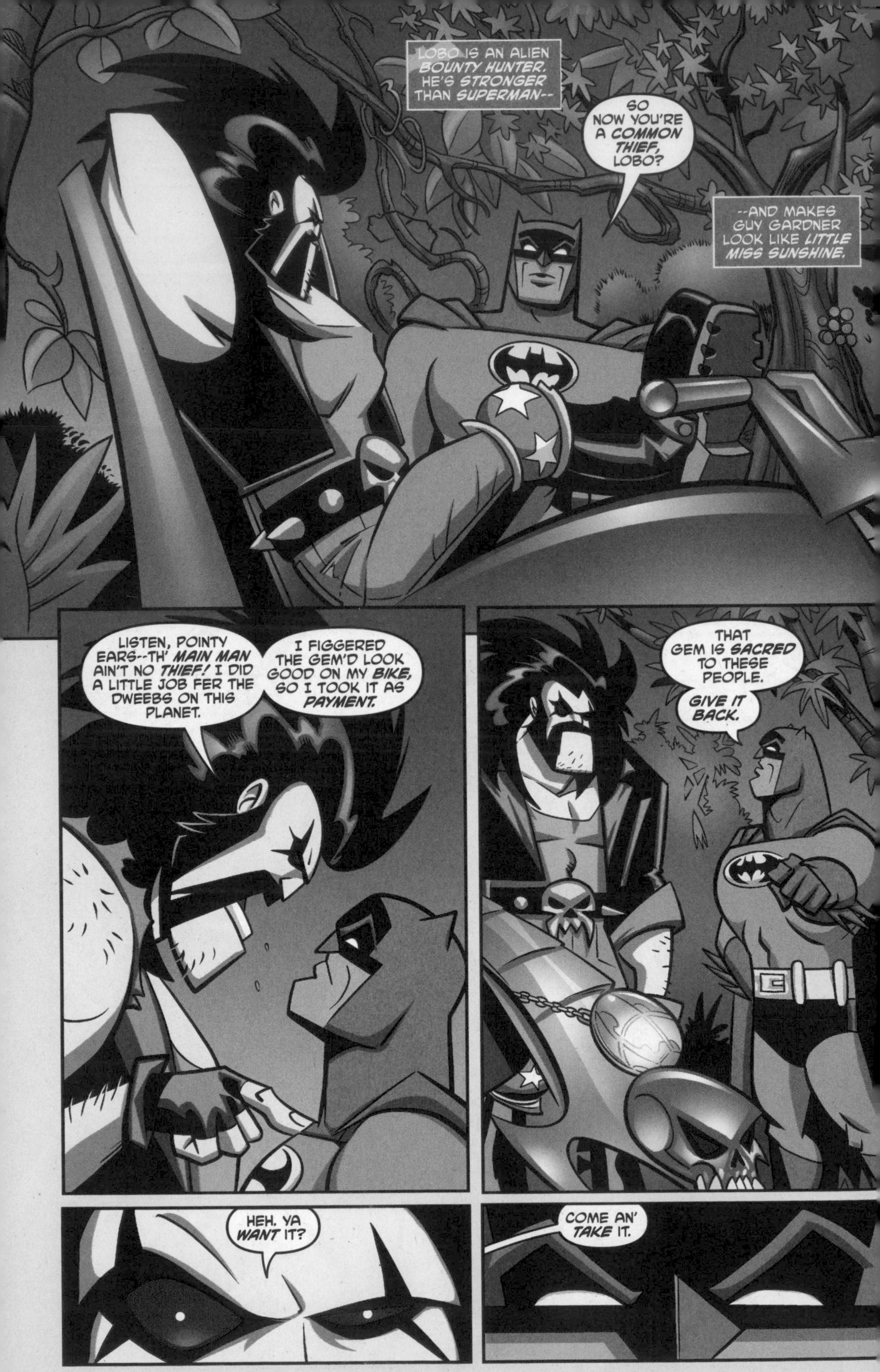
LOBO IS AN ALIEN BOUNTY HUNTER. HE'S STRONGER THAN SUPERMAN--
SO NOW YOU'RE A COMMON THIEF, LOBO?
--AND MAKES GUY GARDNER LOOK LIKE LITTLE MISS SUNSHINE.
LISTEN, POINTY EARS--TH' MAIN MAN AIN'T NO THIEF! I DID A LITTLE JOB FER THE DWEEBS ON THIS PLANET.
I FIGGERED THE GEM'D LOOK GOOD ON MY BIKE, SO I TOOK IT AS PAYMENT.
THAT GEM IS SACRED TO THESE PEOPLE.
GIVE IT BACK.
HEH. YA WANT IT?
COME AN' TAKE IT.

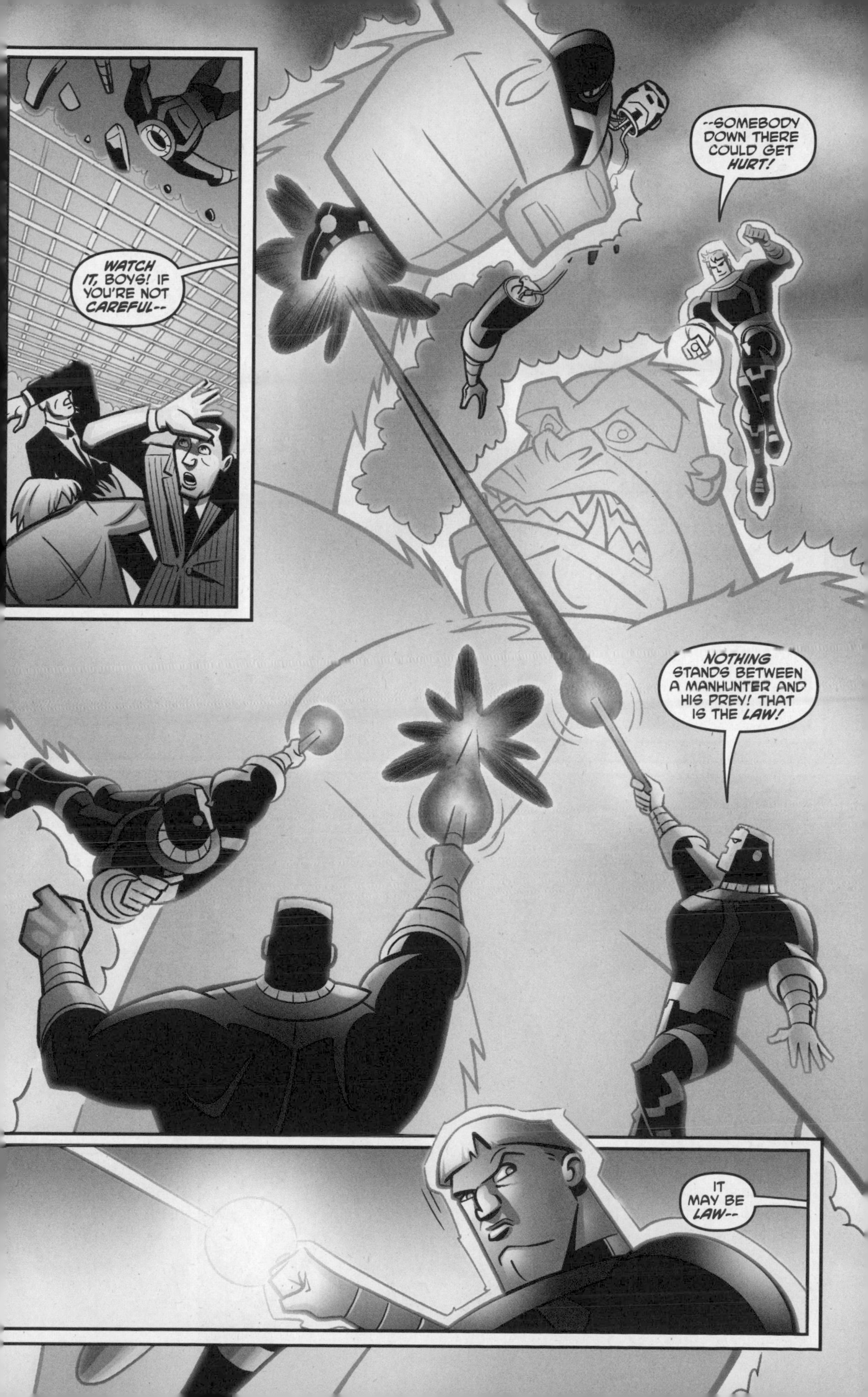
WATCH IT, BOYS! IF YOU'RE NOT CAREFUL--
--SOMEBODY DOWN THERE COULD GET HURT!
NOTHING STANDS BETWEEN A MANHUNTER AND HIS PREY! THAT IS THE LAW!
IT MAY BE LAW--

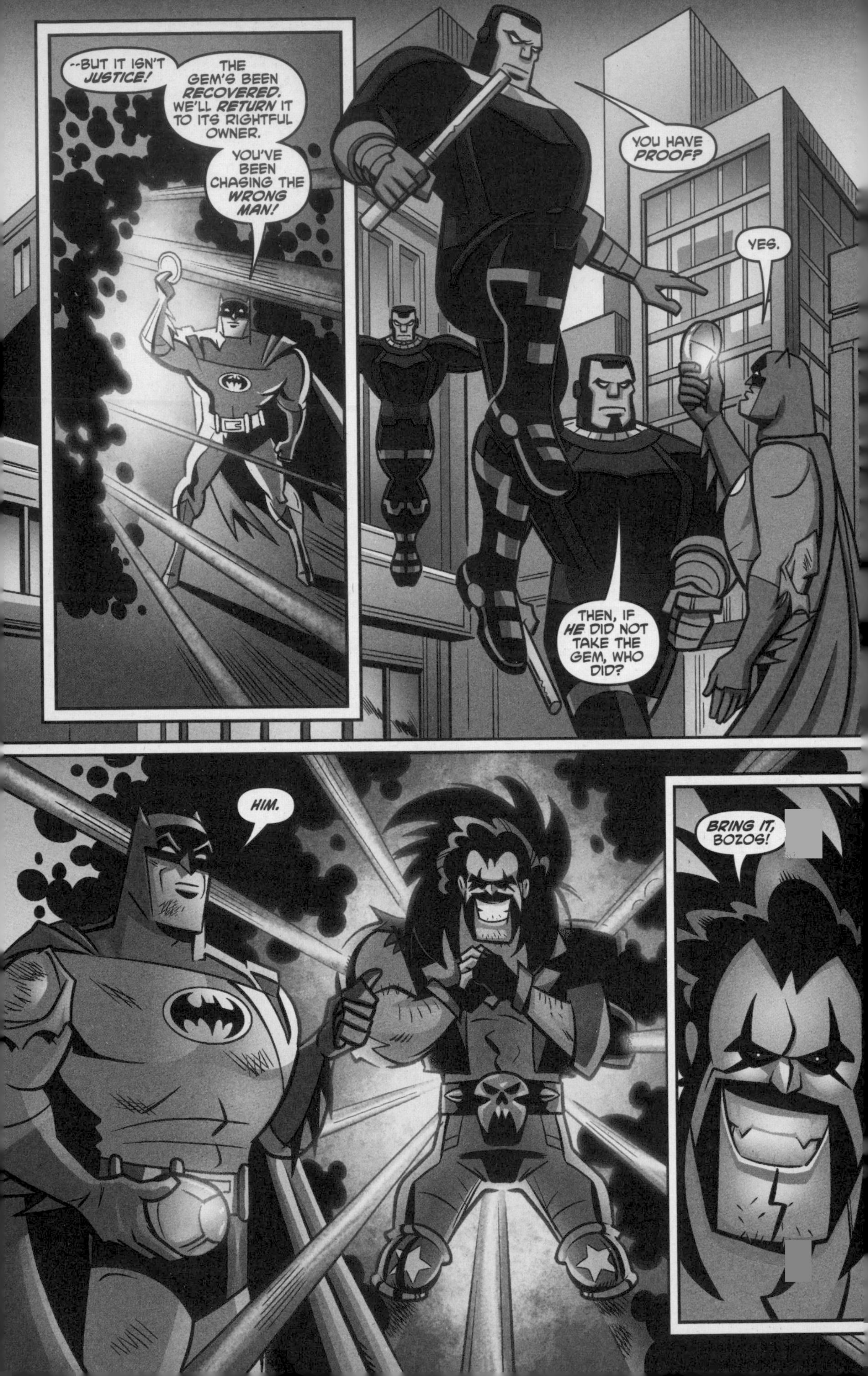
--BUT IT ISN'T JUSTICE!
THE GEM'S BEEN RECOVERED. WE'LL RETURN IT TO ITS RIGHTFUL OWNER.
YOU'VE BEEN CHASING THE WRONG MAN!
YOU HAVE PROOF?
YES.
THEN, IF HE DID NOT TAKE THE GEM, WHO DID?
HIM.
BRING IT, BOZOS!

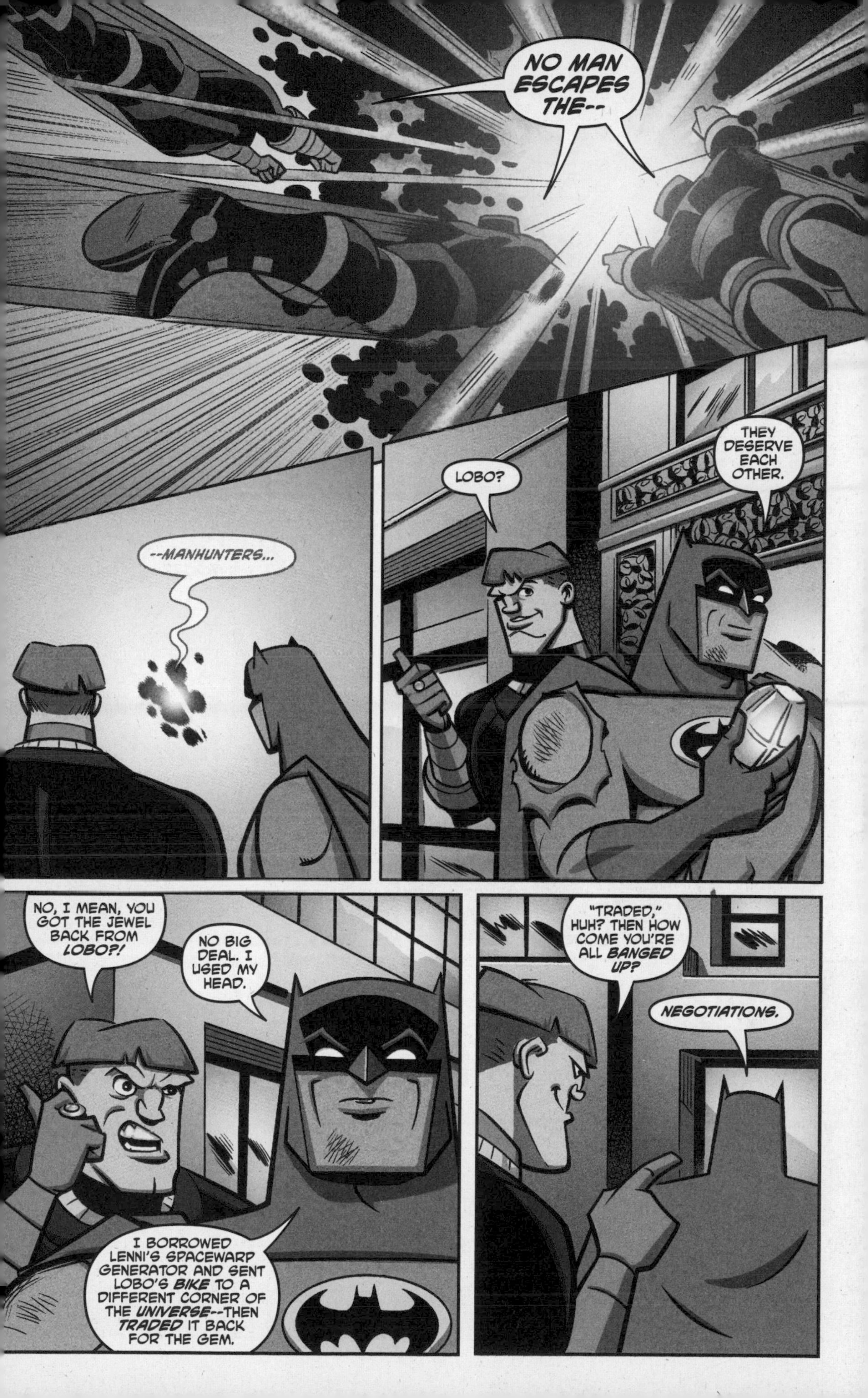
NO MAN ESCAPES THE--
--MANHUNTERS...
LOBO?
THEY DESERVE EACH OTHER.
NO, I MEAN, YOU GOT THE JEWEL BACK FROM *LOBO?!*
NO BIG DEAL. I USED MY HEAD.
I BORROWED LENNI'S SPACEWARP GENERATOR AND SENT LOBO'S *BIKE* TO A DIFFERENT CORNER OF THE *UNIVERSE*--THEN *TRADED* IT BACK FOR THE GEM.
"TRADED," HUH? THEN HOW COME YOU'RE ALL *BANGED UP?*
NEGOTIATIONS.

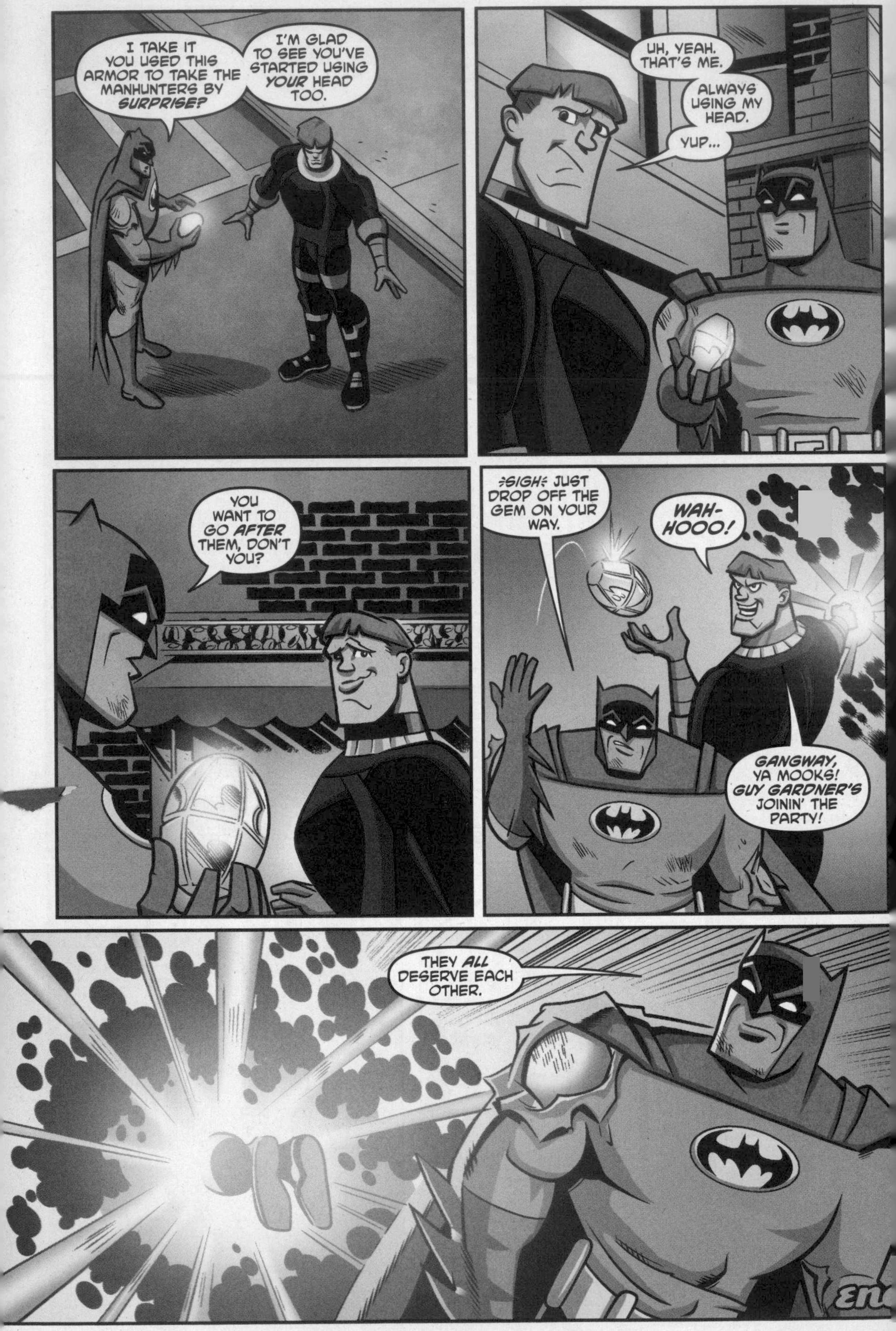
I TAKE IT YOU USED THIS ARMOR TO TAKE THE MANHUNTERS BY SURPRISE?
I'M GLAD TO SEE YOU'VE STARTED USING YOUR HEAD TOO.
UH, YEAH. THAT'S ME.
ALWAYS USING MY HEAD.
YUP...
YOU WANT TO GO AFTER THEM, DON'T YOU?
≠SIGH≠ JUST DROP OFF THE GEM ON YOUR WAY.
WAH-HOOO!
GANGWAY, YA MOOKS! GUY GARDNER'S JOININ' THE PARTY!
THEY ALL DESERVE EACH OTHER.

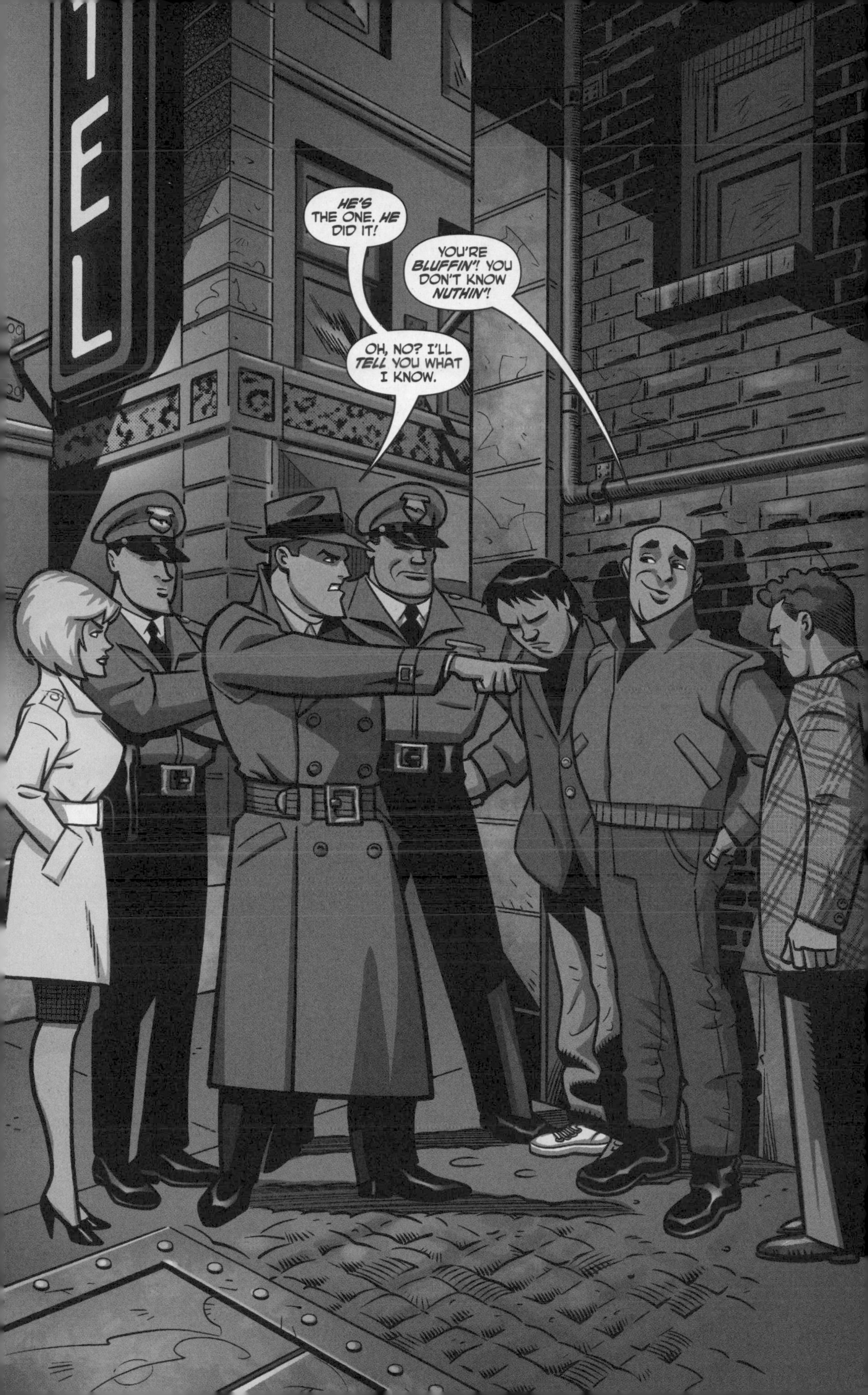
TEL
HE'S THE ONE. HE DID IT!
YOU'RE BLUFFIN'! YOU DON'T KNOW NUTHIN'!
OH, NO? I'LL TELL YOU WHAT I KNOW.

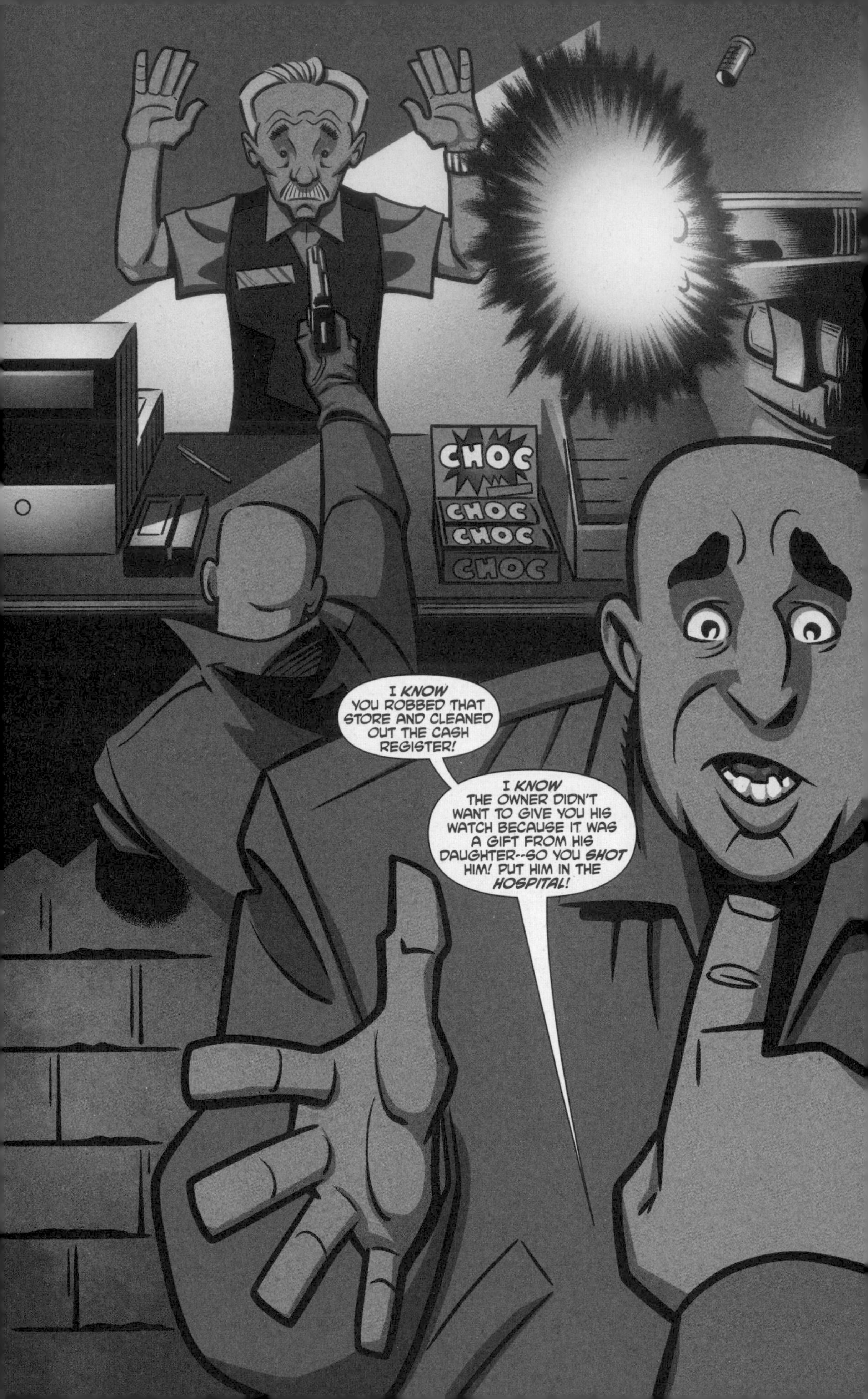
CHOC
CHOC
CHOC
CHOC
I KNOW YOU ROBBED THAT STORE AND CLEANED OUT THE CASH REGISTER!
I KNOW THE OWNER DIDN'T WANT TO GIVE YOU HIS WATCH BECAUSE IT WAS A GIFT FROM HIS DAUGHTER--SO YOU SHOT HIM! PUT HIM IN THE HOSPITAL!

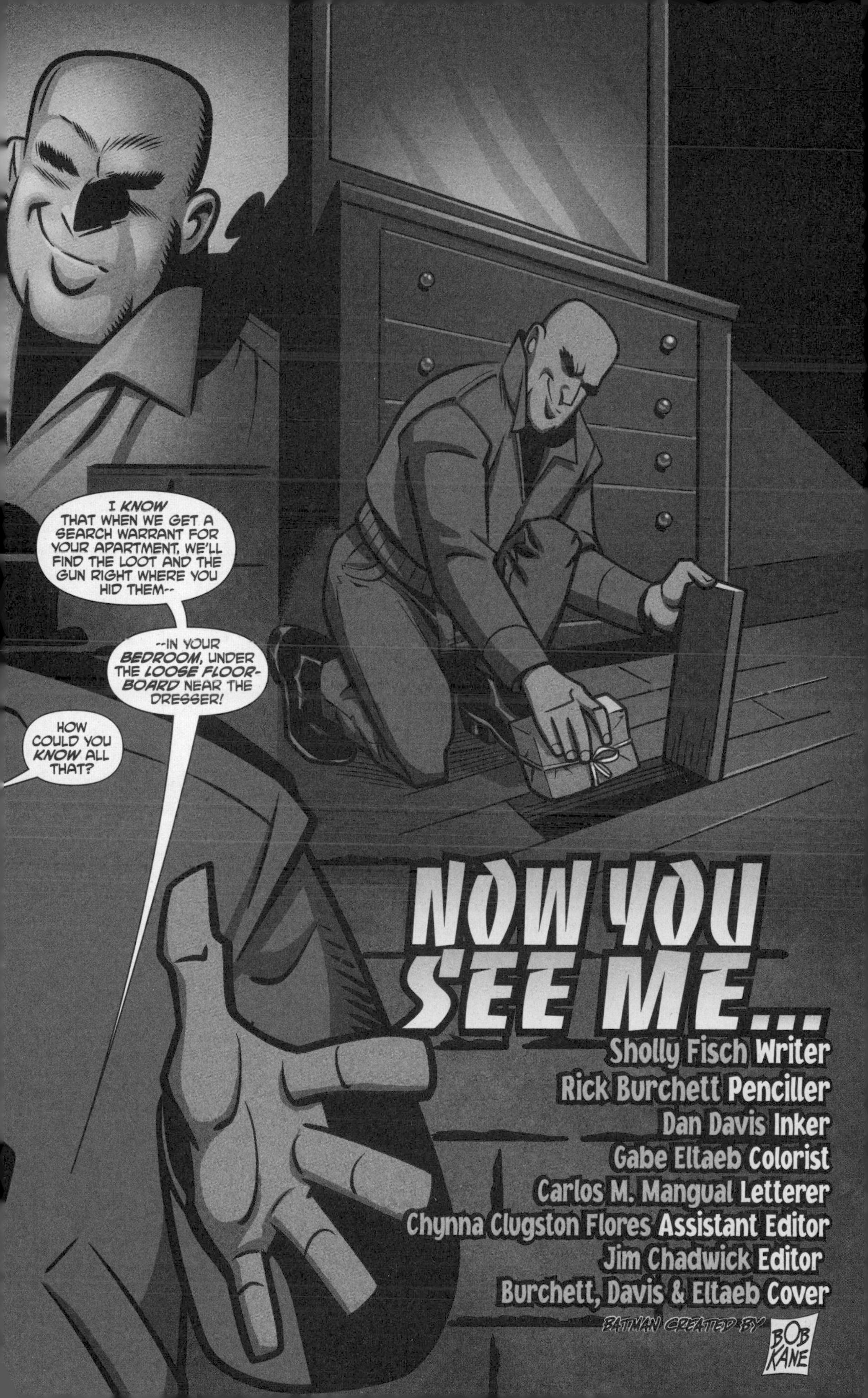

I KNOW THAT WHEN WE GET A SEARCH WARRANT FOR YOUR APARTMENT, WE'LL FIND THE LOOT AND THE GUN RIGHT WHERE YOU HID THEM--
--IN YOUR BEDROOM, UNDER THE LOOSE FLOORBOARD NEAR THE DRESSER!
HOW COULD YOU KNOW ALL THAT?
NOW YOU SEE ME...
Sholly Fisch Writer
Rick Burchett Penciller
Dan Davis Inker
Gabe Eltaeb Colorist
Carlos M. Mangual Letterer
Chynna Clugston Flores Assistant Editor
Jim Chadwick Editor
Burchett, Davis & Eltaeb Cover
BATMAN CREATED BY BOB KANE

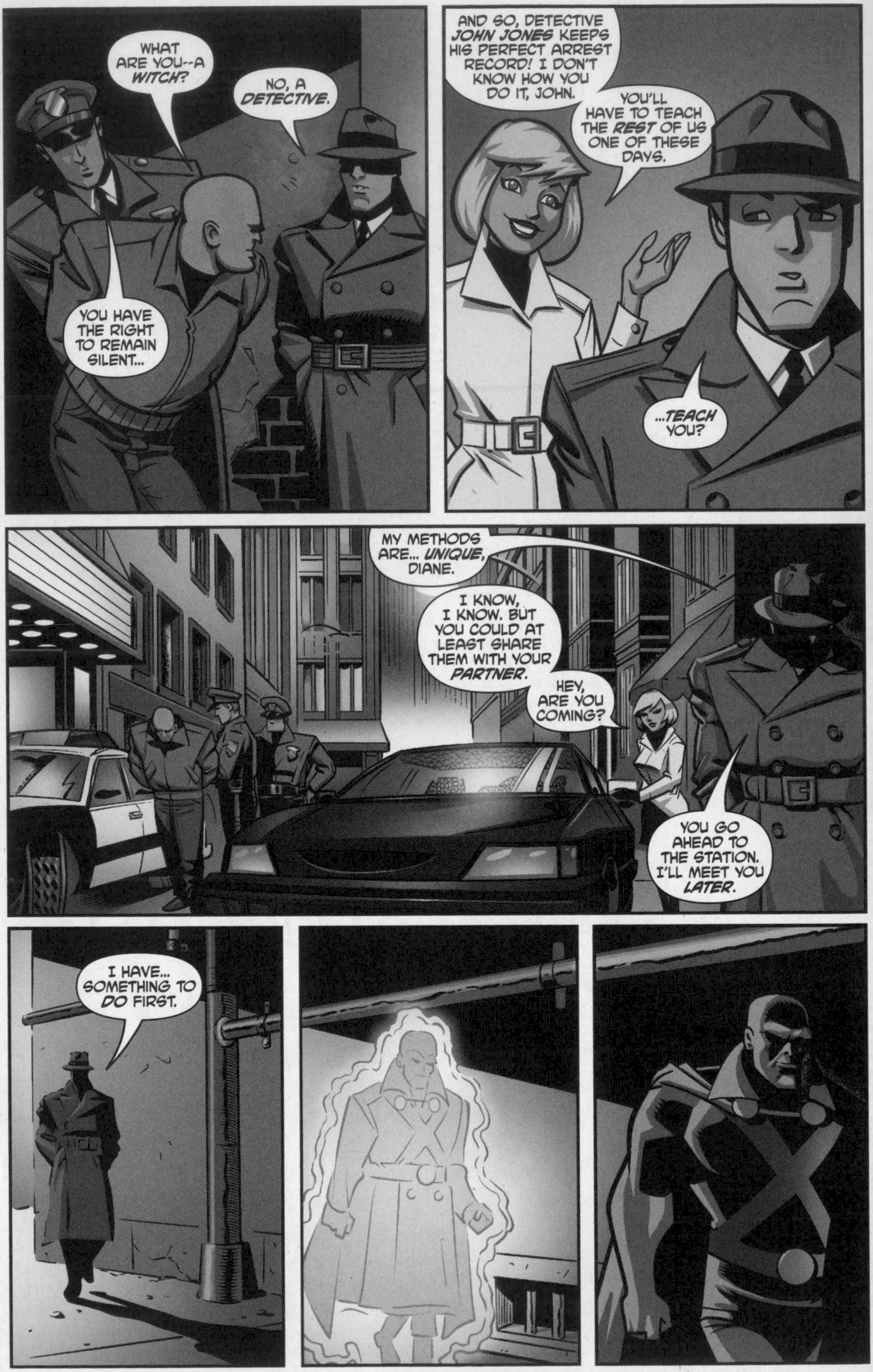
WHAT ARE YOU--A *WITCH*?
NO, A *DETECTIVE*.
YOU HAVE THE RIGHT TO REMAIN SILENT...
AND SO, DETECTIVE *JOHN JONES* KEEPS HIS PERFECT ARREST RECORD! I DON'T KNOW HOW YOU DO IT, JOHN.
YOU'LL HAVE TO TEACH THE *REST* OF US ONE OF THESE DAYS.
...*TEACH* YOU?
MY METHODS ARE... *UNIQUE*, DIANE.
I KNOW, I KNOW. BUT YOU COULD AT LEAST SHARE THEM WITH YOUR *PARTNER*.
HEY, ARE YOU COMING?
YOU GO AHEAD TO THE STATION. I'LL MEET YOU *LATER*.
I HAVE... SOMETHING TO *DO* FIRST.

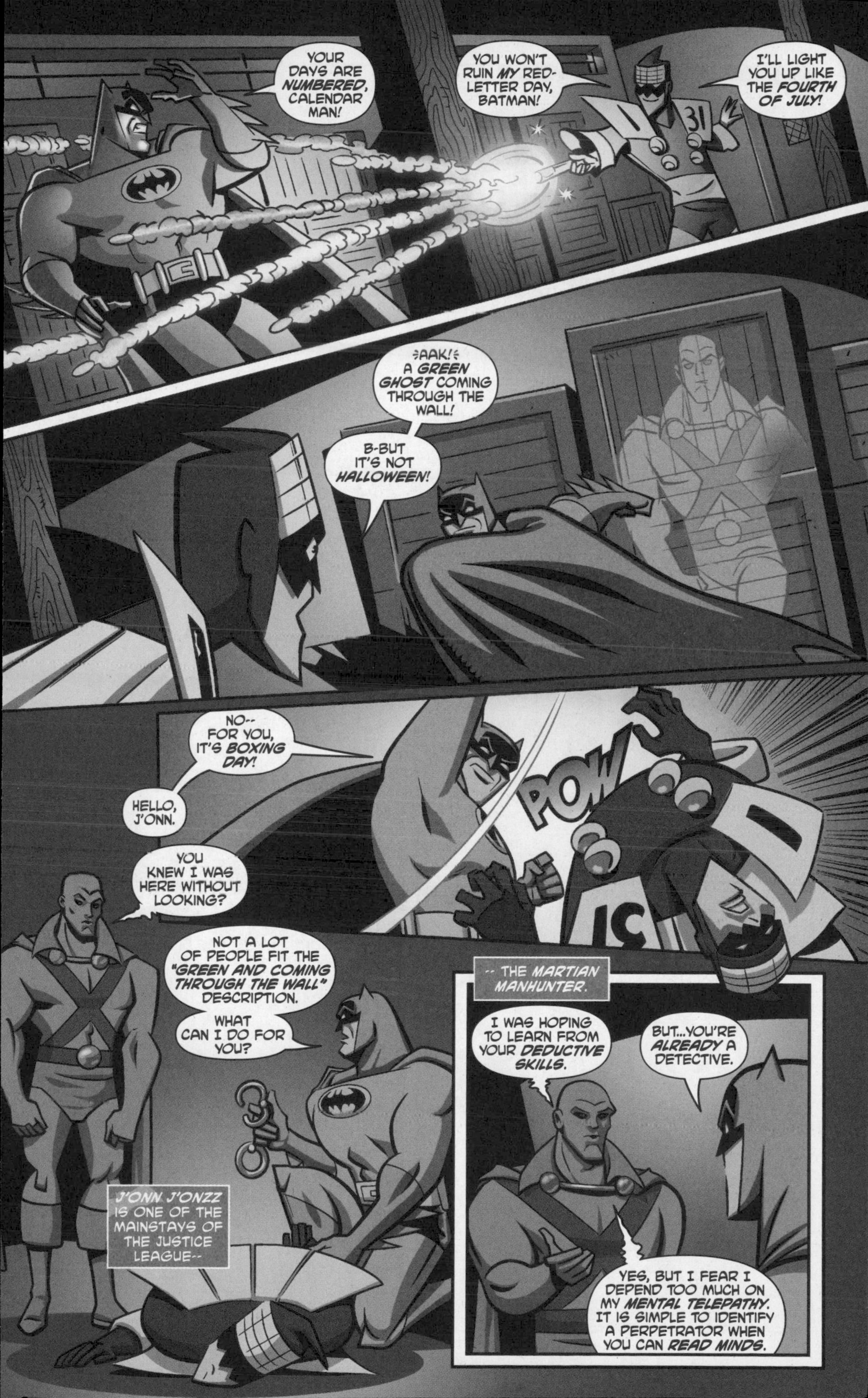
YOUR DAYS ARE NUMBERED, CALENDAR MAN!
YOU WON'T RUIN MY RED-LETTER DAY, BATMAN!
I'LL LIGHT YOU UP LIKE THE FOURTH OF JULY!
AAK! A GREEN GHOST COMING THROUGH THE WALL!
B-BUT IT'S NOT HALLOWEEN!
NO-- FOR YOU, IT'S BOXING DAY!
POW
HELLO, J'ONN.
YOU KNEW I WAS HERE WITHOUT LOOKING?
NOT A LOT OF PEOPLE FIT THE "GREEN AND COMING THROUGH THE WALL" DESCRIPTION.
WHAT CAN I DO FOR YOU?
J'ONN J'ONZZ IS ONE OF THE MAINSTAYS OF THE JUSTICE LEAGUE--
-- THE MARTIAN MANHUNTER.
I WAS HOPING TO LEARN FROM YOUR DEDUCTIVE SKILLS.
BUT...YOU'RE ALREADY A DETECTIVE.
YES, BUT I FEAR I DEPEND TOO MUCH ON MY MENTAL TELEPATHY. IT IS SIMPLE TO IDENTIFY A PERPETRATOR WHEN YOU CAN READ MINDS.

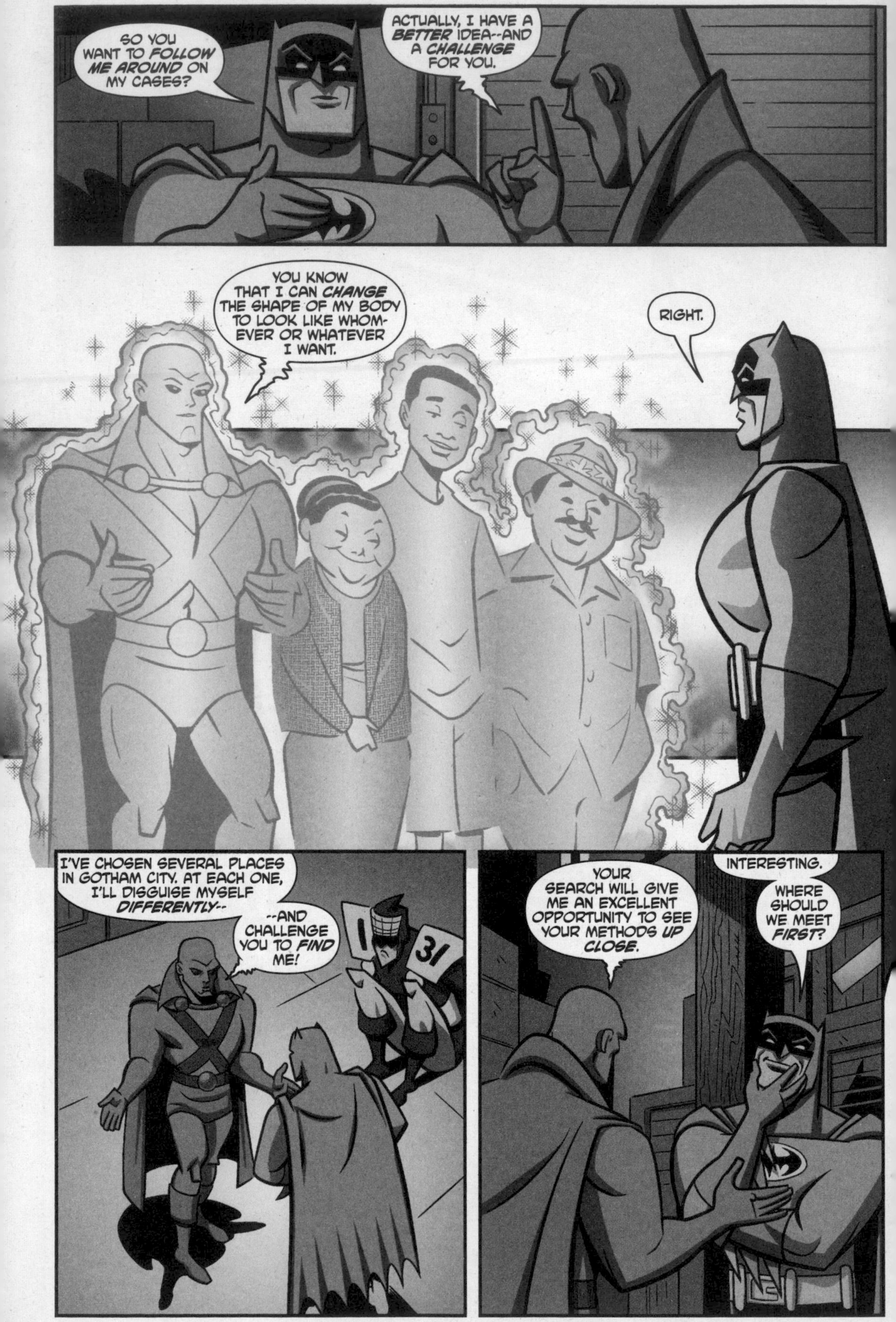
SO YOU WANT TO FOLLOW ME AROUND ON MY CASES?
ACTUALLY, I HAVE A BETTER IDEA--AND A CHALLENGE FOR YOU.
YOU KNOW THAT I CAN CHANGE THE SHAPE OF MY BODY TO LOOK LIKE WHOM-EVER OR WHATEVER I WANT.
RIGHT.
I'VE CHOSEN SEVERAL PLACES IN GOTHAM CITY. AT EACH ONE, I'LL DISGUISE MYSELF DIFFERENTLY--
--AND CHALLENGE YOU TO FIND ME!
31
YOUR SEARCH WILL GIVE ME AN EXCELLENT OPPORTUNITY TO SEE YOUR METHODS UP CLOSE.
INTERESTING.
WHERE SHOULD WE MEET FIRST?

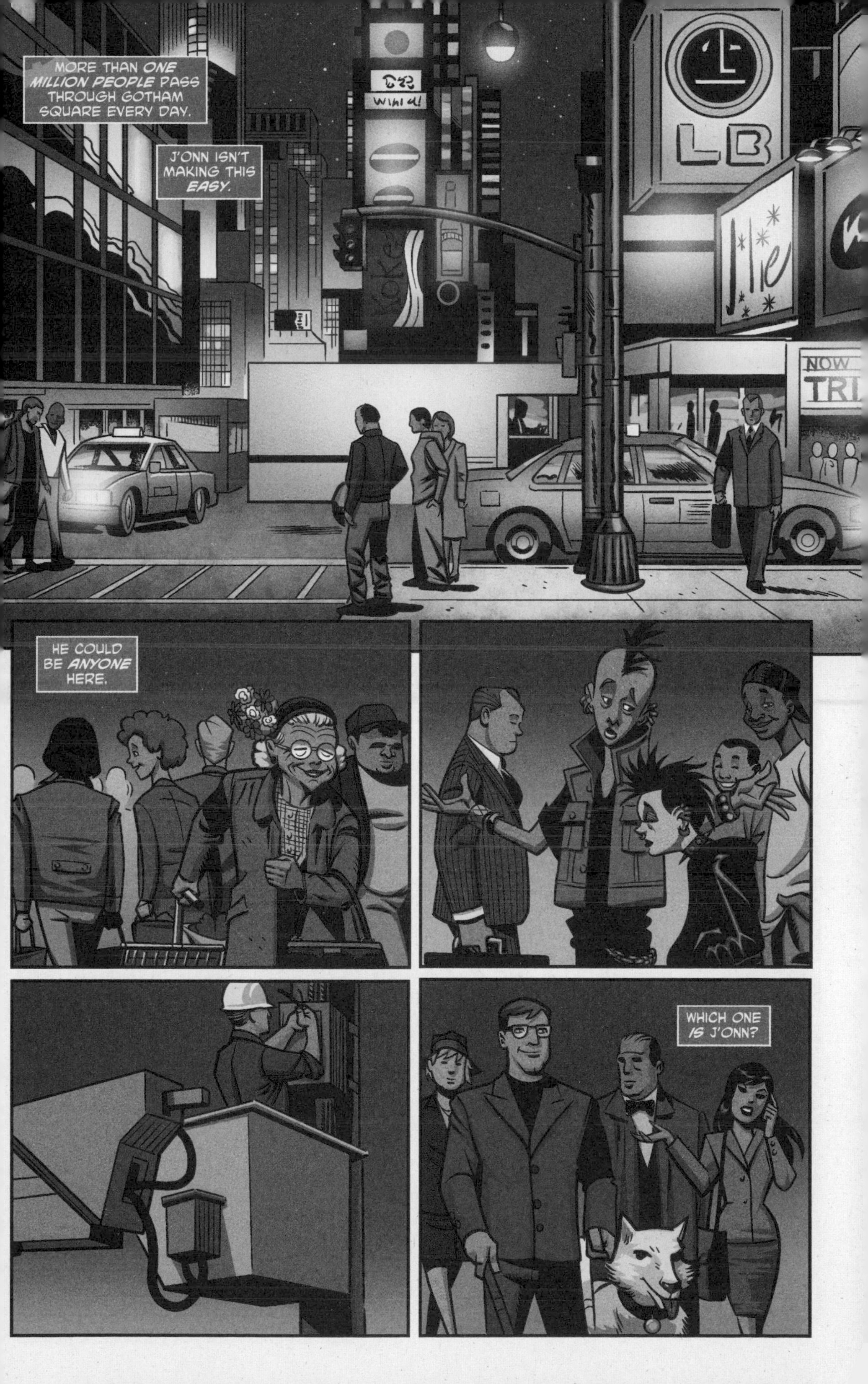
MORE THAN ONE MILLION PEOPLE PASS THROUGH GOTHAM SQUARE EVERY DAY.
J'ONN ISN'T MAKING THIS EASY.
LB
NOW
HE COULD BE ANYONE HERE.
WHICH ONE IS J'ONN?

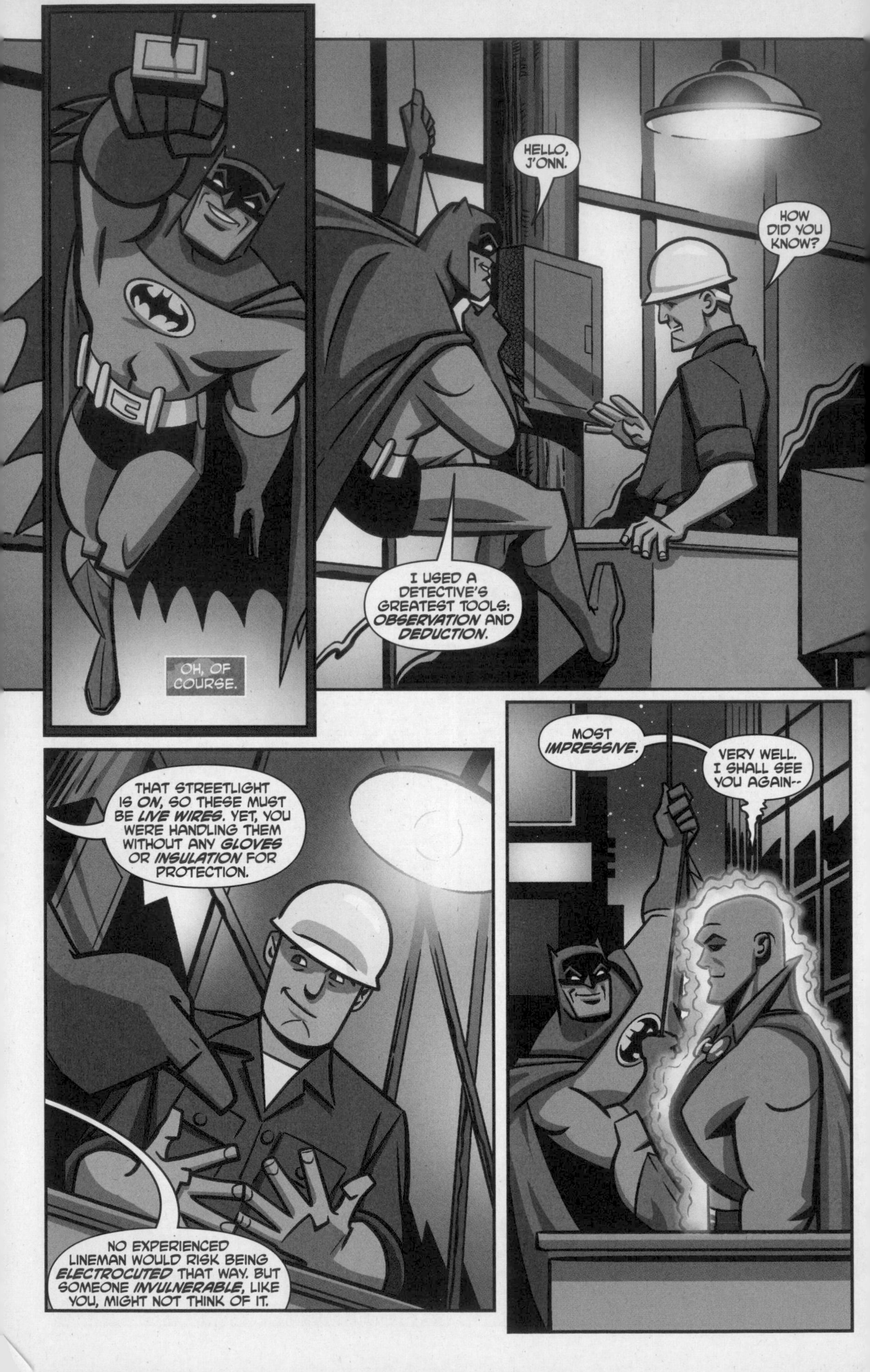
OH, OF COURSE.
HELLO, J'ONN.
HOW DID YOU KNOW?
I USED A DETECTIVE'S GREATEST TOOLS: OBSERVATION AND DEDUCTION.
THAT STREETLIGHT IS ON, SO THESE MUST BE LIVE WIRES. YET, YOU WERE HANDLING THEM WITHOUT ANY GLOVES OR INSULATION FOR PROTECTION.
NO EXPERIENCED LINEMAN WOULD RISK BEING ELECTROCUTED THAT WAY. BUT SOMEONE INVULNERABLE, LIKE YOU, MIGHT NOT THINK OF IT.
MOST IMPRESSIVE.
VERY WELL. I SHALL SEE YOU AGAIN--

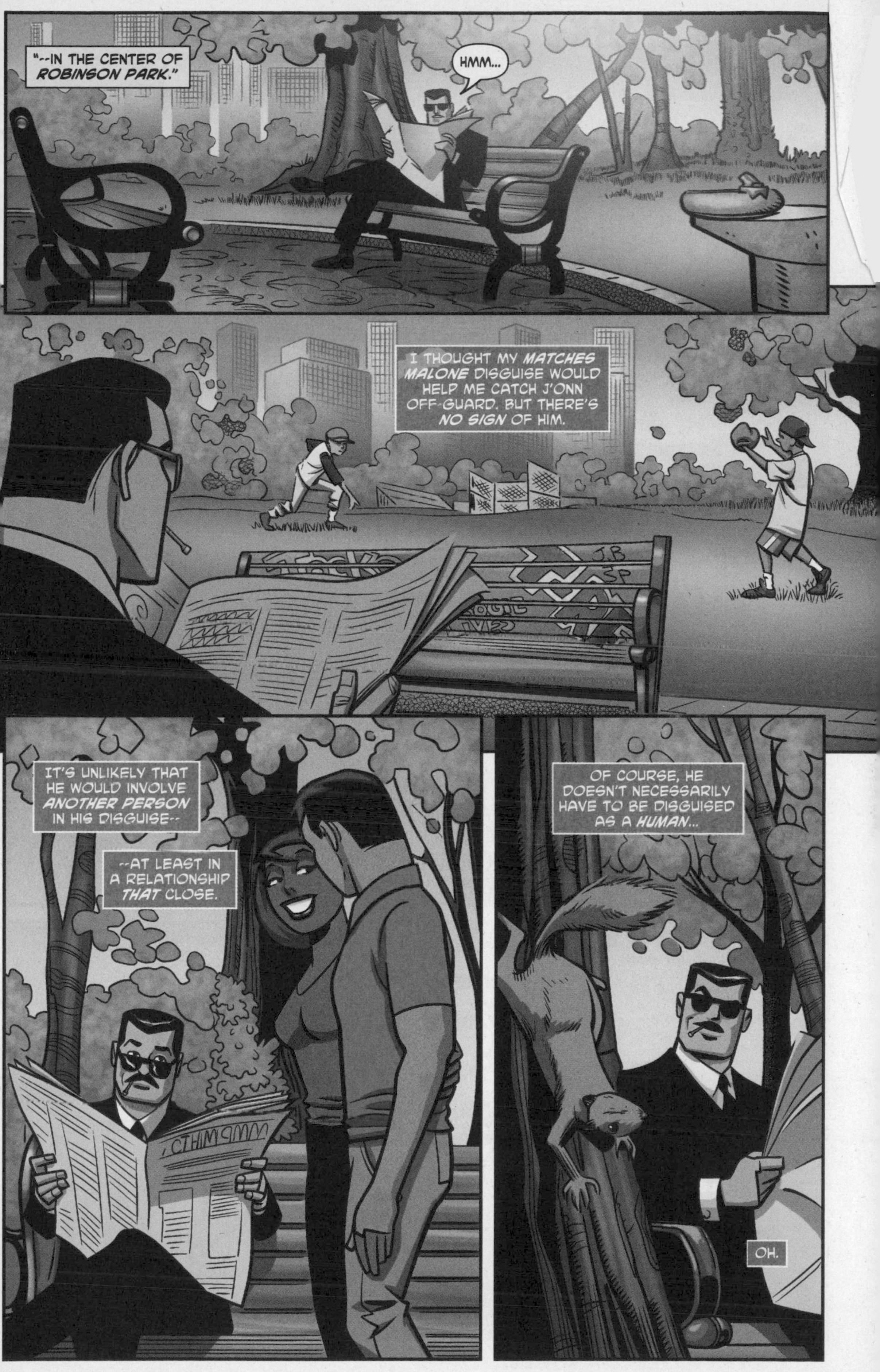
"--IN THE CENTER OF ROBINSON PARK."
HMM...
I THOUGHT MY MATCHES MALONE DISGUISE WOULD HELP ME CATCH J'ONN OFF-GUARD. BUT THERE'S NO SIGN OF HIM.
IT'S UNLIKELY THAT HE WOULD INVOLVE ANOTHER PERSON IN HIS DISGUISE--
--AT LEAST IN A RELATIONSHIP THAT CLOSE.
OF COURSE, HE DOESN'T NECESSARILY HAVE TO BE DISGUISED AS A HUMAN...
OH.

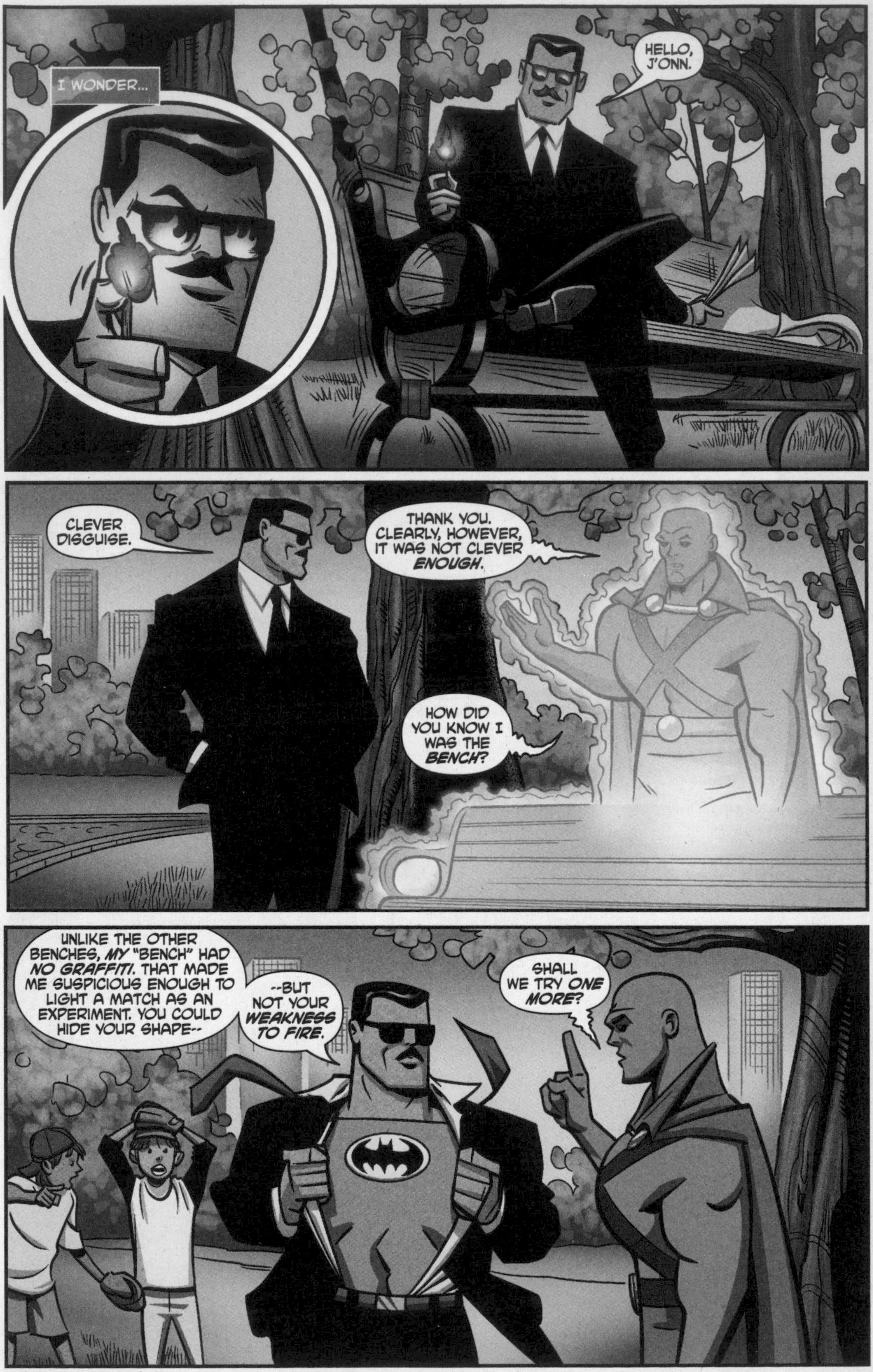
I WONDER...
HELLO, J'ONN.
CLEVER DISGUISE.
THANK YOU. CLEARLY, HOWEVER, IT WAS NOT CLEVER ENOUGH.
HOW DID YOU KNOW I WAS THE BENCH?
UNLIKE THE OTHER BENCHES, MY "BENCH" HAD NO GRAFFITI. THAT MADE ME SUSPICIOUS ENOUGH TO LIGHT A MATCH AS AN EXPERIMENT. YOU COULD HIDE YOUR SHAPE--
--BUT NOT YOUR WEAKNESS TO FIRE.
SHALL WE TRY ONE MORE?

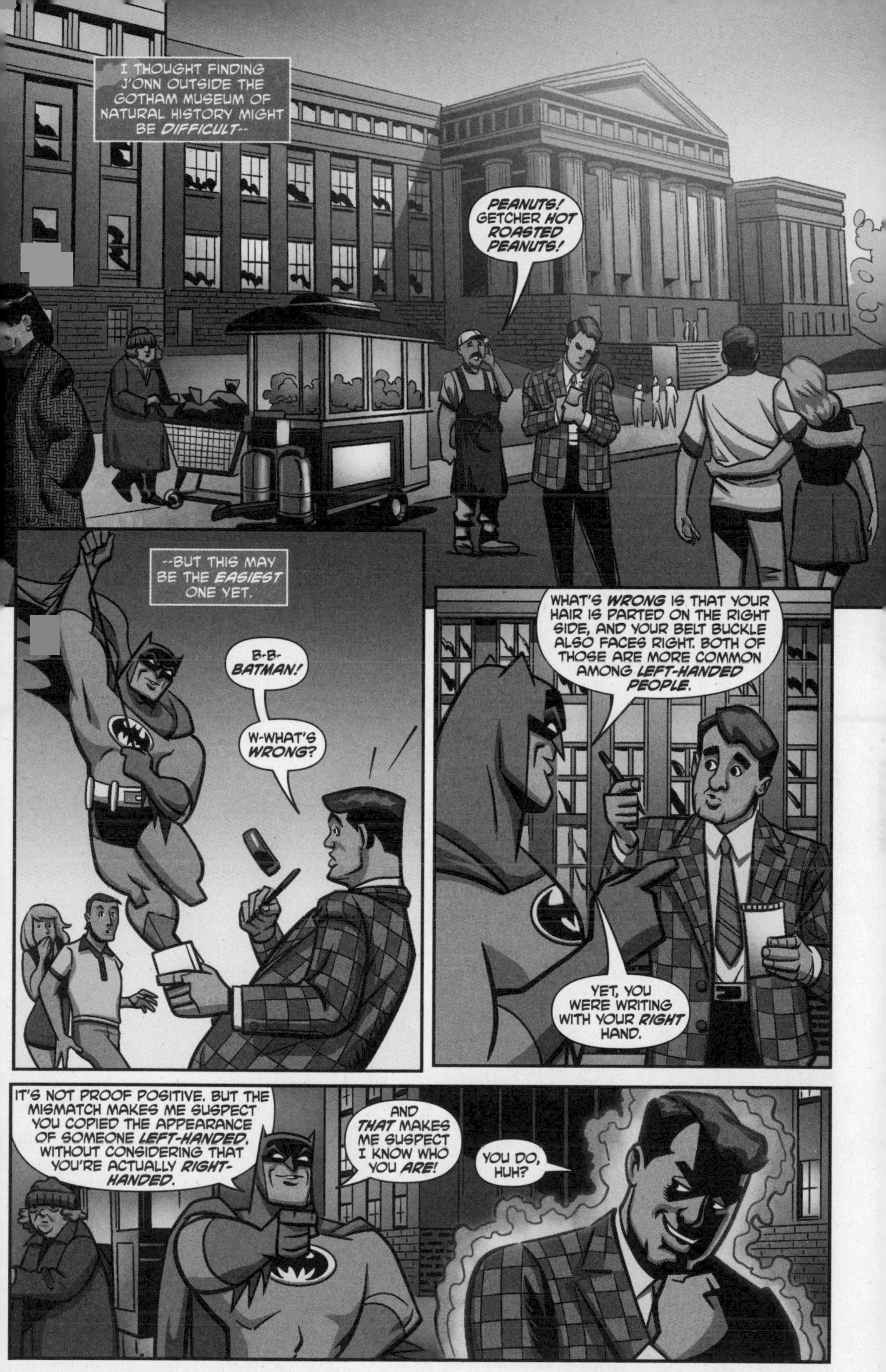
I THOUGHT FINDING J'ONN OUTSIDE THE GOTHAM MUSEUM OF NATURAL HISTORY MIGHT BE DIFFICULT--
PEANUTS! GETCHER HOT ROASTED PEANUTS!
--BUT THIS MAY BE THE EASIEST ONE YET.
B-B-BATMAN!
W-WHAT'S WRONG?
WHAT'S WRONG IS THAT YOUR HAIR IS PARTED ON THE RIGHT SIDE, AND YOUR BELT BUCKLE ALSO FACES RIGHT. BOTH OF THOSE ARE MORE COMMON AMONG LEFT-HANDED PEOPLE.
YET, YOU WERE WRITING WITH YOUR RIGHT HAND.
IT'S NOT PROOF POSITIVE. BUT THE MISMATCH MAKES ME SUSPECT YOU COPIED THE APPEARANCE OF SOMEONE LEFT-HANDED, WITHOUT CONSIDERING THAT YOU'RE ACTUALLY RIGHT-HANDED.
AND THAT MAKES ME SUSPECT I KNOW WHO YOU ARE!
YOU DO, HUH?

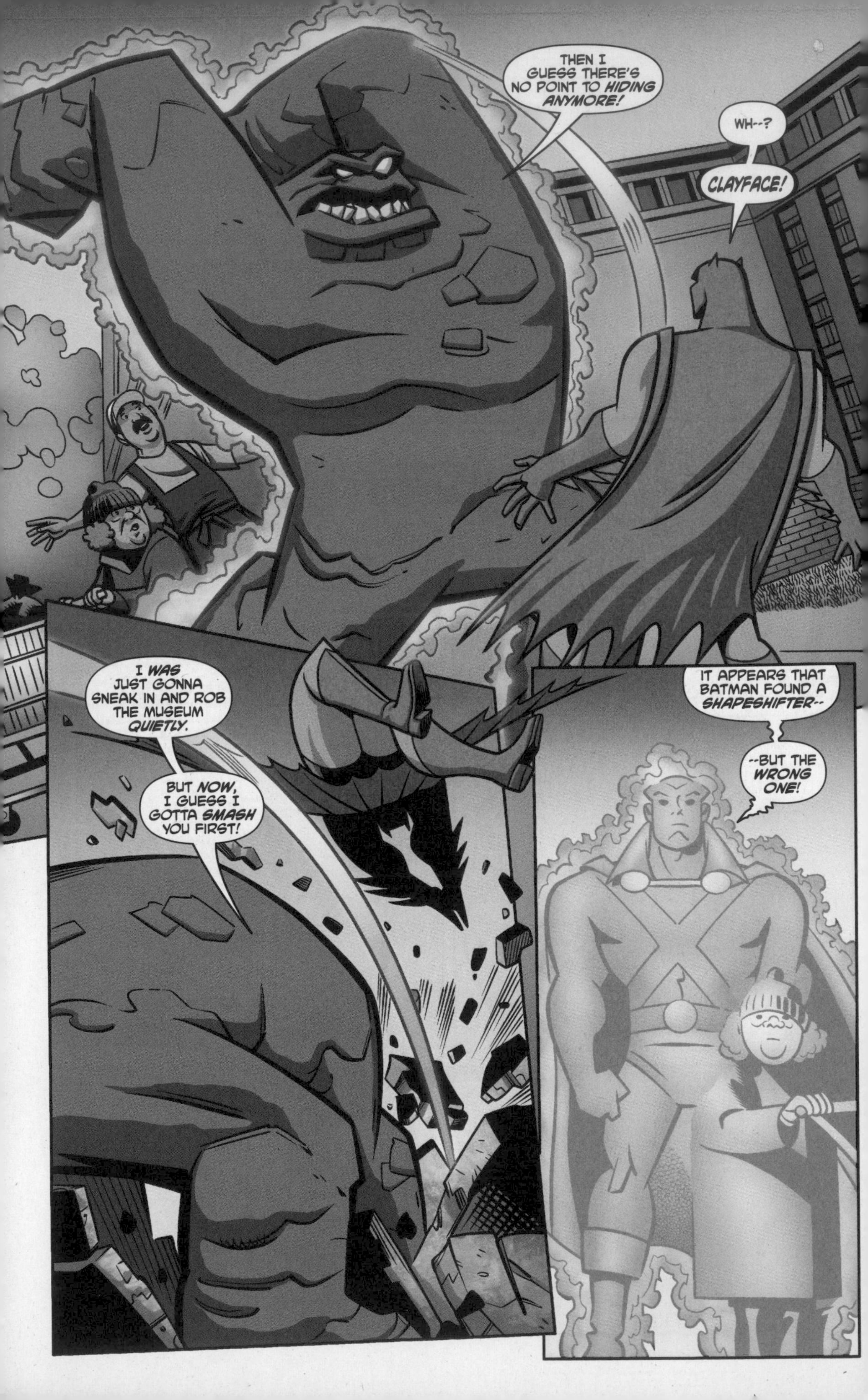
THEN I GUESS THERE'S NO POINT TO *HIDING ANYMORE!*
WH--?
CLAYFACE!
I *WAS* JUST GONNA SNEAK IN AND ROB THE MUSEUM *QUIETLY*.
BUT *NOW*, I GUESS I GOTTA *SMASH* YOU FIRST!
IT APPEARS THAT BATMAN FOUND A *SHAPESHIFTER*--
--BUT THE *WRONG ONE!*

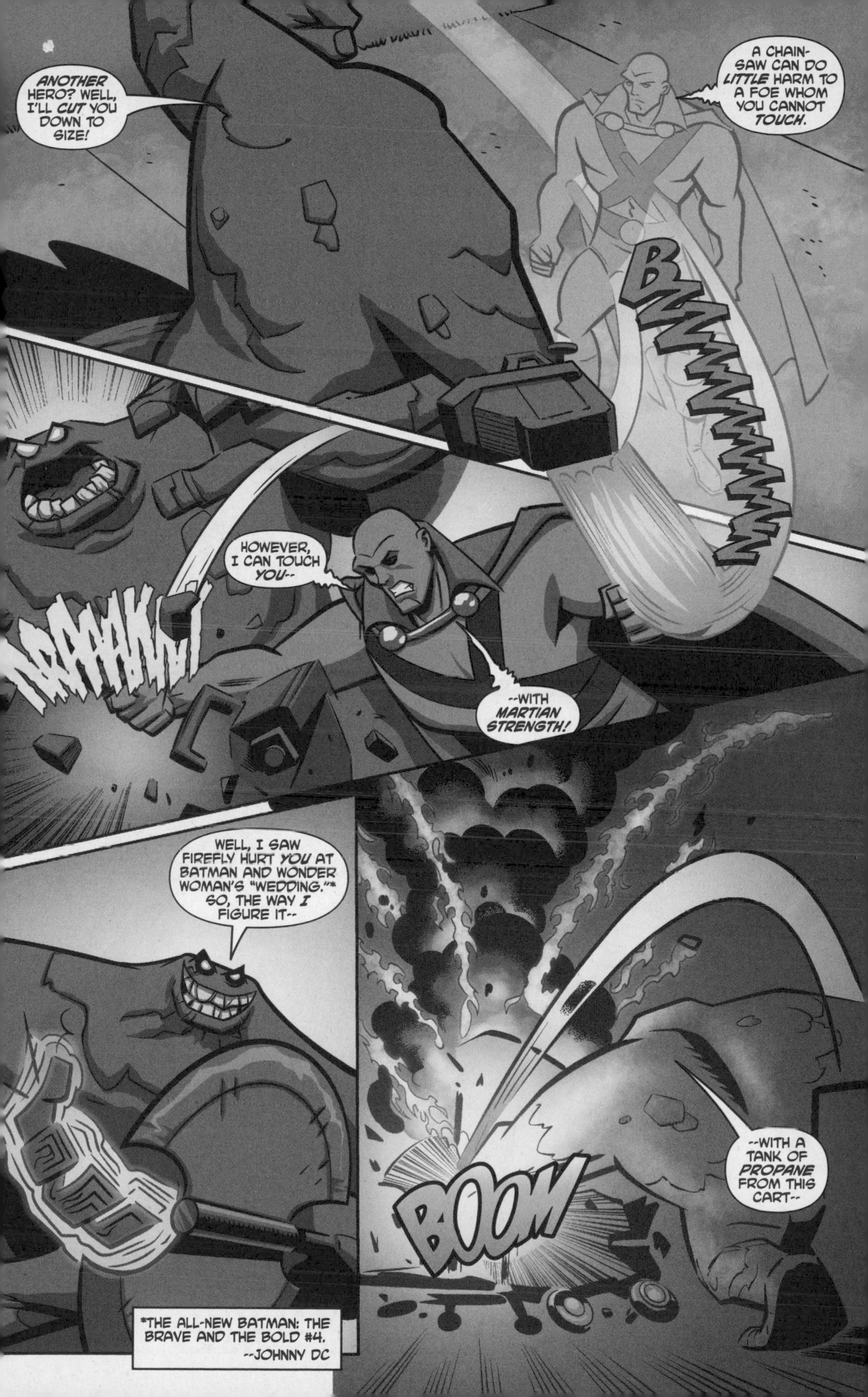
ANOTHER HERO? WELL, I'LL CUT YOU DOWN TO SIZE!
A CHAIN-SAW CAN DO LITTLE HARM TO A FOE WHOM YOU CANNOT TOUCH.
BZZZZZZZZM
HOWEVER, I CAN TOUCH YOU--
--WITH MARTIAN STRENGTH!
WELL, I SAW FIREFLY HURT YOU AT BATMAN AND WONDER WOMAN'S "WEDDING."* SO, THE WAY I FIGURE IT--
--WITH A TANK OF PROPANE FROM THIS CART--
BOOM
*THE ALL-NEW BATMAN: THE BRAVE AND THE BOLD #4. --JOHNNY DC

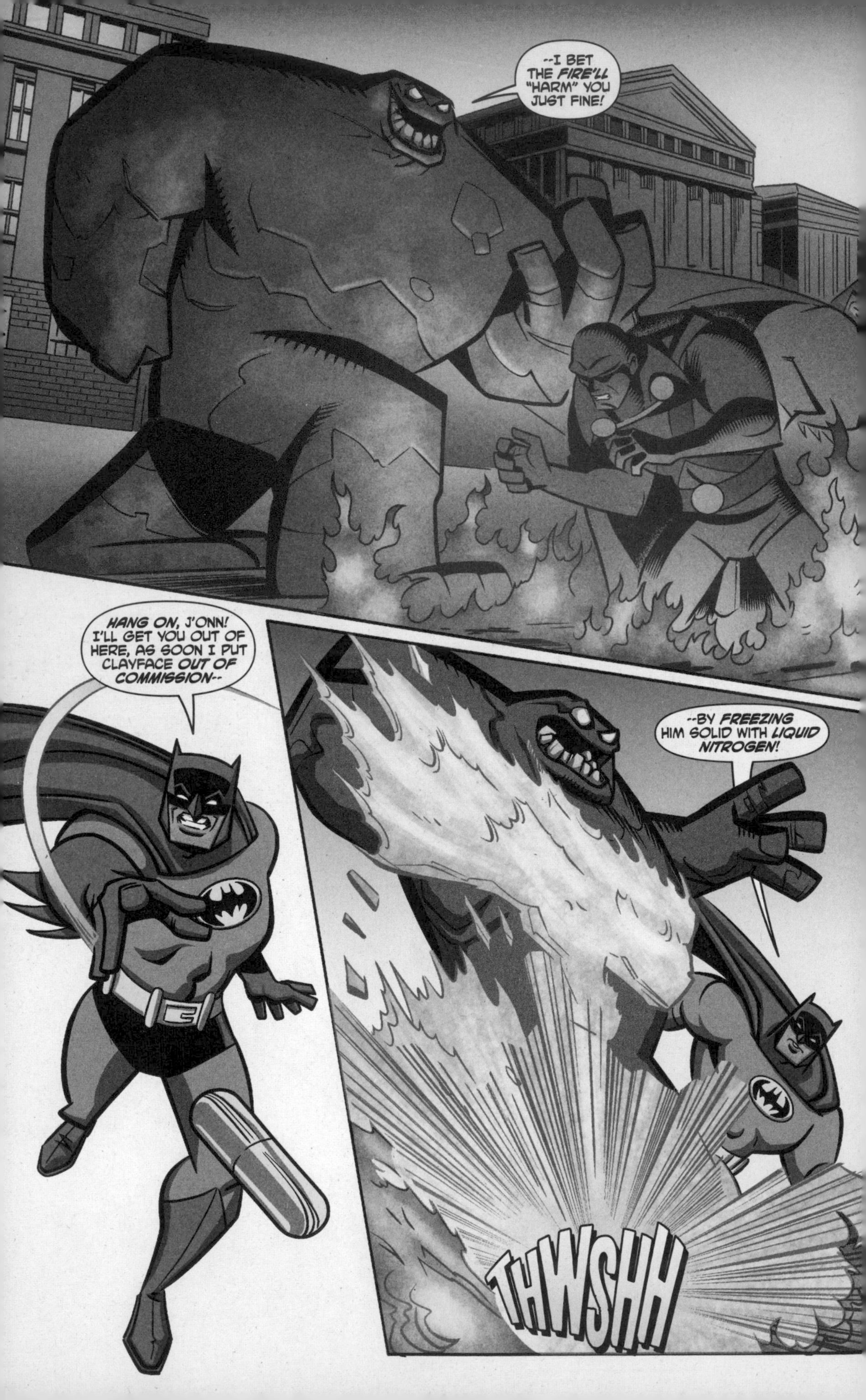
--I BET THE FIRE'LL "HARM" YOU JUST FINE!
HANG ON, J'ONN! I'LL GET YOU OUT OF HERE, AS SOON I PUT CLAYFACE OUT OF COMMISSION--
--BY FREEZING HIM SOLID WITH LIQUID NITROGEN!
THWSHH

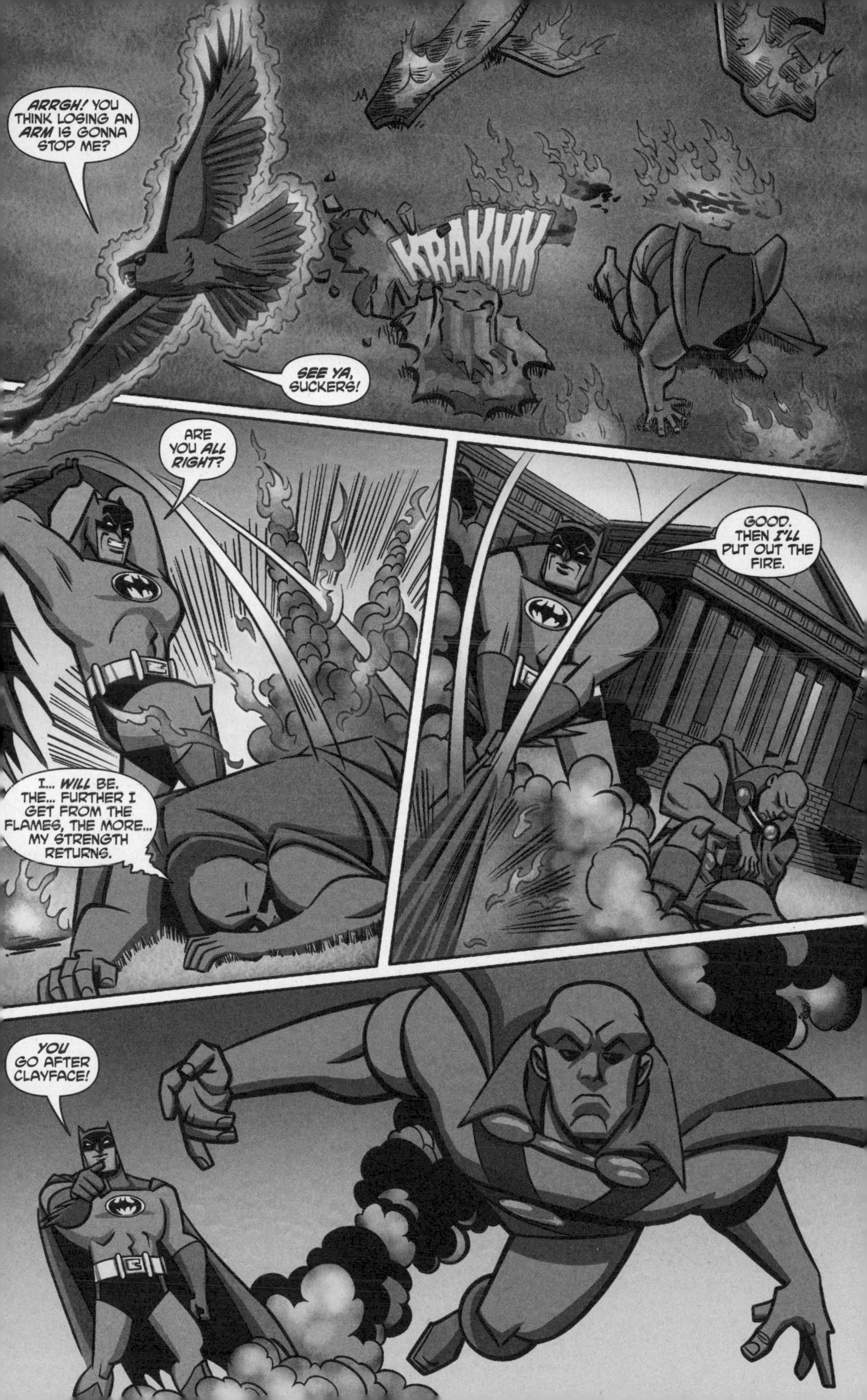
ARRGH! YOU THINK LOSING AN ARM IS GONNA STOP ME?
KRAKKK
SEE YA, SUCKERS!
ARE YOU ALL RIGHT?
I... WILL BE. THE... FURTHER I GET FROM THE FLAMES, THE MORE... MY STRENGTH RETURNS.
GOOD. THEN I'LL PUT OUT THE FIRE.
YOU GO AFTER CLAYFACE!

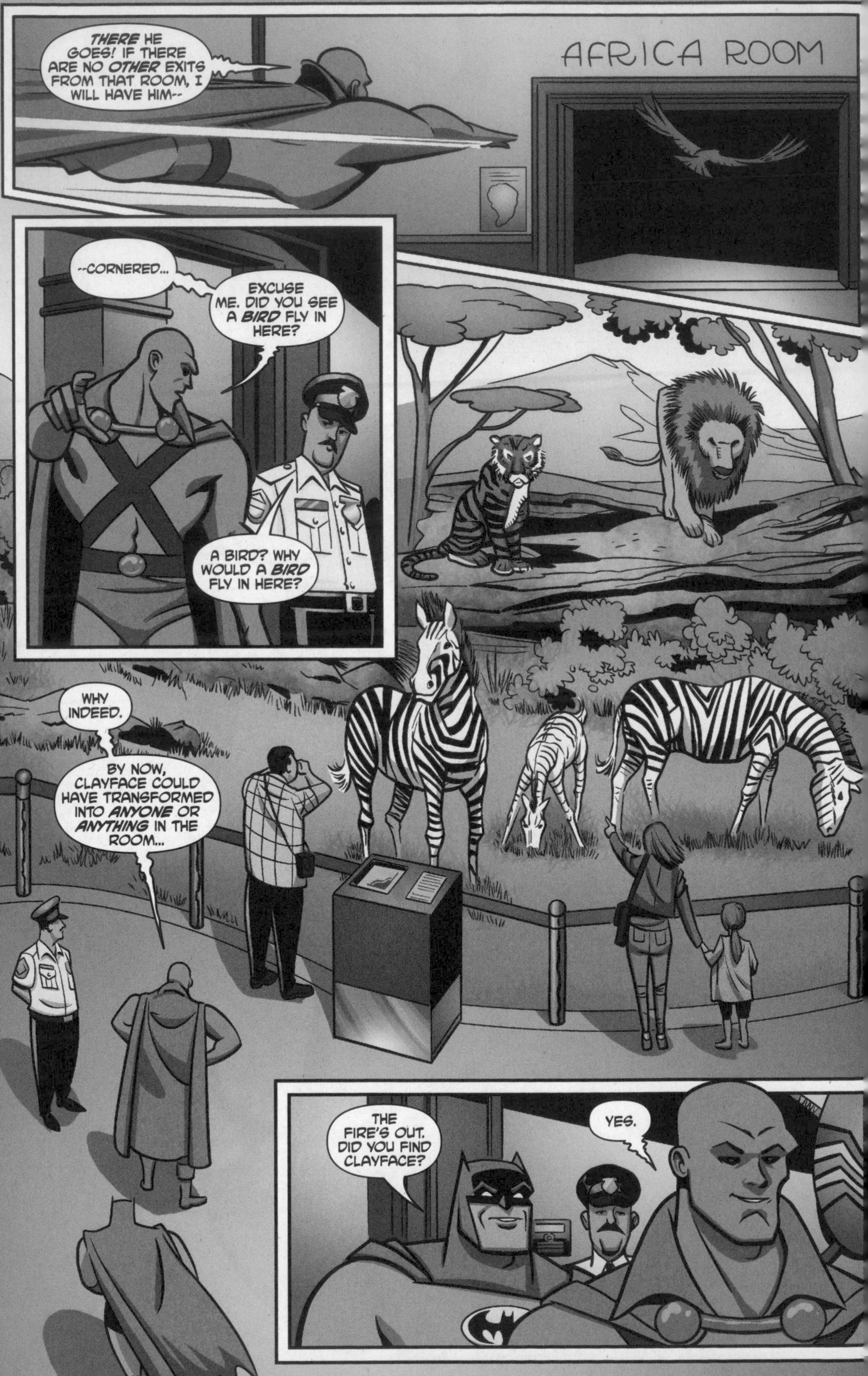
THERE HE GOES! IF THERE ARE NO OTHER EXITS FROM THAT ROOM, I WILL HAVE HIM--
AFRICA ROOM
--CORNERED...
EXCUSE ME. DID YOU SEE A BIRD FLY IN HERE?
A BIRD? WHY WOULD A BIRD FLY IN HERE?
WHY INDEED.
BY NOW, CLAYFACE COULD HAVE TRANSFORMED INTO ANYONE OR ANYTHING IN THE ROOM...
THE FIRE'S OUT. DID YOU FIND CLAYFACE?
YES.

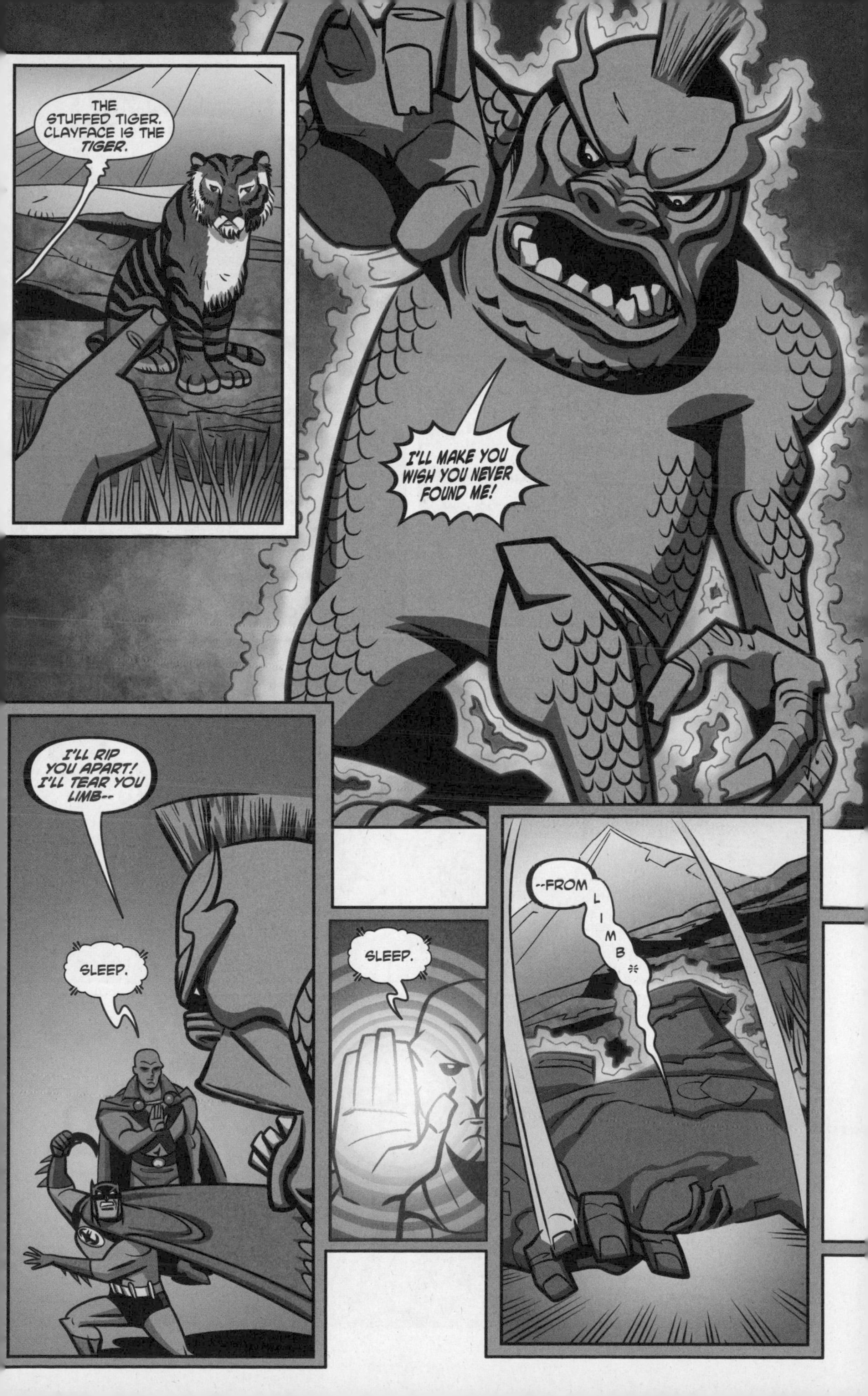

THE STUFFED TIGER. CLAYFACE IS THE TIGER.
I'LL MAKE YOU WISH YOU NEVER FOUND ME!
I'LL RIP YOU APART! I'LL TEAR YOU LIMB--
SLEEP.
SLEEP.
--FROM LIMB*

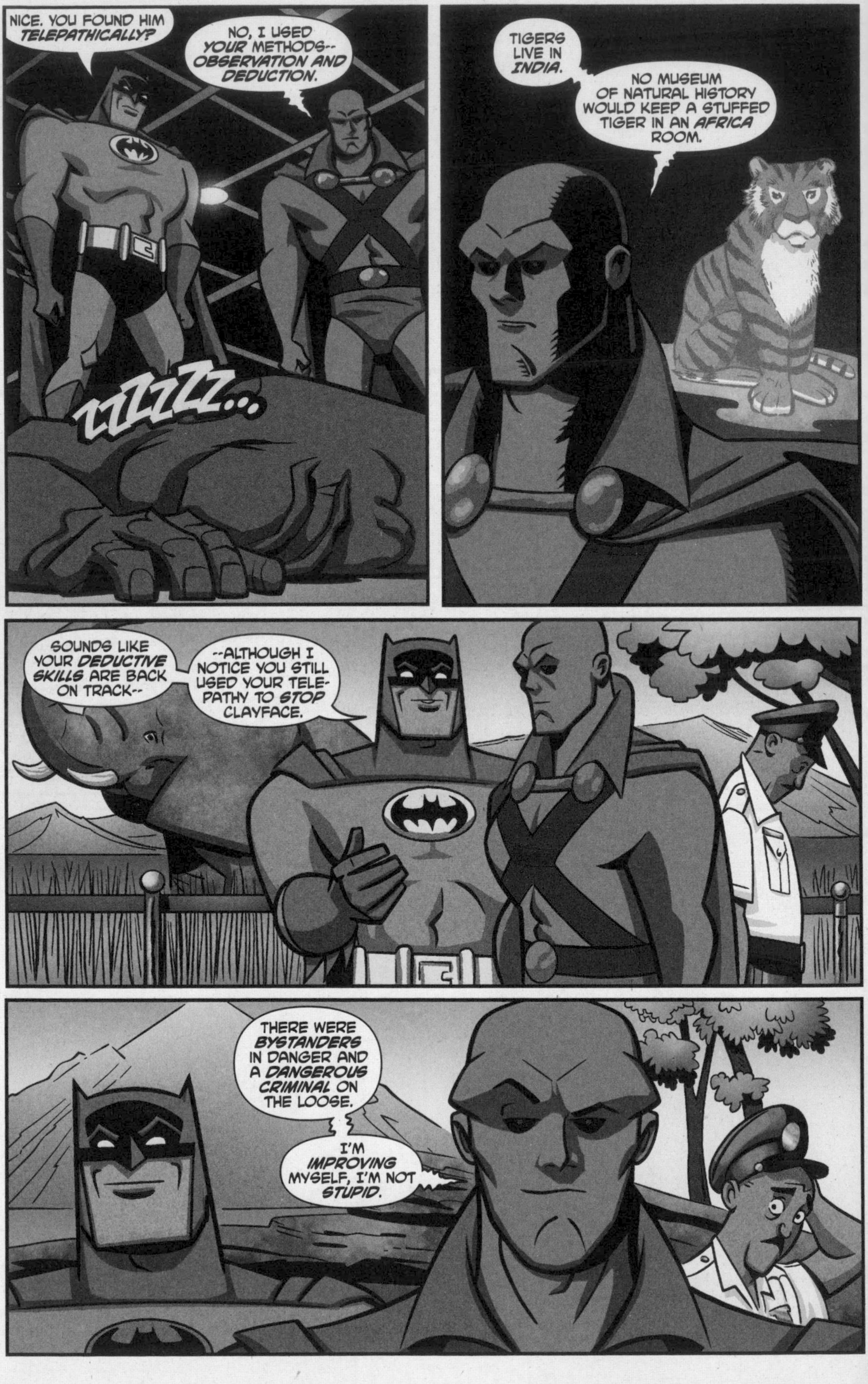
NICE. YOU FOUND HIM *TELEPATHICALLY?*
NO, I USED *YOUR* METHODS-- *OBSERVATION AND DEDUCTION*.
ZZZZZZ...
TIGERS LIVE IN *INDIA*.
NO MUSEUM OF NATURAL HISTORY WOULD KEEP A STUFFED TIGER IN AN *AFRICA* ROOM.
SOUNDS LIKE YOUR *DEDUCTIVE SKILLS* ARE BACK ON TRACK--
--ALTHOUGH I NOTICE YOU STILL USED YOUR TELEPATHY TO *STOP* CLAYFACE.
THERE WERE *BYSTANDERS* IN DANGER AND A *DANGEROUS CRIMINAL* ON THE LOOSE.
I'M *IMPROVING* MYSELF, I'M NOT *STUPID*.

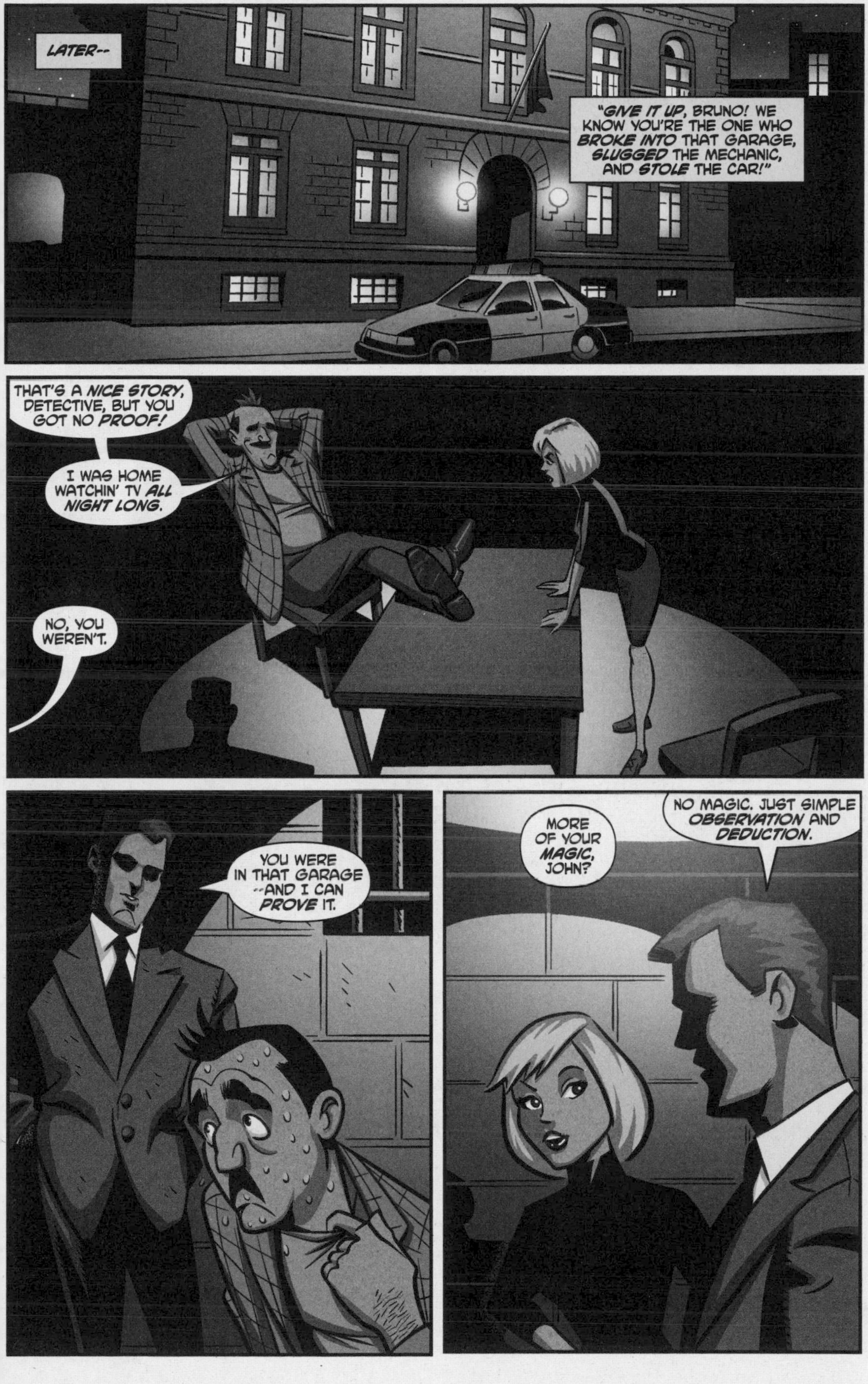
LATER--
"GIVE IT UP, BRUNO! WE KNOW YOU'RE THE ONE WHO BROKE INTO THAT GARAGE, SLUGGED THE MECHANIC, AND STOLE THE CAR!"
THAT'S A NICE STORY, DETECTIVE, BUT YOU GOT NO PROOF!
I WAS HOME WATCHIN' TV ALL NIGHT LONG.
NO, YOU WEREN'T.
YOU WERE IN THAT GARAGE --AND I CAN PROVE IT.
MORE OF YOUR MAGIC, JOHN?
NO MAGIC. JUST SIMPLE OBSERVATION AND DEDUCTION.

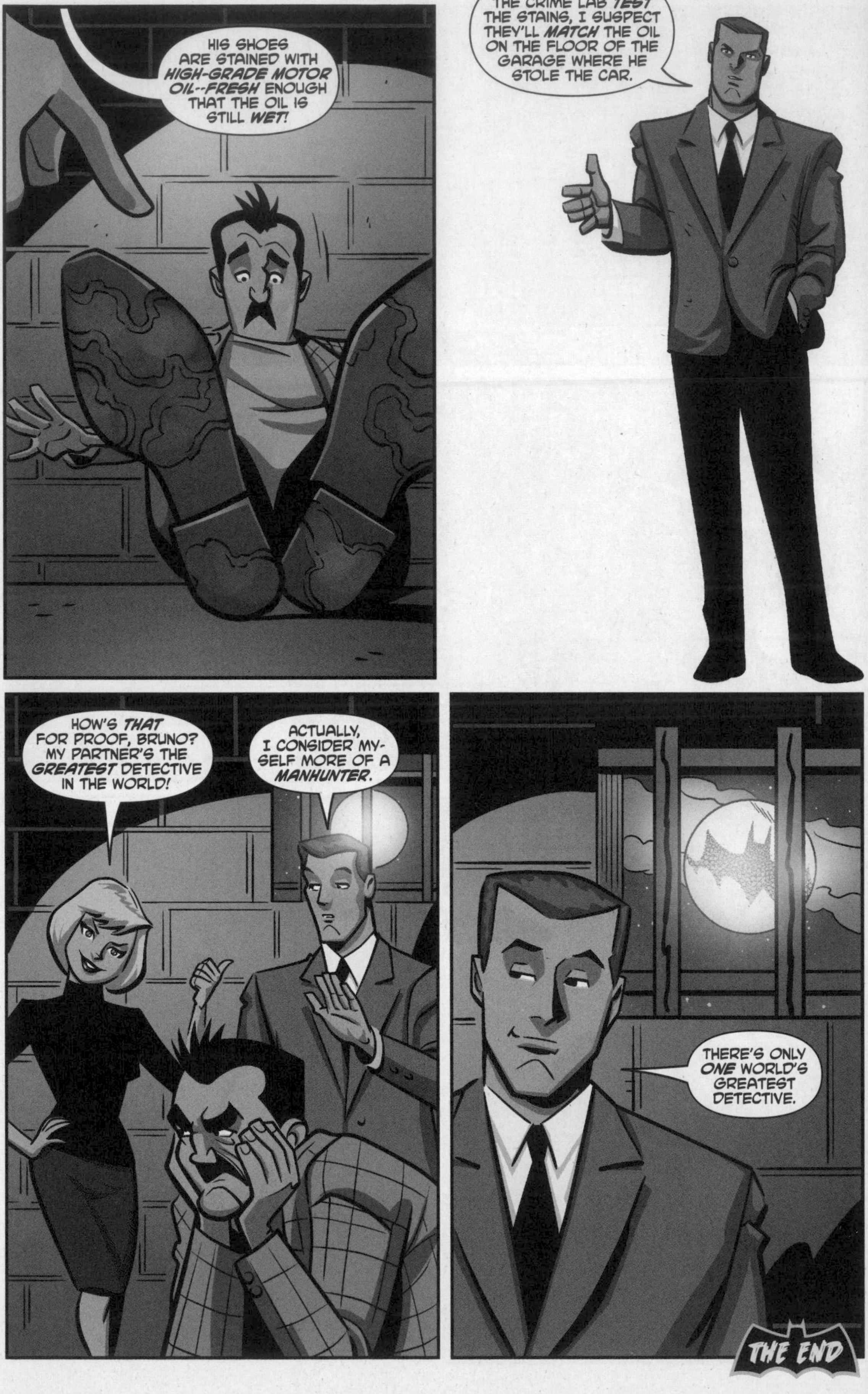
HIS SHOES ARE STAINED WITH HIGH-GRADE MOTOR OIL--FRESH ENOUGH THAT THE OIL IS STILL WET!
IF YOU HAVE THE CRIME LAB TEST THE STAINS, I SUSPECT THEY'LL MATCH THE OIL ON THE FLOOR OF THE GARAGE WHERE HE STOLE THE CAR.
HOW'S THAT FOR PROOF, BRUNO? MY PARTNER'S THE GREATEST DETECTIVE IN THE WORLD!
ACTUALLY, I CONSIDER MY-SELF MORE OF A MANHUNTER.
THERE'S ONLY ONE WORLD'S GREATEST DETECTIVE.
THE END

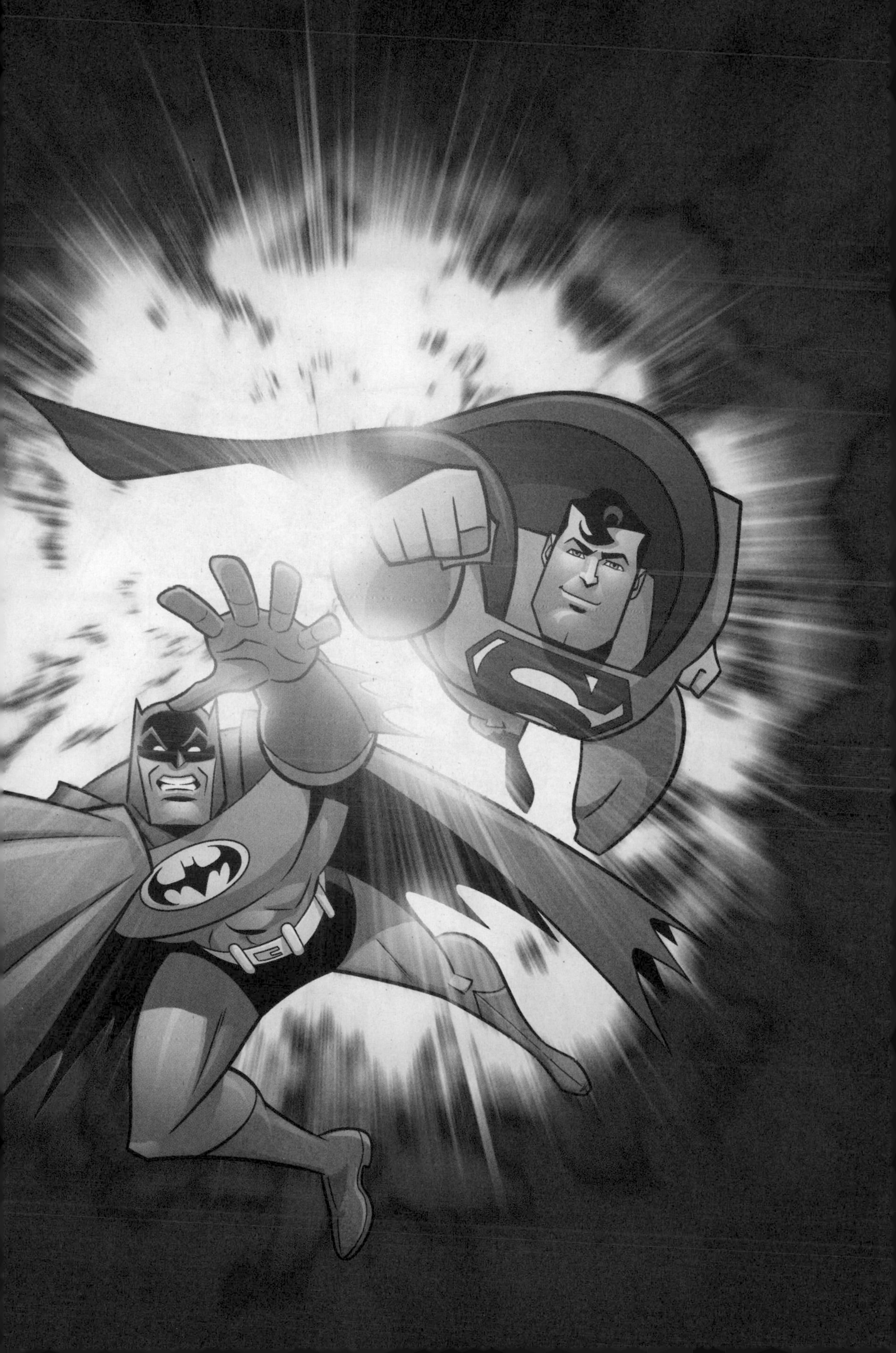

THE ALL-NEW BATMAN: THE BRAVE AND THE BOLD #2

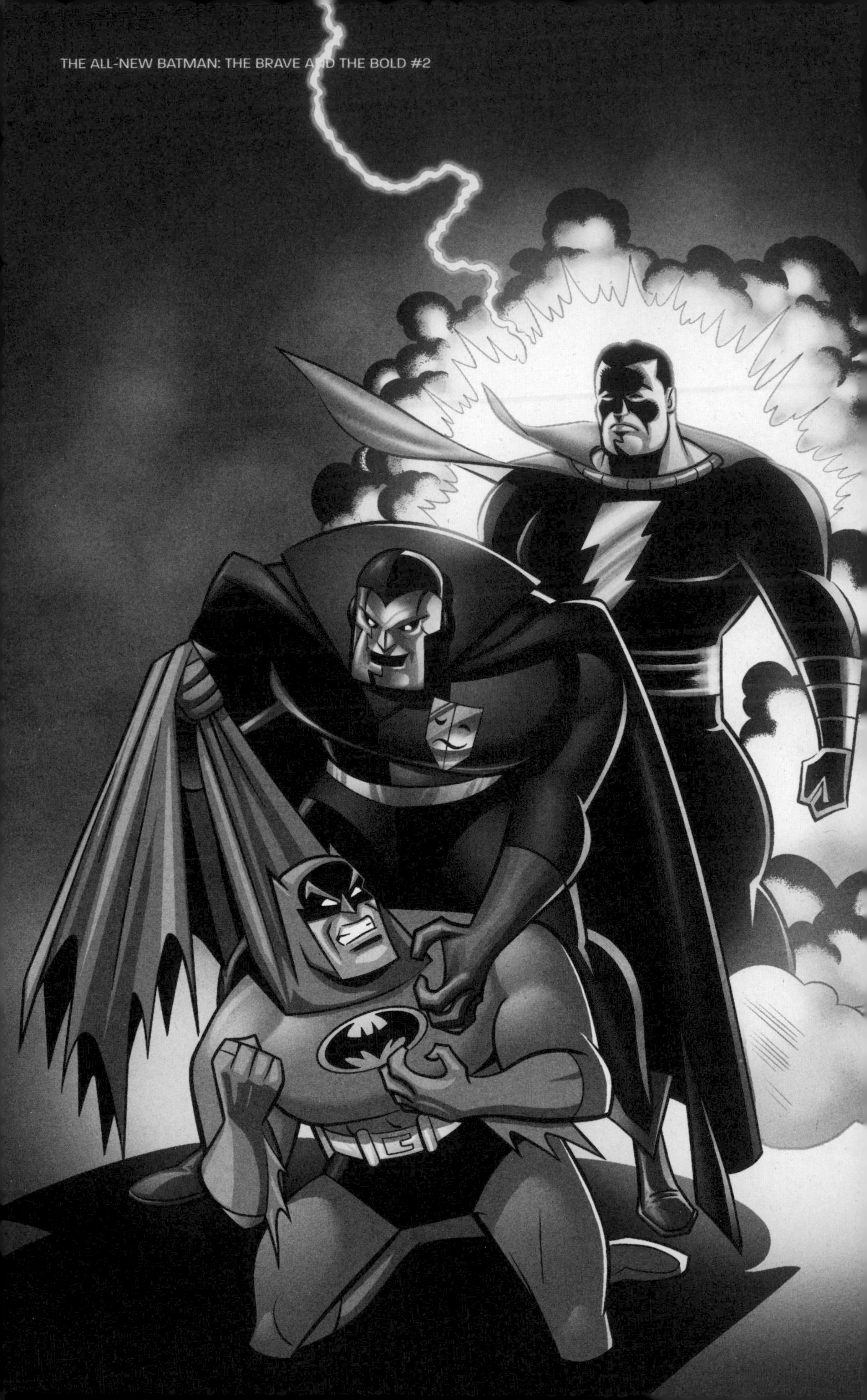

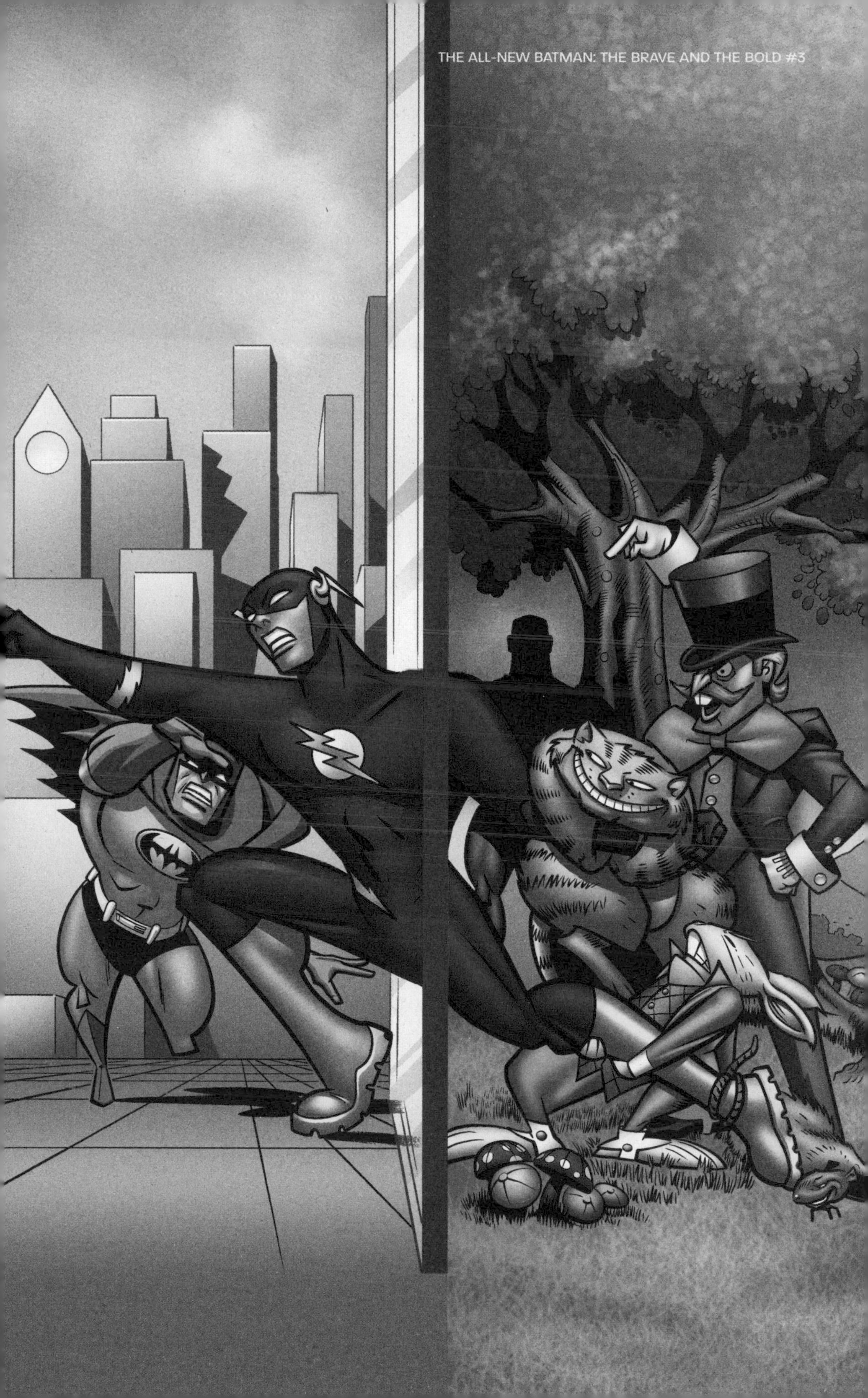
THE ALL-NEW BATMAN: THE BRAVE AND THE BOLD #3

THE ALL-NEW BATMAN: THE BRAVE AND THE BOLD #4

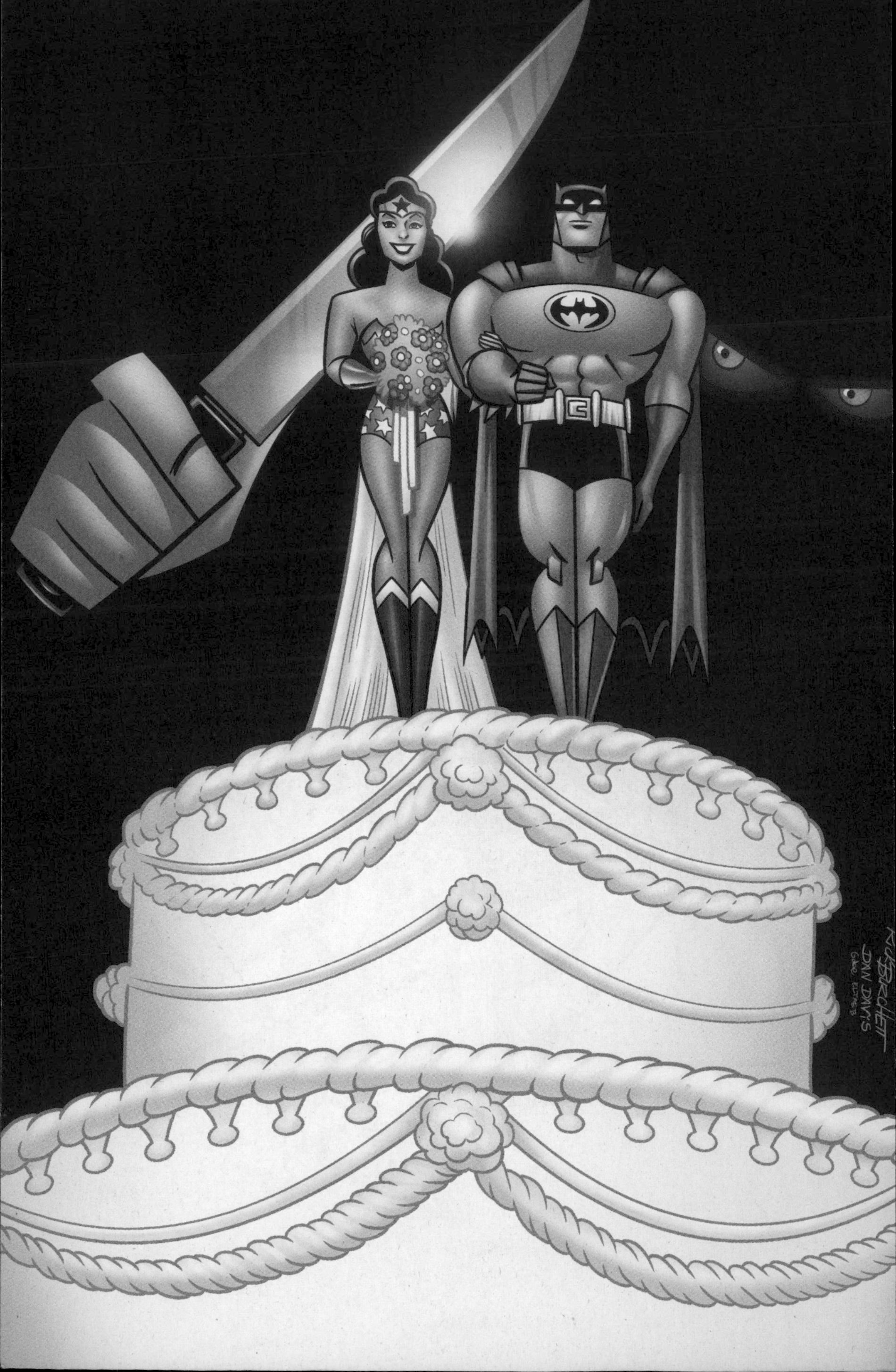

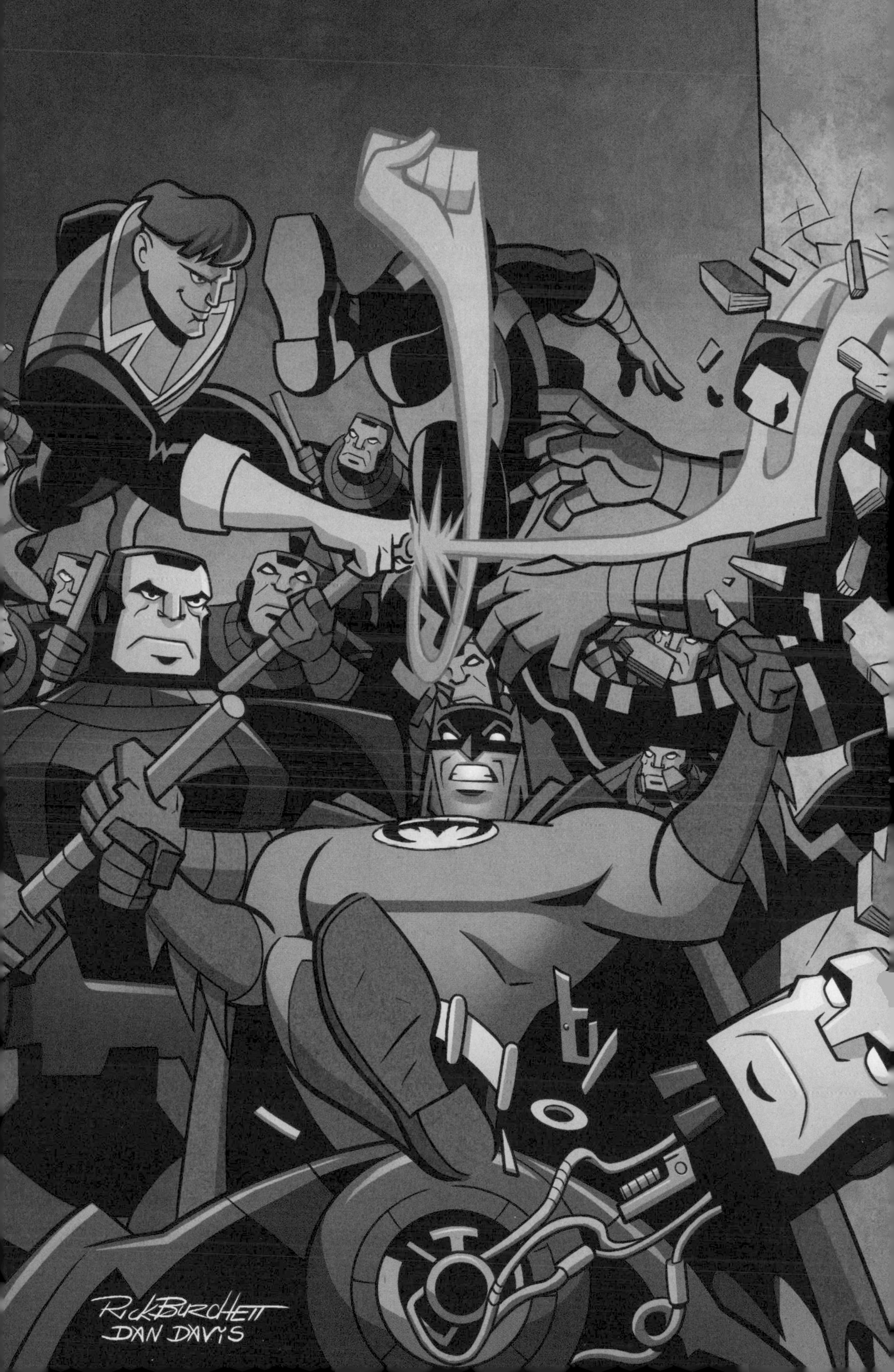
RICK BURCHETT
DAN DAVIS

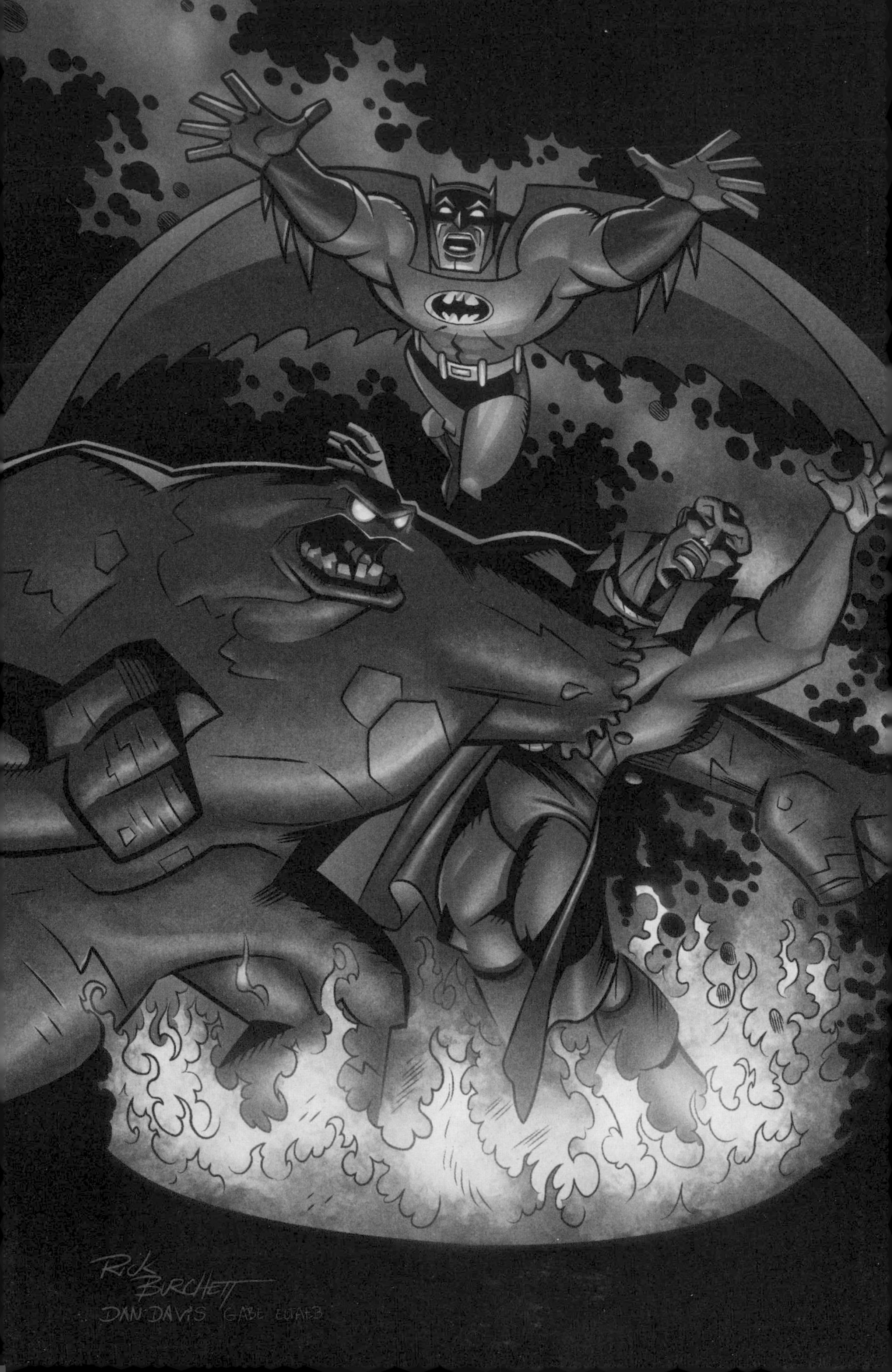
RICK BURCHETT
DAN DAVIS
GABE ELTAEB